A Complete Guide to
JOB Placement

Author
Neelima Vinod

V&S PUBLISHERS

Published by:

V&S PUBLISHERS

F-2/16, Ansari road, Daryaganj, New Delhi-110002
23240026, 23240027 • *Fax:* 011-23240028
Email: info@vspublishers.com • *Website:* www.vspublishers.com

Regional Offi ce : Hyderabad
5-1-707/1, Brij Bhawan (Beside Central Bank of India Lane)
Bank Street, Koti, Hyderabad - 500 095
040-24737290
E-mail: vspublishershyd@gmail.com

Branch Offi ce : Mumbai
Godown # 34 at The Model Co-Operative Housing, Society Ltd.,
"Sahakar Niwas", Ground Floor, Next to Sobo Central, Mumbai - 400 034
022-23510736
E-mail vspublishersmum@gmail.com

Follow us on:

All books available at **www.vspublishers.com**

Printed at : Param Offseters, Okhla, New Delhi-110020

Publisher's Note

V&S Publishers has always been with you. By publishing a series of career books, it has been guiding you to make a fruitful transition from college to working life as comfortable as possible with least amount of inconvenience. You've been in school followed by a stint in college for much of the life you have seen. What will your life be like now that you are graduating from college? How will you adapt? This book will show you steps, through different chapters, necessary to move ahead gracefully to a lively future.

Most students find it difficult, at least during the initial days of work life, to adapt the requirements of corporate environment mainly because of the enormous difference in the way professors and managers operate; while professors focus on increasing learning quotient and improving subject matter understanding, managers want implementation of the knowledge and therefore focus on getting the task done, meeting deadlines, etc.

The move from college to work life affects almost all aspects of your life. Not only will you have to adapt at work, but you will also have to adapt to your new life outside of work. After graduating from college, you may experience a bit of inconvenience to progress into the "real world." Here are some tips to help you out.

Make new friends. After graduation, you and your college friends may move elsewhere in order to pursue careers. You may lose touch with even your best of friends. It's time you build new relationships. Make friends with people you work with or get involved with your community in order to meet new people.

Say bye to your free time in college. Once you have a full-time job, your days off will be few. Spend your weekends wisely too.

A college degree is not the end; you still have many more goals to achieve. What do you want to do with your professional life? Do you want to climb the corporate ladder? Own your own business? Turn your hobby into a career? What about your personal life? Travel the world? Think hard about the goals that you want and strive every day to achieve them.

Once you enter the working life there will be no more staying up until four in the morning. You will have to change sleeping habits. With a standard forty-hour work week, you won't get few hours of afternoon naps anymore. Try to go to bed at a decent hour so you will be refreshed for work. You should try to get around eight hours of sleep per night.

Transitioning from a college to a professional life means shutting out those faded jeans and sneakers for more appropriate attire. If you want to be seen as a professional, you have to look the part. Save the t-shirts for the weekend and invest in appropriate dresses to wear through the week.

Do you know where you are going to live after graduation? A far away town or city rented place or hostel. Or else you could always move back in with your parents and save some money. It's usually hard for a college student, who has been pretty independent for the last few years to move back in with his parents. Just remember: if you want to be treated like an adult, you need to act like one at home or outside.

Learn to manage your finances. As soon as you land a job, learn how to save money. You will also need to budget wisely. If you are low on cash for the month, don't buy those shoes you have been eyeing. Wait until you can afford them.

Be prepared for entry-level jobs. Even though you have a college degree, don't expect to have the perfect job that brings in a big pay packet. Most of jobs available to new graduates are entry-level. These jobs often require long hours and hard work. Most employers want to see their employees start at a certain level in order to better understand the business. Working hard at this entry-level job will show your employer that you are dedicated and thus open up new doors for you.

Network wisely. As you transition from college life to the work world, don't overlook important associations that can contribute to your professional advancement. Stay in contact with your professors, friends, and family members who have connections with people in major corporations and organizations. These people may let you know when they are aware of opportunities that could benefit you.

Knowing what to expect after graduation and following some of the guidelines mentioned above should help launch your post college life on a positive note. It is becoming more and more important to have the correct know-how to proceed in career.

This book shows you ways to bridge the gap that exists between Campus environment and Corporate setting and to help those students who are just about to move to the job world. The transition into the "professional world" may be inconvenient at first, but you will become acclimatized to it after a while. Good luck!

Contents

SECTION I
INTRODUCTION

Campus to Corporate: The Giant Leap
Education: Where is Career Planning?
Your Problems
Career and Life
Making the transition from Campus to Corporate
The Book in a Nutshell

Campus to Corporate: The Giant Leap

Zoom in. Let's go to a college scene.

hang out near the canteen. The girls wear scarves, long t-shirts, and tight slacks. The boys are dressed in loose pants; some of them have iPods plugged in their ears. Some students rush through corridors as they are late for class again. On the way they greet lecturers, and sometimes bump into senior friends or bullies.

Now another college scene.

Students laugh and nudge each other in a dimly lit classroom. The boys and girls are dressed similarly to the kids in the previous scene. One steals a smoke when the lecturer is away. The campus is nothing but a block of concrete buildings with windows looking

In both scenes the student community is smiling. (Since this book is primarily for students, I'll address students as 'you' from now on). College is usually the best time of a person's life. Your college may not be the best college in the city; still there is an aspect to college life that beats all life's blues.

Most Bollywood movies are about college kids – people like you. Have you ever

happens when you are doing your Post Graduation or Degree – that is one reason, of course. The main reason, however, is that you are now part of an exciting phase of life when anything is possible if you want it to be.

When you are a student you have time on your side. You can experiment with subjects and be bold about your job search. This is a time for ideation – you can take life into your own hands and decide what you want to make of it.

A much later scene. Top angle of an office.

Chairs and desks have been neatly arranged. A bunch of former students from the two earlier colleges are sitting quietly with poker faces, listening as their new boss gives them a presentation. The students wear formal clothes; their iPods are tucked away in their briefcases and handbags.

This is the corporate world. Notice anything different? There is a change in everything about those students. Their clothes are different. Their posture is different. Their accessories are now hidden. They are the same people, but in a very different set-up.

Ephin, a Post Graduate student who works with a high-end company as part of her internship programme, rightly says that "College and work are at two ends of the spectrum."

The office environment is very different from the campus. You know all about your campus – the place where you hang out with friends, make comments, try out new dress fads, study, cram for exams, do practicals. College is the place you try to get away from, try to reach. Your experience of college is unique – each of you has your own special successes and failures in college.

College life is all about Angels and Demons. The Angels are your pals or friends, the people who like the same music you do, laugh at your jokes, tell you what's wrong with your outfit, lend you their notes. The Angels are those lecturers and professors who tell you great stories when they teach, guide you when you go wrong and commend you when you do something worthwhile. The Angels are all the opportunities that life in college can throw at you in the form of fests and other extracurriculars. The Angels come in the guise of great ambience, cool campus space, extensive library, and internet access.

Demons come in many guises. They come as seniors who rag even when the law says 'No Ragging'. Assignments and exams are Demons you have to face. Lousy campus infrastructure and low quality teaching are some other Demons you may have to deal with.

Identify your College Angels.

_____

_____

_____

Identify your College Demons.

_____

_____

_____

The *corporate space* has a whole different set of *Angels* and *Demons*. In college, you could manage friends, teachers and assignments easily enough. College is an extension of school, a heavenly combination of work and play. Corporate life is nothing like that.

Corporate life is about work. What is work? *Work is all about reporting to the boss daily, doing what is assigned to you correctly* (no experimental college approach), and being responsible – not just the salary. All the hard work you did to get through the interview comes into action once you get hired. It's a *continuous show of professionalism and performance.* No excuses like *I performed badly this semester, so I'll make up for it in the next. You are expected to be good every day of your work life.* In short, as an employee, you should know what the company expects from you, how to maintain a positive attitude and how to display interest in the company's work.

What kind of changes can you expect when you make the big shift from campus to corporate?

► **Corporate environment:** The office looks different from your campus. Watch out for air-conditioned office space, cubicles, revolving chairs, desks, cabins for senior bosses, etc.

► **Bosses and Team Leaders:** No more lecturers. You enter a class structure where you are new and at the bottom of the ladder. Everyone else is senior to you.

► **Colleagues:** Everyone you meet is not going to be your best friend. You treat your colleagues with respect.

► **Targets:** *Fests and trophies will be replaced by targets. The more targets you achieve, the more chances of you getting promoted and a better salary.*

► **Teamwork:** *Corporate* life is about successful *group effort.* Being good is not enough. In college, you get graded for your hard work and efforts. In the office, being a team player helps. For this, you need good communication skills.

► **Formal wear:** When you work in an office, you have to change your personality and look as well. No more casual college wear. No more satchels, think briefcase.

► **Salary:** No more grading. *Your new grade is currency.* The more you work for your company, the more chances you have of getting a better pay packet.

2

Education: Where is Career Planning?

We live in a country where education is taken very seriously. You must have been reminded several times how lucky you are to have received an education. India faces many broad based challenges when it comes to getting kids enrolled into primary schools and sustaining education through secondary school. Challenges include *good infrastructure, mindset issues, lack of incentives for innovative teaching methods,* etc.

India is a large democracy. *To become a knowledge economy, people need technical skills or hard skills.* These are the skills that you need on the job. A knowledge economy also needs *soft skills,* called *etiquette* in corporate terms or communication skills in plain speak.

expertise but not the soft skills to cope with your new environment. Let's see what some of these problems might be and how to improve soft skill sets to deal with different environments.

YOUR PROBLEMS

What kind of problems do you think the education you received has?

_____

_____

_____

Here are some issues that may have cropped up:

Low on quality

The biggest problems could range from quality of education to inadequate teaching tools. You could be a student privileged enough to study in a huge campus with enough computers and an accessible well-stocked library, or you could be in a concrete building with zero access to computers and books.

Do you use the resources around you? Resources in college include *libraries, computers,* and, if none of these are available, well-meaning teachers who are willing to guide you. If your college lacks even these basic requirements, do you use the facilities you get at home? Do you read the newspaper or watch educational programmes on TV? If you have an internet connection at home, do you use it to supplement your subject knowledge?

You have all heard the story of how American President Abraham Lincoln studied under a street light. You also know how former President of India, Abdul Kalam dreamt of outer space while he studied in a tiny village in Chennai. Instead of blaming your circumstances and lack of resources, capitalise on your biggest resource – YOU.

It is very easy to get demotivated but simple activities *like reading the right material and watching the right programmes can make a huge difference.* Use the resources available to you to *increase your knowledge quotient* and *improve your awareness of potential career choices.*

The corporate world is full of people like you and me. Why worry then?

> **Sangeeth Verghese, founder of LeadCap India and a leadership thinker and**
>
> **India, a system of learning called pedagogy is followed. This relies on a tight hierarchy of teacher and student, meaning that the teacher is supposed to spoon feed knowledge to the unquestioning student. Learning completely depends on the knowledge level of the teacher. If the teacher is not adequately equipped, the students do not learn at all.**

Don't you ask your lecturers to give you notes before the exams? Don't many of you rely heavily on guides? All this is part of the spoon-feeding process that starts from kindergarten. When you rely on this method, it becomes hard for you to think for yourself and make your own decisions. This doesn't have to be the case. There are other options for learning. Unfortunately, this *pedagogical baggage* is carried by the student, even when he is ready to join his new job.

In a corporate environment, Verghese says, "You are expected to hit the road running and take initiatives with minimum hand-holding. If the student depends on the teacher for all knowledge, then he loses his way in the self-initiated corporate set up. The solution? A lot of soft skill training before the job."

► Career confusion

While perceived *lack of resources* and *spoon-feeding* are problems that stem from the the Indian education system, another problem is *zero awareness* when it comes to making the right career choice.

Ephin is a student who has received education at an upcoming college and later in a more established institution. She feels that as a fresher Psychology graduate, she had very little knowledge about how the job market functioned. "I didn't know what my options were. Whatever I had understood during my graduation was not the *real picture*." Ephin feels that students do not have enough exposure to industrial experience. "A student needs to undergo a lot of training when it comes to getting the right soft skill sets. Confidence can be built through workshops and interactions with professionals who can tell us what we can expect when we apply for a job and once we get employed there."

Ephin is lucky enough to have landed up in an institution where she gets access to more avenues. If you are not part of such an environment, then you have to take extra initiative to find out the motive behind specialising in a particular subject.

If you are a BCA student, why did you opt for Computer Science? If your answer is anything like *IT has good scope, Software people get more money, IT people can go to the US*, etc., then you have made your decision based on some vague notions. Do you know the kinds of jobs that specialising in IT can get you? Are you aiming to be part of one specific company? Do you have several options in mind?

► Career and life

A career is an important life decision. More and more people are wedded to their careers. You wake up to go to your workplace and you come home only to prepare for the next day. If you make the wrong career choice, the result could be devastating for you and your loved ones.

Have you thought of your career plan? Whose advice do you seek the most when it comes to this decision?

_____

_____

_____

It is wiser to listen to what your guardians and well-wishers have to say. Listen to people who have more experience and make your decision based on what is feasible.

If you have gained entry into an expensive college, consider whether it is feasible for you to join, what steps must be taken to make your stay there as hassle-free as possible, what loans can be availed of, and what preparation you must make to acclimatize there. Much preparation must go into every decision so that your journey will be smoother. If you know what choices your subject has to offer and the jobs in the current job market that suit your profile, you can have a meaningful discussion with your guardians or career counsellors.

A student Avinash tells his father that he wants to do *Anthropology*. He has completed his degree in *Architecture,* and now wants to change his stream. His father goes blue in the face and asks, "What is Anthropology?" Avinash knows about the subject vaguely but cannot respond satisfactorily. His father then asks him, "What scope does the subject have?" Avinash wants to get into academic research but he is unable to communicate his goals. He ends up taking the subject, but that is after so much heartache and misunderstanding. *If Avinash had been able to communicate his goals clearly, he would have been able to make a smoother transition.*

There are many social pressures you will face. Maybe your family runs a business and you are expected follow suit. You may feel that you lack business acumen and your interest may lie elsewhere. How do you handle this social pressure? By being informed about the choices that are suited for you. *You must educate your family and relatives about the best options for your aptitude. It is no use becoming a doctor because your parents expect you to be one. You must have the aptitude to be a doctor.*

Another problem is comparison. "Look at your cousin brother. He's already earning xxx dollars and look at you applying for a job like this!" This is a comparison that often does the rounds in all family conversations. Do not let the comparisons bother you too much. If you rightly deserve a better job, then do the job you get as best as you can and keep improving your skill-sets so that you can ultimately apply for your dream job. You have to remind yourself that the ladder starts on the ground and not up there in the stars. *It takes time to climb and effort.*

While you must educate and inform yourself and those around you, *you must also remember that your career is your own life partner.* So be mature when you choose. Every person has his/her own unique identity and circumstances. Take a career that aids you to go ahead financially and with confidence. A good career makes you a much better person and a more responsible citizen. At the end of the day, the decision is yours. No use blaming friends and family for the wrong steps you take in your life. *Consider all advice, but decide alone.*

3

Making the Transition from Campus to Corporate

Transition is the natural way of things. Can you imagine a life where there is absolutely no change? Picture yourself in the same house surrounded by the same people forever. Time moves forward. Your degree course is long over. Can you imagine just watching the world pass you by? Can you do it? Isn't that riskier than not making any transitions at all?

remember and what negatives?

_____

_____

_____

_____

friends, and getting a feel of the campus and syllabus.

What would you change if you had a chance?

_____

_____

_____

_____

Maybe, you would be a little friendlier or a little less nervous. This is a clue to how you can better handle the transition from Campus to Corporate.

When you join college, you usually have a *Fresher's Day*, a welcome organised by your seniors. On Fresher's Day, you are welcomed as *initiates*. There will be *jokes*, *a bit of harmless teasing*, and you will feel that the *school is far away, a different world that you have outgrown*.

When your college days are up, very few of you have an idea about *how different corporate life is from life on campus*. Some *colleges have career counsellors* who engage students in discussions about their future plans. When you leave college, however, you are filled with farewell plans and exam tensions. *You don't do much preparation to enter the job space.*

Entering the job market is much more than making a resume and getting a job. It is about being ready enough for the change. This is an important phase of your education that no one prepares you for. There are no textbooks that grade you on your resilience and ability to handle change with grace. *In fact, change management is a structural approach used by companies to help employees make the required transition to the company's changing needs.*

YOUR CHANGE MANAGEMENT

What kind of changes have you experienced in your life?

_____

_____

_____

How well do you handle change?

_____

_____

If you like the thrill of a new experience and feel a sense of adventure every time, there is a possibility of change, that means you are someone who likes to live on the edge.

Gina is not like that at all. She is extremely nervous about leaving college. That is her comfort zone. Her friends are there; her life revolves around her college activities and assignments. She dreads the prospect of leaving college and getting on in the world. She suffers from a phobia of moving out of her comfort zone.

If you have to manage change, you have to start early. Sudden transitions are different. Gina should start working on being open to change. Change is not equal to disaster. Be flexible if you want to adapt – change with change and you will be fine.

Here are a few things you should know before you take the plunge:

➤ **Do you have the stamina?**

What does the corporate world and sports have in common?

The competition. The targets. The stress.

Without the adequate stamina, even if you have the job, it will be hard to keep it. Develop a routine even while you are at college. Living a chaotic life will reduce your chances of having a healthy lifestyle. This will in turn upset your endurance levels. You know that a healthy body has a healthy mind. Know your body and its limitations and choose your work accordingly.

Your limitations should not, however, dictate the way you live your life. Many differently - abled citizens have crossed all physical limitations to achieve their goals. Limitations are, as the adage goes, in the mind – you are young enough and elastic enough to create a better lifestyle for yourself. The key to being productive is to be determined enough to increase your stamina. If you feel you have a limitation, work on it. Consult doctors, eat healthy foods, change your lifestyle, and be health conscious on a day - to - day basis – not just when you feel like it.

When you are new on the job, you will need to be alert at all times. If you are sluggish, you will lose out. *A combination of right exercise, right diet, and the right attitude will give you the stamina to become a Corporate Sprinter.*

➤ **Do you have the right mind frame?**

No one is prepared for all eventualities. You know what college life is and you may have read up on the corporate scenario. All the preparations that you do for the job interview must be added up with a **Positive mind-set**. *Without a positive thought process, you will find the transition from campus to corporate life uncomfortable.*

Joining a new work place is all about being willing to cooperate with new people from diverse backgrounds. Corporate offices with all their glitz and glamour can be scary, especially if you come from a small town. You could get a **culture shock.** In cities, relationships are handled differently. But you have enough exposure to TV. So don't be too surprised. Just be accepting in the beginning. Learn from the company – be prepared to let your cultural notions and ideas take a back seat for a while.

Another stumbling block will be **Language**. People from all over India and the world working in one office space. How will you communicate? Some offices train you in soft skills. Other times, you learn on the job. Every action you take on behalf of the company is part of your learning curve.

To develop the right mind-set, you have to unlearn everything you know and be enthusiastic about making a new you. Don't worry about losing the old you.

▶ **Do you have the emotional IQ?**

Having the right mind-set translates into the right kind of emotional intelligence. You may be feeling sad, panicky, or over excited. But you must learn how to behave in a balanced manner if you are to be taken seriously. *Emotional Intelligence IQ or EQ is as important as IQ.* It helps you to navigate through society and all its constructs. If you can understand not just your emotions but the emotions of those around you, and you are able to use all that data to make good decisions, then you have a good EQ.

Nobody teaches you EQ. It is the ability to identify, use, understand and manage emotions in positive ways to relieve stress, communicate effectively, face challenges and diffuse conflicts. Emotional intelligence helps you to relate better with other people and achive greater success. In school, you are graded for your IQ. Nowadays, many schools are focussing on creating well-rounded individuals.

You must have gained your EQ without knowing it – in school, at home, with friends and family. Circumstances give you opportunities to understand your EQ.

You can check your EQ in moments of stress. Suppose you wanted to wake up early but the alarm didn't go off. You are in a bad, snappy mood in the morning as you had so many things to do and you weren't able to complete them. You snap at your family members. When you keep reacting to the situation, you end up getting upset.

Suppose you had watched how you felt. You wake up in the morning. You are late but if you hurry, maybe, you can get things done in time. When you watch your emotions, you automatically look for solutions. When you don't look inward, you tend to put the blame on someone.

▶ **Are you able to handle your emotions?**

_____

_____

In a work place, handling emotions is very important. When you work, be a good 'me-manager'. This means that you must know how to manage time, deadlines, stress and emotions.

► **Do you react to situations or do you respond?**

When you react to every situation, you are at the receiving end. Any incident can make you upset, any phone call can make you sad, any comment can make you lose your confidence. When you respond, you are in control. This is important during an interview - your interviewer wants to know how much thought you put into each decision. If you handle a phone call based on a sudden reaction, the company could lose a valuable customer. So a thoughtful approach works.

► **Can you understand how others feel?**

The art of understanding others is called empathy.

Venkat is a man of average intelligence. He is pleasant and acknowledges everyone and everyone at his workplace likes him. They don't know why – maybe because he smiles, maybe he is kind, they can't point out exactly why he is so likeable. People turn to him during crises.

One reason is that Venkat is a good judge of other's emotions. He is able to put people at ease. This quality is admirable – what Venkat consciously or unconsciously does is that he reads other's emotions through their facial and body language, and he expresses himself with enough confidence to be trusted.

Are you shocked when someone misunderstands your motives?

Ayesha is an intern. She gets a phone call in the office and she is delighted that her friend has called her. She speaks loudly and enthusiastically, for a good fifteen minutes. Her superiors are unhappy with the call – they scold her and give her a lesson on manners.

What did Ayesha do wrong? Nothing, if you think about it. Her managers should probably lighten up. Right? Wrong. Ayesha thinks she is still in college and doesn't know the do's and don'ts of office life. She should have spoken in a low voice and cut the length of the call. She should not have given the office number to her friend in the first place. She is not sensitive enough to understand what is expected of her at work.

When you are new to the job, you have to be aware of what is required from you. You must be observant and understand how the office works. *Don't compare college life with corporate existence*. They are two different worlds, where the sets of rules are different.

Whether you have to give a presentation or deal with clients and colleagues, you must be ready with a smile on your lips. It is possible to be a reliable employee only when you have mastered yourself and don't lose yourself to the moment. The phrase *lose your temper* shows that *you lose your cool. There is loss, no gain.*

When you are in a stressful situation, can you navigate yourself and your colleagues out of any clear and present danger? So stress in the workplace affects not only the person in stress, but also the situation and the associates or colleagues with whom he/she is working. The output is also affected. Hence, we need to change our attitude or behaviour as well as mental make-up to deal with stressful situations at the workplace.

To deal with change, you need *presence of mind.*

4

This book is all about getting the job and being successful the right way. You will be taken through various aspects of a job hunt from identifying your skills to acing the interview. You will identify "*Brand You*". Every step of the way, you will review your strengths and weaknesses, and identify aspects of yourself that you have been ignoring

Campus to Corporate is all about staying in the corporate world long enough to become a one hundred per cent experienced professional.

Every book has a protagonist or a central character. The protagonist of this book is *You – the fresher making an entry into the coveted job scene.*

There are many self-help books out there. What makes this one any different? Well for one thing, you write the book along with me. I've given you a lot of space to express yourself and be honest about how you feel. What you take from this book is "*Brand You*" and "*how to sell yourself*".

This book is not about formulae, but more about knowing who you are and getting to the place where you deserve to be.

Instead of referring to several books to understand all the things about the job hunt, this book aims to be a *one-stop address* for all things that are job-related. Experts from

All that is expected from you is a pen to jot down your thoughts. Look out for the **Fresher Shoot section** where questions from students like you have been answered.

The book is divided into six sections. Each section focusses on one aspect of the job hunt.

Section 1: Test Yourself deals with *Assessment Tests*. Answering these tests give you an idea about your verbal reasoning and analytical abilities; your personality and career aptitude.

Section 2: Know your SWOT deals with knowing your strengths and weaknesses. It is only by *knowing yourself, your circumstances, your family expectations,* and *your goals* that you can create a *career blueprint* that fits you.

Section 3: Polish Your Skills is an extremely important section, where I give you a comprehensive overview on how you should polish your existing skill-sets within the college scenario and also in the corporate scene. An entire part of this section deals with communication skills. Building soft skills is the aim of this section. You will also understand how important self-branding is − even if you have all the qualifications, you must know how to present those effectively face - to - face, in a resume, a cover letter, a presentation, or your style quotient.

Section 4: The Job Hunt Begins - will help you find out where the jobs are and how you can write *effective resumes* and *cover letters*. I have broken down resume writing into small chunks where you get a chance to showcase your strengths. You will understand the dynamics of *group discussions* and go through *mock interviews* and *real interview* types.

Section 5: Corporate Communication is what you do once you get the job. Once you clinch the interview, you must prove yourself on the job. Section 5 deals with surviving your first day at office and creating a work ethic that will be useful in the long-term. *Corporate etiquette* is not taught in college and must be learnt on the job − work is as much about dealing with people and cultures as it is about achieving targets.

Section 6: Career Switch and Career Graph is your guide through the four stages of your career graph. I give you tips on what you should know about career change − it is another transition that is a part of corporate life.

Read this book to understand *Career in a Nutshell − decide to have a career and excel*. You are on the threshold of leaving campus and entering the corporate world. It's a long journey, so let's prepare ourselves! Breathe in and welcome…

Recap

Campus to Corporate – A Comparison.

Identify College Demons and Angels.

Lack of Emphasis on Career Planning.

Do You have What It Takes to Succeed?

Summary of the Book.

SECTION 2
KNOW YOUR SWOT

1. Finding You: Your SWOT
Swot You
Project your Future

2. Identifying You
Your Priorities
Your Parents
Your Circumstances
Your Motivation
Your Personality
Your Experience

3. Branding You
Are you a Brand?
Before the Career Plan
Career Plan
Career Expectations
Career Boosters

Finding You: Your SWOT

SWOT YOU

Right now you may be a fresher, just out of college and thinking about getting a job

work will be far away from your thoughts. Yet you are curious. *What is the job hunt all about? How can I get through it?*

First, you have to know who you are. This means that you have to understand certain things about the kind of person you are. *"Hey we all know about ourselves!"* you may tell me. Right? Well, wrong. *At this point in your life, you may not be the best judge of your own personal and professional goals.* Others could have more clues about how capable you are. I am going to help you get to know more about you, or help you with your *self-assessment*. Many times, when we assess ourselves, we come up

Many freshers get into careers without thinking it through. They take whatever comes their way because that's all there is or they assume that they have zero choices. Do you want to take the road ahead just because it is there, not because it will help you succeed? I hope not.

This section is all about you getting to know you, your good and *your not so good points, your awareness of yourself, and your possible future.* If you get into your college

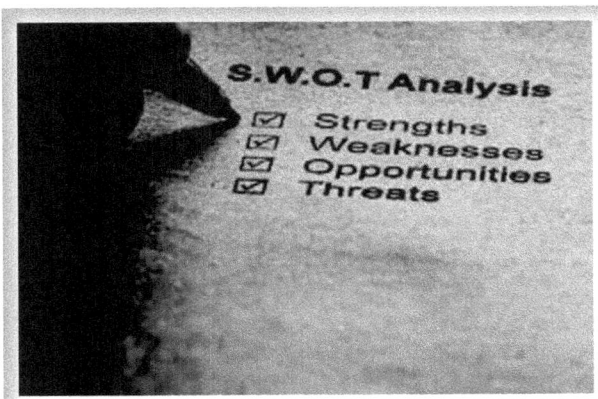

S.W.O.T Analysis
☑ Strengths
☑ Weaknesses
☑ Opportunities
☑ Threats

course, career and other aspects of life blindfolded, without thinking things through, you will face the consequences. The mantra today is *to be prepared.*

Knowing yourself is the best way of knowing where you can go. When you understand yourself, you know what kind of job you can search for and what kind of environment you can work in.

Once there was a man who thought very highly of himself. His friend, however, was an ordinary guy, who hadn't achieved anything in life yet. Once the two of them were travelling in their SUV up a steep road – suddenly without word or warning the ethical man hit a labourer woman who appeared out of the blue. The woman fell down dead. His friend screamed at him to stop the car – so he did. His friend got out and tended to the woman – in the meantime, the ethical man drove away at top speed. He was shaking and praying to God that he would not get caught.

What does this tell you? The ethical man did not know many things about himself. You only find out who you are during a crisis. Even your judgement about yourself can go wrong in a sudden stressful situation.

Sometimes what works very well for others cannot work for you. Just because your friend got a job in a BPO, what makes you think that you will do well there? You may have other strengths that can be used better in another kind of setup.

Throughout the book, we get to see the viewpoints of students like you who are on the threshold of job search. We also get some expert advice from professionals who can help in their respective areas. Remember, before setting out to do anything, there are immense resources today in the form of *CDs, websites, professionals, and books* like this one. *Use these resources.*

LOOK AT THE MIRROR

What do you see? *In this section, we explore the Angels and Demons in you.* Take a good look. Most of you like what you see.

When you look at a mirror, you see your physical appearance. You also assess various aspects of yourself like the way you look, the clothes you wear, your facial expressions (are you smiling or not), your posture, and your potential. You compare yourself with your peers or your friends. What makes you stand out? What makes you unique? This is your **USP - Unique Selling Point** – your Key to Success.

Remember to focus on the good things that you see, but you must not ignore your weaknesses. *You are a package of both positives and negatives.* When you do the *Fresher fitness exercises* below, be as honest as possible. That is Rule Number 1 of any *self-assessment exercise.* If you feel really shy, then say that you are shy. The first step in dealing with any issue is to understand that there is room for improvement. Then there is no stopping you from achieving your dreams!

Fresher fitness

Write one adjective or descriptive word about yourself. I've provided some adjectives to help you…you don't have to use these if you have any other ideas about yourself.

Confident Shy Smart Average   Successful   Loser Proud

_____

_____

_____

_____

Not very difficult was it?

Companies conduct SWOT analysis to evaluate the Strengths, Weaknesses, Opportunities and *Threats* involved in a venture or project. You can do your own SWOT and identify your positives and negatives.

First try to figure out the *positives or the good things about yourself. Those are your strengths.* You could be a good narrator or an athlete. The *negatives or things you don't like about yourself are your weaknesses.* These traits could be laziness, aimlessness, anger, etc. Write in short sentences or use simple adjectives. Be as honest as possible – don't be too humble or too showy. Just be yourself.

STRENGTHS or POSITIVES

Each one of you has a special something – call it a gift, a blessing, your USP, the magic ingredient that makes you tick. The funny thing is sometimes you have qualities even you don't know about until someone comes along and says, "Hey you are one of the most confident people I've met"….and you say *Really*? Is that me you are talking about? Answering these questions gives you some clues about the direction *Project You* must take.

What do you think makes you unique? Do you have any particular skill-sets or qualifications that you are proud of?

_____

_____

What do people around you think is your strength? (These must be people you respect.)

_____

_____

What is your one achievement you would like to talk about if given an opportunity?

_____

_____

Are you a cool networker – do you have relevant contacts or resources that will get you ahead?

_____

_____

WEAKNESSES OR NEGATIVES

Each one of us is notoriously bad at something. No one, and believe me no one, not even your favourite celebrity, is perfect. Being perfect goes against all laws of nature. Having weaknesses is a positive as it gives you the motivation to work on yourself. That is the biggest career of your life – improving yourself is a never-ending process that keeps giving you results.

There is a story about a man who was caught in the rain one day. He came across someone in the storm. On looking closer, he noticed that the figure in the rain was a leper; the rain poured down on his bandaged fingers. The man ignored the leper and rushed home. Why did he leave that way? He was afraid and went home but the image of the leper's bandaged fingers troubled him. He could not sit in the comfort of his home. So he went back in the rain to help the leper.

The man managed to help the leper build a shelter - although he was afraid, conquering the fear and going out of his way for someone else gave him great joy. He was transformed at that moment and found his calling. This man became the much revered and much loved Baba Amte.

 He was ashamed by his terrible fear when he saw the leper. That troubled him all the way home – he became aware of his weakness. Once he examined his weakness, he gained the confidence to overcome it.

You have to stop clinging to your weakness. Weaknesses are actually messages that tell you which areas of yourself you can improve. So don't hold on to the things that you think make you 'You' - get rid of the bad things and you will be a better 'You'.

What are you least confident doing?

_____

_____

What weaknesses do people around you think you have? Does your mom say that you have to work harder or your lecturer say you have to speak up?

_____

_____

What don't you like about your education? Is there any subject that you really think you need and have to work on?

_____

_____

What are your demons according to you – temper, laziness, fear? Is there any experience you have had that shows this weakness?

_____

_____

What is your biggest weakness according to others? (Are these people whose opinion you value?)

_____

_____

You want to be a teacher but you are dead scared of speaking before a crowd. What are you going to do about it? Will that stop you from becoming a teacher?

_____

_____

OPPORTUNITIES

The subject that you specialise in and the positive aspects of your character give you chances. It is up to you to be watchful and alert. The old story of the hare and tortoise still makes sense today. The hare is a quick runner – like the college student who is tech savvy and ahead of others, but the tortoise considers all options and reaches the finish line. He does not try to take too many short-cuts and makes it to the end. Will you use the chances given to you? In _a world, where there is so much opportunity, the only thing you should know is to look in the right direction and work single-mindedly towards your goal._

What kind of scope do you think your subject has?

_____

_____

Are you making the most of the resources available to you?

_____

_____

Are you aware of the job opportunities that your subject has to offer?

_____

_____

Are you comfortable with technology?

_____

_____

What kind of service do you want to offer to the world? No matter what the contribution, every person has something unique to offer.

_____

_____

THREATS

There are many threats around you – bad company can ruin your future; parents can force you to take up a subject that you dislike just for the sake of prestige; financial issues can force you into studying in cheaper institutes with low - quality resources or even abandon studies altogether.

It is said that the biggest enemy you have in your life is yourself. If you are plagued by fear, then no matter how talented or wealthy you are, no resource can take you to the top. If you have communication problems, even admission in a top-notch institute will not guarantee success. But remember there are solutions to these threats.

What obstacles do you think you have in your own personality? An example could be communication problems.

_____

_____

Bosses, colleagues, and competition – do these things worry you?

_____

_____

Do you have the positives to wipe out obstacles around you and within?

_____

_____

If you see technology as a threat, are you willing to change your attitude?

_____

_____

WHAT SWOT CAN TEACH YOU:

See how your answers reflect a lot of things about yourself?

Doing SWOT regularly teaches you the value of self-assessment. Keep asking yourself questions. It makes you more responsible and accountable to yourself. Instead of worrying about what others think and how others judge you, observe how you can keep track by understanding your feelings. You can change the questions to reflect the day.

Being observant about your day-to-day happenings helps you keep track of your changing positives and negatives. Ask questions like _"What did you do today that you didn't like or was out of character"?_ If you are honest with yourself, you will find that each answer you give opens a new possibility to change yourself in a positive way.

PROJECT YOUR FUTURE: MAKING THE BLUEPRINT

A good way of identifying who you are is to find out more about who you want to be. You may not know now what exactly it is that you want to be but you can make your dream a reality.

Former President Abdul Kalam speaks about how a teacher inspired in him his love of flight. This love is what turned him into India's missile man. Steve Jobs had a dream of bringing a computer into every home. Martin Luther King had a dream of equality for people of all races.

This is a good time in your life to read biographies of achievers as one fact comes out of every story. Successful people start out with dreams. The dream is the centre towards which they work with single - minded devotion. They do not count the money they may receive or the days that they take to achieve change. This dream is powerful enough to become the Blueprint.

So first you need to have a dream or a goal. Once you know what you want to achieve, you have to be ready for it. You have to dedicate a great deal of time to making your dream come true. Winning is not just about getting the lottery, good fate, or being lucky. Being successful is all about hard work. Ask any celebrity or sports person if success came easily to them and they will say, No way! Remember what author Malcolm Gladwell says about needing 10,000 hours to master your skills. No shortcuts in polishing your skills!

Who has inspired you and why? Write about someone besides your family members.

_____

_____

Now write about the family member you look up to and why.

_____

_____

I won't ask you to identify your dream right now. This is a long-term goal that you have to think over deeply. Answer these more specific questions and see if any goal is forming in your mind.

Where do you see yourself when you are old? What kind of house do you live in? Where? What kind of people do you want around you? Are you happy?

_____

_____

_____

_____

_____

Use your imagination a bit. Anything is possible.

Where do you see yourself ten years from now?

_____

_____

_____

Now this question is closer to home. Some of you see yourselves working in important companies or doing the things you love, like riding motorcycles or being happily married.

Where do you see yourself five years down the line?

_____

_____

Alert! This is an important interview question and one that we will return to later in the book. This is also a question that you may have been asked many times by your parents, and even yourself.

Within five years, you will have completed your degree, maybe post graduation, what then? What kind of a job have you searched for? Are you doing the right course to achieve your goals? Are there any additional skills you need to do to achieve your Personal Five Year Plan?

At the interview, you will have to talk about your career plans that you want to achieve in five years. This is a make or break question that can determine your future. You will have to answer diplomatically and with confidence.

Where do you see yourself in two years?

_____

_____

Always start with long - term goals. Then go backwards. This way you can identify what you have to do to achieve your goals. In two years, you will probably be thinking of doing your post graduation or getting a job. How are you going to get the job that will get you ahead?

Where do you see yourself at the end of the year?

_____

_____

_____

Every year people talk about *New Year Resolutions*. This is an over-hyped concept but a very good way of gaining more positives or strengths. You can make a resolution like *I will read two books a month*. Personal goals are more important than goals that others set for you. If you follow through this resolution you will end up reading twenty-four books in a year – far better than reading nothing at all!

Where do you see yourself today?

_____

_____

Set yourself one or two daily goals. If you have an assignment to complete two weeks from now, set baby step goals to complete this assignment on time. This kind of day - to - day goal setting helps you stop postponing things. If you are regular about assignment completion, you will have more confidence in the corporate world where daily targets determine your success average.

Here are some answers that are negative.

I have enough time to decide.

Not really. It's always better to start thinking about realistic goals early on. You can have big dreams but how do you get there? What kind of planning do you need to do now to be another Steve Jobs? Think about it instead of postponing a good future.

I'm living in the present so I won't trouble myself with these thoughts.

That's lame. Living in the present means being happy now – it doesn't mean putting off decisions that you can make today for tomorrow.

Living your dreams is about *effective time management*. **Managing time is too important to be casual about since time is the only asset that you have!**

2

Identifying Yourself

Your identity depends on a lot of factors. The question, *Who are you* answer. You are so many things to you and to so many people – a daughter, a son, a student…what makes you *You* to a large extent is a whole bunch of social constructs. In this section, we take a look at how ideas can shape you. You have priorities that make you special. Your parents have ideas about you that also help create your identity. You are from a certain kind of set-up – a village, a city, – all

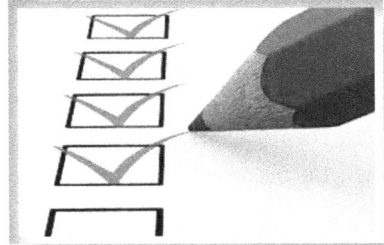

dreams that you have for yourself.

YOUR PRIORITIES

We live in a *heliocentric universe*, with the planets revolving around the Sun. Let's do

the Sun. The orbits around you are your priorities. Here are some priorities you could have.

Family, Money, Education, Ambitions, Interests, Travel

Take a look at this solar system.

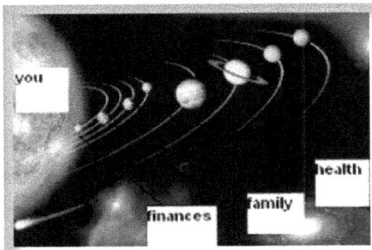

Now make your own solar system, where you are the centre and your priorities range from the most important to the least important.

Each of you will have different priorities. Knowing which priority is important helps you create a plan to achieve your goals. *It's all about your life choices.* These indicate which direction your life will take. Of course, everything may not work out as planned, but you can work towards your goals

Also understand that priorities change. When you are a student of literature, you may not want to teach. But once you pass out and look at your career options, teaching may seem like an ideal option as it is convenient for you. Do not be too rigid – options keep changing. You can keep redrawing the solar system we designed just now.

Now work out your subject priorities in your solar system. Which subject does your life revolve around? Which subjects interest you the least?

_____

_____

Looking at your analysis, decide whether you have made the right subject choice. Choosing a subject is an important decision that takes you one step closer to your career. If you choose Economics when the love of your life is Literature, all is not lost. You can get into a writing career with Economics as the focus. If you want to be a doctor and you get a rank in the All India Medical Entrance that qualifies you to join Veterinary College, think long and hard. Treating animals and treating humans are two unique professions. One is never a substitute for another.

If you are dissatisfied and do not think you have a qualified veterinarian in you, wait another year and rewrite your entrance test. Never make a hasty decision to please your parents or to keep up with your friends. Time is too valuable to lose – it is better to study for one or two more years to get the subject of your choice than to dedicate an entire degree course to a subject you dislike.

YOUR PARENTS

Things are changing. Nowadays youngsters in urban areas have more freedom to opt for careers of their choice. While initially there was stigma about careers in fashion designing or performing arts like dance, now parents are much more open and even encouraging about alternate career choices.

In the movie *3 Idiots*, you saw how the character Farhan (actor Madhavan) became a photographer in the end. His father forgives him once he understands how badly his son wants to clicks pictures for a living. The problem that Farhan faced the most was that he was trying to please his father. He never tried to communicate with his father about his dreams. The generation gap goes both ways. Why don't you try being more honest with your parents? Tell them what matters to you. Articulate your ideas with clarity.

Very often students blame their parents and grandparents for being regressive and backward. Think about the time they grew up in - it was a time before mobile phones and Google. It was a time when they respected their elders and did not question decisions that were made. It is your responsible attitude that can change their attitude. If you waste your time and take life too casually, you cannot expect their cooperation.

But I feel more comfortable talking to my friends.

That's what most of you feel. Life would be much easier if you communicate with your parents. Keep them informed about your choices. Why don't you want to be a doctor or an engineer like they tell you to? Is the option that you have practical? If you want to be an animator, understand what minimum qualifications and skills you need to pursue this as a career.

My parents are too strict. They don't understand me.

Why are they so strict? Have you broken their trust at any time? Is your family background more conservative? If your calling is so strong, then take all this opposition as a challenge.

There is the story of a boy who was beaten black and blue as a child because all he loved to do was to watch mimics and clowns performing in street corners. He faced a great deal of poverty and hardship. Today he is a famous comedian. He went against all obstacles and fought for his love.

Sometimes you have to fight for your career, if you are sure about what you want.

My family is too poor. What's the point of dreaming big?

The only way you can lift yourself out of poverty is by getting into the work force. You may be poor financially, but you can be rich in dreams. Take the course that is most affordable and try to avail of scholarships and grants. There are many opportunities for economically depressed people but what is needed is extreme hard work and awareness. You also need a mentor – someone who can guide you. Explain to your parents how important it is that you get an education and a career. Whether you are male or female, you must be financially independent.

I studied in a rural school. My parents don't think I can cope with studies in a good college.

If you believe in yourself, half the battle is won. You may face the hurdles of communication problems as students who have studied in rural areas may not always have good language skill sets. This could be a barrier when you listen to lectures or try to communicate with urban students. But language skills are very easy to pick up. Look at the resources around you – watching English programmes on TV and listening to the news on the radio can perk up your skills faster. This book will help you tackle many of your communication skill issues. But you have to believe in yourself first, then your parents will.

Do your parents encourage you?

_____

_____

If they do, consider yourself lucky and take advantage of their support. Do not expect your parents to make decisions for you – you have to scout for details about careers and new courses. You can expect your parents to support you but they cannot spoon-feed you all the way to your job desk.

YOUR CIRCUMSTANCES

Each of us is a product of our circumstances. This means that you are born into a family from a certain community with certain resources. You may be from the creamy layer or you may be from a family that has struggled a great deal to get you a good education. Once you get to college, your attitude will get you into the circumstance that you desire. Consistent hard work and focus give you the grades you need to compete as a level player in the field.

What kind of family do you come from – upper class upper - middle class lower - middle class?

_____

_____

Is your income badly needed to supplement the family income?

_____

_____

Your circumstances are a barometer of how much you really want to succeed. "Lots of success stories come from villages. Not a good example. Not too sure but I think they were robbers on somethin in the movie shouldn't give such ideas to young minds!"

If your circumstances are bad, it is in your power to make them better. If money is a huge problem, then don't think twice about working. Make the money first and gradually aim to achieve your specific career goals. Nowadays students have many part - time opportunities. They double as students, receptionists, BPO trainees, and sales reps. These kinds of efforts translate into **experience** – the most useful word when it comes to getting hired in a company of your choice.

YOUR MOTIVATION

You might have heard of **Maslow's Hierarchy of Needs Pyramid** – a triangle that explains human priorities. The basic priorities start at the bottom – self-actualization happens from the bottom up.

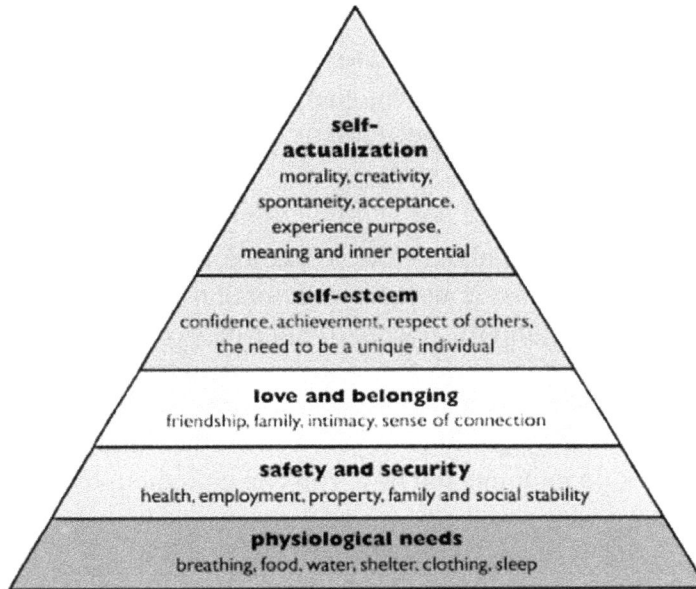

As a young student you have to focus on your basic needs first. Your parents may support you but the first step towards achieving your goals is being financially independent. The rest of the pyramid deals with all your other priorities in life – relationships, health, and creativity.

Being independent gives you a much stronger ability to make crucial decisions. Then you can gradually move in the direction where your motivations lie.

Find out what motivates you and work towards it. Even if it is a hobby, eventually you could become a professional. Anil has a convenient job in Abu Dhabi - he works as an accountant for a reasonably good firm. After his B.Com, he struggled a great deal to get a job and when he finally got an offer letter he did not turn it down. He followed Maslow's law - he wanted to be financially independent. Now he has the financial security and confidence to take his creativity seriously. He has enrolled in a photography course. He is even thinking of turning it into a profession.

Creativity does not have to take a back seat. If creativity is as basic to you as food and water, then enroll in a course in design, visual arts, or the performing arts. Be serious about your craft and your craft will take you seriously.

What motivates you? Is it creativity, money, family, or rank?

_____

_____

Knowing who you love, what you love, and where you want to be, gives you a **Career Vision**. Again these are not permanent – changing circumstances lead to new motivation. Keep examining your goals and what excites you. Make your decisions based on your analysis.

YOUR PERSONALITY

Identifying who you are is also about how you come across. Revisit your college life and ask yourself some questions about your participation or non-participation in various aspects of college life. Knowing the degree of your involvement helps you understand your own preferences. When you look for a job, you must try to find a place for yourself where you will feel needed and where you will learn. Before you start scouting the papers or the internet for the right kind of job, know what kind of skills you have, the skills you should work on gaining, and how you can gain them by taking specific steps to achieve them.

Are you likeable?

_____

_____

How do you come across to other people…do you give out positive or negative vibes? The way someone else behaves with you is a clue about what kind of relationship they wish to maintain with you.

Every person you meet is an opportunity. So smile and be yourself!

Your Likeability Quotient

Are you open while talking to people or do you prefer to stay aloof or apart? Why?

_____

_____

_____

_____

It's no use being a rank holder, if you can't show it. If you keep to yourself, you will miss out on so many opportunities. A corporate career requires you to have good networking skills. Stop staying away and get involved. Don't care about being rejected or accepted. Just step in and gradually you will be accepted.

What kind of ideas and interests can you relate to?

_____

_____

_____

Figure out what interests you. Is it creative things like arts and music? Are you more goal oriented and keen on entrepreneurship? Do you read? Do you like gaming? If you know what interests you, it is easier to match your career with your interests. If you have like-minded friends, it helps you develop your speaking skills when it comes to your interests. Discussion is a healthy way of learning new things and new ways of expressing yourself.

What kinds of reactions do you have towards people with issues or problems? Why?

_____

_____

_____

Knowing how you react to difficult situations enables you to deal with potential challenges in the future. Do you get frustrated, angry and tense – worst of all do you show it?

Are you artificial when you talk to people or are you real?

_____

_____

_____

If you are artificial, then that means you have to work on feeling comfortable wherever you go. Be yourself. Don't get too tense if you are going for an interview. That makes you artificial and you will be judged for a character that is not your real one but a mask!

Being likeable is about spreading out your interest base. Do you know that people who have denser social networks have more grey matter in their brain? It's scientifically proven. This means to have friends you also have to be smart. Your interests should be wide and you should be willing to enthusiastically exchange ideas about any subject. You should also have *empathy*. Having empathy means you are able to understand the other person. That is an important part of making friends and making impressions. When you go for your group discussion, instead of being scared of other candidates, befriend them and understand them. This will make you calmer.

Being likeable helps you a great deal even when you enter corporate life. Important decisions your bosses make are sometimes based on how far you come across as likeable to the entire team. Understand that before you go to office.

YOUR EXPERIENCE

What kind of academic and work-oriented experience have you gained on campus?

_____

_____

_____

Campus life is an explosion of experience. College gives you a whole range of subject-related acumen and communication skills as well. Capitalise on it…what I mean to say is **make the most of it!**

Which job-based skills have you gained?

_____

_____

_____

_____

Every moment you have spent in college has been an opportunity to grow. It is not the size and prestige of the institution that matters. What matters is your level of enthusiasm. Did you take advantage of the competitions that were hosted there? Did you do complete justice to your assignments? Did you go on the college tour? What about friendship – did you have many good friends?

College is a place where you learn so many things about yourself. Being there gives you a sense of **identity**. *It's a time of self-discovery.*

SO ARE YOU A BRAND?

The saying goes that you have three seconds to make an impression on your interviewer or even at a gathering, as much time as a customer needs to gauge a product. If you want to reinvent yourself or change in a positive sense, there is no harm in imagining that you are a product in a supermarket. A customer heads your way and looks at you, thinking whether or not to invest time and money on you. The customer mentally asks these questions:

Is this the best one on the rack?

Why would anyone choose this?

What makes this product stand out?

Will this product have any value once I purchase it?

So many things go into making any product – be it a boring thing like a lighter or

initially that you are all raw material. What you need is a lot of polishing and proper packaging to create the desirable outcome.

Being able to package your strengths into three seconds (or to be fair ten minutes) involves a lot of preparation. The preparation must continue throughout your work life. Job hunting becomes successful if you make the right kind of presentation. To sustain

minimized.

Rohan hasn't got his degree yet. He does the night shift at a call centre. He gets a call for an interview from one of the best BPOs in the vicinity. Rohan is the kind of guy who wants to get ahead in his life. He knows how important money is and how much

good grades.

It's because he couldn't play *dumb charades*.

"What do you mean?" you'll ask. *Dumb charades is just a pointless game*. Someone says the name of a movie and the other acts it out. It's a great way to kill time.

But this game is a test of nerves - it speaks about how you relate to other people, something very important when you need to get a job, pass an interview, and stay on in a company where you have to get your message across on a daily basis. If you can emote or show your emotions when you stand before your classmates, your worst critics, it means you are comfortable about who you are. It means you have the right body language.

It means you have the X-factor.

X-FACTOR

This term is used a lot these days in reality shows. Why do some people make it big while others don't? Some call it luck. Some call it destiny. Others call it the "X" Factor.

A good recruiter's experience: "What we look for the most today is a **can-do** attitude. There is no time to deal with people who are not equipped to deal with stress. I'll give you an example. Once I asked a fresher during campus recruitment to describe herself in one word."

"Genuine," she said.

Of course, she got the job.

Fresher Shoot

I don't like the idea of being a brand. Then how can I sell myself?

Why do you use certain brands more than others? Some quality of the brand attracts you and makes you want to dig deeper into your pockets to purchase it. Brand equals value. When I tell you to see yourself as **Brand You**, what I mean is that you must always represent yourself in the best possible way. Your value as a brand comes across in everything that you do and the personality that you are made of.

Imagine you are a vegetable seller. You sell your vegetables to the poorest woman and the richest, most sophisticated woman. Your product is the same. The only thing is that you have to present it differently to both kinds of clients. You are the same person - you have to effectively package yourself to different people in different situations.

The bottom line is that people have to have the same belief that you have in you. How much do you believe in yourself? If you can't answer that question, then start believing in what you do and what you aim to achieve. Your conviction is what others make of you.

To a certain extent, you are responsible for how you are judged, particularly when it comes to interviews and the work place. You have got to get people to trust you. If you keep yourself at a distance by your posture or lack of eye contact or nervous voice, your interviewer will not get a positive enough signal from you. You end up selling yourself short.

Being a brand means being true to yourself and to the work that you do. Then success is not far behind!

How do I know about Brand Me?

Take a cue from people around you. Your parents may tend to over estimate or under estimate you. But their judgement can be very valuable.

You could learn about yourself from your lecturers. They can mould you if you are willing to learn from them. Some lecturers can give you a sense of worth or maybe appreciate your efforts. By paying attention to them, you may be able to find out what kind of career choice you want to make and get a sense of positive appreciation from them about your efforts.

You can also learn about Brand You from your friends. They tell you when you are shabbily dressed or when you are emotionally stressed. They appreciate you when you have achieved something. Their belief in you can help you move forward in so many ways. If you are straying from the path, a good friend always warns you.

Even your worst critic is valuable. The feedback you get from this unpleasant source helps you the most as someone who doesn't like you tells you what you don't want to hear, but what can help you grow.

When you go for an interview, you get feedback on your **Brand Quotient**. Remember that every product has its defects and the challenge that every manufacturer faces is modifying the product and improving brand value. Companies invest so many resources to perfect their brands. You must invest in yourself as well.

I am what I am. How can I improve myself?

You are special, no doubt about it. But when you want to enter the job market, you will have to make small changes in every aspect of your behaviour, look and attitude. This book aims to help you sort out what those changes are and how you can do it. Each student will have to focus on various aspects of change.

BEFORE THE CAREER PLAN

When you plan to have a career, you are investing in yourself. Money has been invested in your education, so your parents are shareholders in your success. You invest your time in your school and college education. You have already begun to lay the foundations of your future.

Get organised. Making a career is all about taking steps to reach the place where you have the most skills and you are most comfortable in. You did the Assessment tests in Section 1. You have an idea now about where you want to go and what kind of person you are. You understand how your expectations can be different from those of your family or the people around you. You have also learnt how important it is to change to achieve your own goals.

Now what you need to do is create a plan. In order to create a blueprint, you need to know a couple of things about what you are looking for in a career.

How soon do you want to get a job?

_____

_____

Time and career matters are closely linked. If you are in your final year of college, you have time to prepare yourself meticulously. If you need the job in a month, then you will have to speed up the whole process. Advisably, take your time and do things as correctly as you can. Don't worry if you goof up – learning is all about goofing up!

Does your family depend on you for your income?

_____

_____

It's one thing to be idealistic. It's another to really need the money to run the house. Never be a burden on the family if you have the education. Try in your best capacity to help your family by using your education. No easy money please! Be serious about your ambition to make money and there is enough opportunity today to earn good salaries.

Can you adjust with people from any culture or do you prefer people belonging to your own community?

_____

_____

When you work in the corporate sphere, you will interact with people from all over India and even the world. It may be a culture shock for you in the beginning, especially if you are from a small town. But just think of the contestants who compete on programmes like _Indian idol_ and _Dance India Dance_. They go to any length to participate in programmes where their talent can get noticed.

If you are deeply committed to getting a good job, it does not matter who you interact with as long as you can learn positive things from your new friends. You can be global and local at the same time these days!

Are you comfortable commuting for the job or are you limiting yourself to nearby options?

_____

_____

These questions help you narrow down your job search options. Some students like to travel and are encouraged to learn new things in new places. Others will be discouraged. Take the job that is convenient. This is best left to you.

See how many things go into making a career? A career means different things to different people – for some it is about achieving a dream, for others it is about having enough security to run a household, for some it is all about the prestige of working for a particular company, for many others it is all about the most convenient learning experience. What goes into your career choice? Write it down. You can choose from the options below or come up with your own options.

Travelling comfort , Ambience of office, Salary and perks, Improving learning curve

_____

_____

All options are important. Even if you don't think so, a job is not just a job. You build most of your life around office once you get employed. You wake up early and commute to office. You have your meals there and spend a great deal of time in the office. You meet colleagues and even make friends. You come home and prepare again for the next day.

So much of your life revolves around office – unlike college when you had the option to cut classes and even take an extra day off. Since you spend so much time there, you have to see your job as something more than just money, travel, and perks. It is a career and you have invested yourself into it. So you have to pick the right one and make the most of the opportunity. So the option **learning curve** is important as all the fun lies in learning and not the routine.

FRESHER SHOOT

Everyone can't be a brand. Why should I try?

Branding means perfecting yourself – if you can become even 45% better, why not give it a shot if it will help your career?

Let's have a look at a student called Deep. Deep is nervous as hell. He wants to change but he can't. He's frozen in front of crowds. His solution is to avoid crowds at any cost. If Deep wants to get a job, he'll have to loosen up a bit. Imagine how he will feel when he is no longer afraid to speak! It's a much nicer feeling than the feeling of being left out and afraid.

Deep can achieve this by making a few sacrifices on his part. In order to achieve his career goal, he will have to spend some time learning how to overcome his fears. We will get into dealing with fear in a little more detail later on in the book. Nowadays ample help is available in the form of books, mentors, CDs, tutorials, counselors, etc.

The question is will Deep be willing to go the extra mile to solve his own problems? Negative emotions like fear, laziness, and anger can be tackled only with whole-hearted focus on your part. Your book or guide can show you the way up to a point. Ultimately, the child must walk alone.

Will you work on your problems? Will you admit that you have a problem with your English (if you really do) and try to solve it? Or will you say Chalta hai, I will pass no matter what.

Pass mark is not good enough. To ace an interview, you have to excel.

CAREER PLAN

When you decide to get a job, you have to work on yourself first. Understand your aptitude and get the qualifications that the job of your choice requires. Students normally get into the course that they like or that they have the cut-off marks to get into. If you work backwards, from the job of your choice, you will see that if you have the right qualifications and the right skill sets, then getting the job of your choice is easy.

A soldier trains himself for combat. When he is ready he enters the field – he is ready to lead only once he has enough experience. The same goes for the corporate warrior who must discipline himself or herself and sharpen all existing skills and gain desirable skill sets before she or he enters the corporate arena.

The soldier is willing to make sacrifices.

This stage of your life is called **Preparation**.

So get the

★ Qualifications

★ Skill sets

★ Exposure to the job market

★ Confidence

JOB MARKET: AN INTRODUCTION

Now you have an idea about where you are and the possibilities that lie ahead if you work on your strengths and cut down your weaknesses. You must be aware of your own potential and also the job market. Many freshers today are confident and capable but where they lag the most is their knowledge of market expectations. Fine-.tuning yourself to the demand around you is the only way you can become a part of that market.

Where are the jobs that you are looking for? There are jobs spread out in the public and private sector.

★ In the public sector, jobs are available in the Defence, Education, Healthcare, Oil and Gas sector, and Banking. It is hard for entry level candidates though.

★ Private sector jobs have many options besides engineering and health care. Choices span across Information Technology, Manufacturing, Finance, Hospitality, Education, Real Estate, and Media.

Do you know what kind of jobs are available for the subject that you are pursuing a degree in? Write down the specific job titles if you know any.

_____

_____

_____

If you haven't started looking already, time to start thinking on these lines. Today education is equal to a job. You may love the subject but all the money that you invest in a course is usually with a purpose in mind. Your course should help you live an independent life. So start zeroing in on the kinds of job roles that suit your subject.

What is the main subject you have opted for?

_____

_____

What are your secondary subjects?

_____

_____

Look at this table and see what career choices match your subject choice.

English: Copy writing, content writing, technical writing, editing, teaching, publishing, media (journalism – print, radio, TV), dramatics

History: Civil services, archaeology, anthropology, restoration and conservation, teaching, writing

Sociology: Social work, special education, teaching, research

Economics: Banking, chartered accountancy, cost accountancy, chartered financial analysis, foreign trade, law

Psychology: Counseling, management, teaching, special education, public relations

Commerce: Business management, banking, chartered accountancy, statistics, operational research, foreign trade

Physics, Chemistry, Mathematics: Engineering, computers, architecture, construction, civil aviation, armed forces, agriculture, food processing, leather technology, footwear technology, plastics, packaging, gemology, meteorology, astrophysics, mining and metallurgy, oceanography, pharmaceuticals

Physics, Chemistry, Zoology/Biology: Medicine, dentistry, veterinary science, paramedical services, nursing, traditional medicine, biotechnology, genetics, food processing, dairy farming, agriculture, poultry, horticulture, aquaculture, marine biology, environmental sciences

Physics, Chemistry, Computer Science: Information technology, multimedia, engineering, industrial design

Political Science: International relations, politics, law, journalism, social work

Do you follow the job market? If you do, how? If not, why?

_____

_____

_____

Well, it's not too late to start. Following the job market is as simple as keeping your senses alert for any new opportunities that connect with your skill sets. This is where you can use the media including newspapers and the internet.

CAREER EXPECTATIONS

Now you have an idea about who you are, what kind of skills sets you have, the kind of job on your mind, and where to look for it. Once you figure out these things, you have to chart out a plan for your future.

Now where do you see yourself five years from now?

_____

_____

_____

_____

I have already asked you this question. But now you will have a better answer since you can match your subject with the career option available. Having a long term idea about how you like to spend your time and what your goals are, makes short term planning easier.

You must move step by step towards the greater goal. When a company employer asks you this question, you will have to modify your answer a bit and talk about a more challenging role. You don't discuss all your personal ambitions during an interview – you follow a **script** that works.

What do you want to achieve in the next six months?

_____

_____

_____

_____

Short-term goals should help you achieve your long term goals. Right now you want to get a job! Everything you do now should move towards achieving this goal.

No plan is foolproof and goals keep changing but if you are able to set some kind of guidelines, you will have more realistic expectations and you can chalk out an exact method to work towards it. By knowing what you want to achieve, you are creating sign posts that help you move forward. To achieve your dreams, you must know your dreams first.

FRESHER SHOOT

What should I expect from work?

_____

_____

All of us have great expectations from the job that we do. It is good to be enthusiastic but you should also be realistic. College life is full of fun and fests. The real world is about challenges and adapting yourself.

Why should I change for others?

_____

_____

Change is natural. In college, you had a different set of realities to deal with. When you work, you have a new set of rules. It is easier to adjust if you are open to change.

I don't like working under anyone. How can I do it?

_____

_____

Unfortunately all jobs require you to work under someone. Be constructive about it. Some day you may be heading your team. You can learn a lot from your employer about how the company works and it is those tips that will help you lead when the time comes.

My boss should be cool, right?

It would make sense if you keep your cool instead. You may not meet the ideal boss, just the way we can't choose our lecturers in college.

I want the best pay. What should I do?

That's far too ambitious. You have just started your job search and already you want to be a millionaire? That's what I mean when I say be practical.

I don't like work pressure - How do I tackle that?

You didn't like exam pressure either, did you? If you are being paid, there are bound to be expectations. Yes, you will have to be punctual. Yes, you will be asked why you logged out early. Remember when you start out, you follow the company's terms.

Won't my salary go up every year?

That's not for you to decide. You've just started out. When you build your career, what's more important is what your resume looks like. Is your job productive when it comes to increasing your skills and improving your personality? If the answer is yes, try to stick to it.

I get bored easily - How can I stick to my job?

If you keep jumping jobs, your resume will not be impressive. Future interviews will pose the uncomfortable question 'Why do you keep changing jobs?' Stop boredom with focus.

Career Boosters

The question you really have to ask yourself is how good you can get. What are the areas you need to deal with to become the ideal candidate?

Be ready to be rejected

Are you afraid of rejection? Does being rejected make you angry?

You could be rejected on your first interview. Analyse why. Many times, you will know the reason. If it has to do with lack of confidence or poor communication skills, these can be fixed. Just because you are rejected by one company, it doesn't mean that success will not come your way. Every failure is a lesson.

Work hard, and then work harder.

There is really no substitute for hard work. When you are looking for a job, you are organisational goals. In order to sell yourself, you have to work hard on improving all

to face the panel. Focus on your positives. If you are a good student, try to score the maximum grades to get your resume noticed.

Become a You Manager

Use your time management skills and organizational skills to the maximum. Plan how you will improve your learning curve. If you read about achievers, you sometimes wonder how they were able to achieve so many things in such a short span of time. The reason is because they were completely focused and dedicated to their work.

Believe in Yourself

Think about all the people who believe in you. Everyone has in them a special potential.

rejection are part of the game. Know when to stop making the same mistakes and carry on with your head held high. Communicate well, create a good resume and impress the

---

Recap

Find your SWOT- Strength, Weaknesses, Opportunities and Threats.

Find out about your Priorities, Expectations others have of you, Motivation, Circumstances, etc.

Create a Brand, 'You'; make a Career Plan and Think Ahead.

SECTION 3
GROOM YOURSELF

1. Polish your Skill-sets or Growing wings
2. Will your Skills
3. Kill your Demons with your Skills

PART A: Basic Skills

a. Comprehension Skills
b. Study Skills
   The Study Process
   Job Connect
c. Participatory Skills
d. Management Skills
   Good Organiser
   Good Time Manager
   Good Stress Manager
e. Computer Skills

PART B:

1. Communication: Verbal and Written Skills
   What is Communication?
   5-Step Immersion Course
   Fix your Communication Skills
      Verbal Skills

POLISH YOUR SKILL-SETS OR GROWING WINGS

Once there was an art historian, who came across an entire room's worth of ignored brass utensils, ancient swords, and coins. The antiques were in a dingy room covered in cobwebs. These trophies were part of a family heirloom and after they were polished and restored the antiques became extremely valuable, and assets worthy of being part of a heritage museum.

Your skills are your trophies. You know what you are naturally good at-you may have a knack at making friends, you may be good with children, you may be good

whatever you are good at is wasted if not put to use.

How do you use your skills? You use opportunities of course. Don't miss an opportunity to do what you are good at. No matter what the circumstances, you have to follow your skill, otherwise it will be lost in a dingy room covered with cobwebs.

You must not just use your skills - you must perfect them. Human beings are capable of perfecting their skills to a high degree. A singer does riyaz, a player practises, a writer writes. To increase expertise, continuous practice is essential. The best actors have been in the industry for years together. Didn't we all see Vidya Balan, National Award winner, talk about her road to success? She was rejected several times before she could succeed. Why she is successful today is because she polished her acting skills even when she was rejected.

you are unsuited to the role or that the competition is stiff. This should not stop you from investing in yourself, because *under every inexperienced fresher is a competent successful individual. Believe that.*

WILL YOUR SKILLS

Skills just don't exist in some people. You must be thinking that a successful person is lucky or more talented than you are. The truth is far from this.

You've seen how the actor Jacki Chan trains his student in *Karate Kid 2*. The boy is asked to do the same thing a million times. He doesn't understand why until his master shows him that the same movements can be used to defend himself.

Skill is the result of a lot of hard work. If you are a good painter, you can become a better painter only if you give more time, dedicated study, and practice to your art. Van Gogh was an obsessive painter - he painted all the time, even when the sun beat down on him and he was prone to epilepsy, he would take his easel and paint. The same goes for writing, accounting, sales, or marketing. Every professional who has experience has gained skills through the number of productive hours that she or he has put into the job. Don't believe that?

How productive do you think you are?

_____

_____

_____

_____

I said *productive*.

You could be sitting at your desk for three hours and trying to study, with the sound of the television in the background, a pair of earphones blasting music, and a cell phone that keeps you updated on your friend's latest texts and their current Facebook status. Do you call that studying?

I wouldn't. To polish skills, you need **Focus**. It's your life we're talking about and polishing your skills can help you make a mark in whichever industry you choose. All of the world's most talented professionals and creative thinkers have started from the bottom. What makes them different from the average person is that they have worked doubly hard for their success.

Always remember it is not only luck, but also your effort that can make you crack the job market. Many skills add up to make you a better candidate and a more efficient person. Remember, various components make a whole.

_____

Fresher Shoot

I have what it takes and I know what I want. What is the most important skill I must polish to get there?

Whatever field you may be in – sales, accounts, finance, design, hospitality, health, media, let's face it, we need good **communication skills**.

You may be a good conversationalist but you may not know when it's best to keep your mouth shut. You may be good at face-to-face meetings but helpless when it comes to writing an email. Again, you may be very good at making presentations but lousy at putting together a good business letter. Oral, listening, comprehension, and written skills are intertwined or connected.

Companies are now looking more and more for people who have the kind of mindset, skill sets, and tone of voice that can convince a customer - they are looking for people with a certain style. Take for instance a BPO - the place where most of you will probably get your first experience certificate. A BPO is like a communication factory. Here communication is the skill set that you need most - you must know how to talk, particularly talk on the telephone. You will probably have to deal with over 50 to 75 calls in an hour.

A lot of employee time is also dedicated to meetings. Here again communication is important; otherwise those meetings will turn into unproductive day-dreaming exercises. What is the mark of a good contributor in a meeting? A good contributor always gets noticed by decision makers for great verbal skills, excellent judgement, attention, and homework done on the subject. Along with communication skills, the employee should know when to speak and to whom. Being distracted during a meeting means that you are wasting your time and everyone else's. Always be prepared. An unprepared employee will have nothing useful to contribute to a meeting.

Work culture today requires what has been described as 'verbal hygiene' - clear, efficient, and decent articulation of language. These skills have their written counterparts in writing and the electronic media.

Communication is not just about being perfect. It also requires enthusiasm and the ability to convey excitement about what you do.

Suppose a salesman came to sell products - he looks aggressive and he orders you to buy the product. You would just slam the door on his face - you will mimic his aggressiveness and react by rejecting him. If the same salesman comes to your door with a smile and positive body language, reflected in his facial muscles, tone and body language, you will consider buying the product.

It is a performance that is expected of the salesman, nothing less. The same goes for you, the potential employee.

Haven't you seen how some companies have a good rapport with the customer? Customers are made to feel good when they enter certain hotels or supermarkets. When you join a company, you are expected to represent the company ethos and please your customers or clients. You will be trained to inculcate a certain kind of work ethic. The faster you are able to pick up these skills, the easier it will be to adjust in your new workspace.

Besides communication, you need a whole bunch of other skills to become a success. We will be looking at these as we progress in the book.

KILL YOUR DEMONS WITH YOUR SKILLS

Here are some skill sets we will examine. For your convenience I have divided skill sets into three broad sections. The first section deals with essential skill sets in college and at work. These skills are important in all stages of your life. Once you acquire them, you will be more confident to face the corporate world once you are out of college.

The second section deals with communication in its verbal aspect - both written and spoken. Another aspect that is touched on is body language.

In the final part of this section, we deal with grooming in looks, voice, presentation, and perspective.

You can create test-based skills with practice. You can also create oral and written skills by polishing the grammar you are already familiar with from the high school level. The fundamental rule is to have good social behaviour, clear correct pronunciation, and clear direct writing skills. For that you have to know a bit of where you could go wrong in pronunciation and how you can correct it, and a little bit of grammar so that you can write in a clear manner. Fundamental computer skills are mandatory and don't forget your GK - 'general knowledge'. You need a little bit of grooming and must be polite at all times. All these skills turn you into a perfect fit for any company. It's up to you now to have the will to learn.

Let's examine each skill step by step. This section is important as it helps you work more on your strengths and weaknesses.

a. Comprehension Skills

By comprehension, I mean the art of understanding. Communication is a continuous cycle – the sender sends out messages, which the target receives and analyzes. If there is no understanding, then communication has not taken place.

A student with no knowledge of English sits in class day after day – he becomes disillusioned and regrets taking the course. He forgets that he was selected because of his merit – so the potential is there. What is lacking is the ability to understand.

The hardest part for a fresher in the corporate space is to understand what is expected of him or her. You have to be patient.

Let's see how much you can understand. Listening doesn't mean you have followed every word. There are times when you may have sat through eighteen classes of English. In spite of your presence in the class, you are unable to write a proper essay on one chapter that has been explained. Why is that? Is it because you are **physically present and mentally absent**? Or is it because you have a **problem understanding what is being taught?**

Do you understand what your lecturers say in class?

_____

_____

Analyze why you follow certain lecturers and not others. Are you more interested in body language or content? Try to pick up clues about how you can improve your behaviour and accent from lecturers you admire. Watch how attentive you are in class. If your focus is bad, then you can expect the same lack of clarity at work as well.

_____

_____

If you don't particularly enjoy a subject, you can rule out any career option with that

subject. If you hate math, no need of considering a career in finance! It is an opportunity to narrow down your choices.

Identify why you find those subjects difficult. Is it because you don't know the basics, or you are unable to follow the lecturer, or you are plain not interested?

_____

_____

Whatever the reason, make an effort to score well in the subject as your scorecard should not reveal that you are very weak in any subject. Poor marks mean that you are not up to the challenge.

Sometimes you dislike the subject for the simple reason that you do not like the lecturer. You should not allow your personal likes and dislikes to influence your love for the subject.

If you are not interested in the subject at all, it is never too late to think of changing your stream. Don't wait until after your post graduation to make new choices.

Are you able to convey your ideas well? Says who?

_____

_____

Maybe your friends say you are terrific at something. Don't get too excited though! The corporate space is extremely competitive and you are constantly trying to prove yourself there. You may not please everyone but that's okay as long as you are good at what you do. Once you shift out of college, you will realize that existing standards are way higher than you imagined. So learn about new standards and then compete. Change is the only way ahead.

Can lecturers understand your essays and your conversations?

_____

_____

Here I mean your English lecturer. If your lecturer is highly critical of your work and speech, it is high time to work on perfecting your English skills. Once you are told about your problem areas, try to fix them immediately instead of postponing the change. Criticism is an opportunity to improve.

Why can't you answer questions when asked?

_____

_____

_____

Sometimes in class a student is asked questions and there is a long silence. Maybe the student doesn't know the answer or maybe she or he didn't get the question.

If you don't follow the question, you could request for some time to think of a good answer.

Contestants for the Miss India Contest sometimes ask their judges to repeat the question just so that they can come up with an impressive answer.

Fresher Shoot

What should I understand before I go corporate?

Understanding involves so many different aspects. It can get a little complicated. Getting through an interview is really an exercise in comprehension. As a student you have to **understand different accents, ideas, and modes of questioning.**

You must also **understand the corporate world** around you – how does it work? What problems exist? What solutions can you come up with? Once you begin to

people in the corporate space.

Understanding also involves having enough communication skills to follow concepts and explanation. **Understanding body language** is as important as understanding verbal language. Slight variations in tone, voice, and rhythm can convey different meanings. To understand this, you have to develop awareness and sharpen observation skills.

b. Study Skills

At college, you are able to zero in on the kind of study skills that you have. At school, you are guided by your

the degree level, you gain a lot of freedom when it comes

can perfect your study method. All students do not necessarily respond well to the chalk and talk method used in many schools. Remember a degree is just a beginning as far as academics go – this is the best time to find your interest and how you can pursue it.

How do you usually study for an exam or test? Why?

Last minute   Day-to-day basis   Study in class itself   Have great memory, don't need to mug up

_____

_____

_____

_____

Usually college goers joke about how studies are pushed to the last minute. *We will pass Ma'am* is a regular response. Of course you will pass. The question is *Are corporates/ offices okay with just pass*? If your communication skills are raw and you have limited or zero experience, your mark list is your only asset. Why kill it with complacency or *chaltha hai* attitude?

What is your opinion about studies in general?

I'm studying to get a job   I'm studying because I love my subject   Boring

_____

_____

_____

_____

Remember how you assessed what you liked and disliked. If you like mountain climbing, no matter how hard it is, no matter how many sacrifices you make and risks you take, you will enjoy every minute of your climb. When George Mallory, a famous mountaineer was asked why he climbed mountains, he simply said "Because it's there."

It is important to know *why you study*. This gives you much more clarity about why you have joined the course and how you plan to use your scores. Are you doing the course for yourself or for your parents? Do you enjoy what you learn? If you don't, you will find it hard to understand it as well. Then you cannot excel.

Studying is not boring if it's a mountain you want to climb. You have to try studying in an interesting and creative way. If you think about it, cricket is just a game – but why have players like Sachin Tendulkar made the game what it is today? They have been playing the same game for years together, making thousands of runs and breaking records. *Kaha cricket or kaha padai*? You will say.

Anything done with dedication becomes worth the trouble.

The Study Process

What kind of learner are you?

Visual (watch and learn)   Auditory (good at listening)   Kinesthetic (spatial and doers)

_____

_____

_____

_____

The reason that you may be finding it hard to cope with studies is because you are still not sure about what kind of learner you are.

★   A visual learner is more comfortable with presentations and reading.

★   An auditory learner does well by being attentive in class.

★   A kinesthetic learner is more in tune with the practical aspects of learning. There are students who do well in the practical aspect of science as compared to the theoretical aspect.

Once you identify what kind of learning method suits you, the learning process becomes easier. If you keep studying using a method that does not suit you, you waste a lot of valuable time. Even when you join office, you have to employ the best way to achieve the right results quicker.

Do you take guidance and make use of the resources (however limited) that your college provides?

_____

_____

_____

_____

Most of your lecturers will be happy to help, provided you show interest and clear your doubts when required; maybe, they have suggestions that could help you find the right course or job. If you show a general lack of interest, you cannot expect your lecturer to inspire you. Teaching is a two-way process. You give the lecturer respect and your attention, and they will compensate you in return. If you are distracted and disinterested, do not expect quality education. Quality comes only when both sides respect each other and listen.

Do you use the library in your college? If not, why? If you can't use your college library, try registering yourself in any lending library in your town. Reading as many books and magazines as you can will change the way you approach learning. Remember how enthusiastic you were about learning when you were a child? Children are naturally curious. As you grow older, you figure the easy way out and lose interest in knowledge building. Seeking knowledge is the most important skill that mankind has; if you have the necessary foundations, money will automatically follow.

The same precepts work wonders in the office as well. Instead of criticising your boss and infrastructure, try to make the most of the time you spend at the work place. If you treat every job opportunity as a personal adventure where you stand to gain, then you will make that extra effort to succeed.

Are you better off doing group study or studying solo (on your own)?

_____

_____

_____

_____

Sometimes group study is a great way of doing a bit of teamwork and making the entire study process more fun. It is advisable to follow the method that works best for you. Group study works for some, not all. Doing a reasonable balance of both kinds of study will make learning a less boring and more stimulating exercise.

Job Connect

Why have you opted for the particular stream you are in?

Everyone did it   I like the subject   It's a money-making subject   I had no choice

_____

_____

_____

The point is are you studying this particular course for any valid reason? If you are then you have a definitive goal to achieve and it is easier for you to focus. It is when you are not convinced about why you have opted for the course that you become confused and aimless. That makes you less motivated and automatically you will not try extra hard to make your resume more interesting. So start getting convinced about the subject you have chosen and if you are not, why not rethink your choices and act accordingly?

Did you do research/read extensively on the subject before you chose it?

_____

_____

_____

Some students mistake Communicative English for Optional English. When they start making sense of Phonetics, Print Media, and Film Making, they are shocked. "This is not English"! they say and some of them even regret taking a course that needs a high degree of creativity and strong English skills.

Make sure you have done your share of research on the course syllabus before you enroll for it. The Internet is a good place to search for course material. You could also read up on the subject so that you develop a strong foundation and knowledge of the theoretical aspects.

Did you seek advice from people who have majored in that subject to understand career options?

_____

_____

_____

You must learn to clear doubts and find out information. It's like going for a party that no one invited you to. Why do you want to walk into a room full of strangers, and even if you do, can you make the most of gatecrashing or will it be an exercise in embarrassment?

"I didn't even know why I took Commerce until I realized later that I had a natural business acumen." says Hafsa, a Commerce student in her final year. Hafsa is lucky.

Before you opt for your core subject, you should know if your interests match your choice. If your heart is in medicine and you opt for dentistry just because that is the only seat available, you are wasting your time.

Good scores = Good job. True or False? Why?

_____

_____

_____

_____

Well it depends on how you scored. Do you know what your subject is about or have you scored marks by mugging up? Marks are an indication that you have a strong foundation. Marks measure how much time you have invested in the subject. If your scores are good, it does help your resume to reach the top of the pile.

How do you know you are in the right course?

You are motivated by the subject.

You don't feel stressed when you deal with the subject.

You are willing to do research on the subject on your own and you enjoy it.

You are excited to wake up in the morning just thinking about the possibilities that your subject has to offer. (That is rare – but there are people who simply love what they do! You **can** be one of them.)

Fresher Shoot

That's the story of this book – nailing the job that suits who you are. If you like your subject, there are more chances that you will know a lot more about the trends related to that subject. In this Information Age, information is everything and you can't say _Okay,_
. **You need a head start**. Start looking now so that you will be way ahead of everyone else when you pass out.

What kind of job are you looking for? Be specific.

_____

_____

_____

When you try to write down that answer, you will probably be stuck on the exact job title. You may have a clear picture about the kind of company you want to work in or maybe you have an ideal company in mind. Once you figure out the job title then you will have to see if the role matches your skill sets. Research your subject by reading books, talking to experts, and doing internships. Understand the options available and zero in on the best option.

For example, a Commerce student should know that the options ahead are auditing, tax - related services, banking, revenue collection, and sales posts. A language student should know that there are opportunities in content writing, editing, and translation.

Connect your skills to a prospective job role

You have picked up many skills at college. Now connect the dots. There are so many professional options these days. Gone are the days when you had to be a doctor or an engineer to be respected. Every skill you pick up has a corresponding job opportunity.

★   Are you a good emcee for college events? That means you are a good speaker and could get into the media space.

★   Are you a good essayist? That means you have writing skills and organizational capacity. Many options for you in content writing and copy writing.

★   Are you a sports person? Utilise it to become a physical instructor. Trainers are in immense demand these days.

★   Are you chatty, sweet voiced, and full of fun? Ever thought of being a DJ?

There are so many choices today. Your personality carries the clue to the kind of job you will do.

Fresher Shoot

Do I work for money or for the love of the job?

This question is about the kind of values you have and the kind of life you can afford. Be honest with yourself. Each of us has different needs. Says Guna who works in an NGO, " I never got into my career for the money. I loved travelling on my social work projects. I would visit villages and interact with homeless children. I would talk to street kids. It gave me happiness."

On the other hand, the objective of work is earning a decent amount and being independent. So decide whether money is a priority. Then work towards the goal.

Good reasons for having good study skills

Having good study skills helps you get good scores necessary for you to get into the profession of your choice. While you are in college it is a good idea to be as enthusiastic as possible about assignments and examinations. You must be thinking that I'm kidding. "Which student likes assignments?" you might say. **If you are looking for a job, you are asking for work and work at college is assignments.**

get around this problem is to make learning an interesting process. Assignments are a kind of preparation and you need as much practice as possible before you enter the workplace.

Good study skills = Focus. Being able to concentrate and deliver good scores is a plus point on your resume. Employers believe that candidates who appear focused and have good grasping powers are more useful to the company.

Every test you prepare for is an aptitude test preparation. People are always doing things for you – either it's your parents who give you security or it's your teachers who give you notes.

Do you work on your projects on your own or do you depend on your friends to complete the work assigned to you? Then you are a victim of spoon-feeding. Do your work on your own. You'll learn better.

Be honest about what you do – if you look towards your friends for the assignment, remember they won't be there when you try to crack that interview. Learning doesn't have to be hard. We have many resources today to make learning more interesting. There are CDs, books, and professionals who are willing to help

seriously, only you stand to gain from your effort.

c. Participatory Skills

College spells out one word – Opportunity. If you weren't outgoing in school, college is the best time to do all the things you were afraid of doing. The *funda* of college life is *Participate, Participate,*

Participate! This *funda* extends to all other areas of life – lack of participation or involvement is what can limit your experience.

In college, there are two kinds of students – the participators and the non-participators. Quite surprisingly a great many students come in the non-participator category.

Answer these questions.

Are you a participator or a non-participator?

_____

_____

Why don't you participate in group activities? Look at the options and frame your answer. If there are other reasons, mention those.

**Hate to work within a group   Stage fright   Not interested in group activities
I prefer to watch**

_____

_____

_____

Group activities are the best opportunity to learn the benefits of teamwork. Take any job and you will find that being a good team player is an important job attribute. Any kind of group activity like a debate, group dance, drama, or athletics is an opportunity to learn how to work with people. When you work as a team there is the excitement of getting everyone to coordinate with each other, the tension of things going wrong, and the final enthusiasm of a job well done. If you prefer to watch the group, learn from your observations – don't feel bad about being a loner. Many observers excel in various other fields.

Benefits of teamwork

★ No one can achieve anything alone; in a company a team is more effective.

★ Each person in the team gets an opportunity to use his or her skill effectively.

★ You learn from others on the job. Every person you meet is a learning opportunity.

Why don't you participate in solo activities? Again look at the options and choose the appropriate one.

Poor writing skills   Not artistic   I like to be where the action is

_____

_____

_____

If group activities are tougher for you, tackle an individual activity like an essay competition or a greeting card competition. Always challenge yourself. You have to keep pushing yourself until you fall off that dangerous cliff and _find that you have wings_!

Working alone is an advantage, as you get totally absorbed in your work. When you do your own solo performance, you are entirely responsible for every aspect of the show you put on. Pleasing the audience is your job entirely and unlike group activities, you have no one to blame but yourself if you go wrong.

Benefits of going solo

★   Doing a solo act is an opportunity to promote 'Brand You'.

★   This is a confidence builder you can't beat. When you are responsible for your performance whether it is on stage or on paper, you have already done your share of homework on the subject.

★   Canvas yourself on stage. If you already have the confidence, college is a great place to build up that confidence.

Fresher Shoot

What's the use of being athletic?

There's a case for sportsmanship. Ask an NSS cadet. Those of you who have a physical streak will be loaded with confidence. Being good at games also means you know the importance of teamwork. Plus you gain a lot of discipline, resilience, and stamina – qualities every job requires in plenty.

Weakness is not considered a plus point when you go job hunting. Build your stamina if you want to brave the long hours and be efficient!

d. Management Skills

Doing well in college or in the workplace is linked to being organised. Suppose you have an interview scheduled and forget

search, until time's up and you are late for the interview. Bad impression made!

Managing your time, emotions, and space can help you declutter your life. Good life managers may not have superb IQs but they know how to work smart.

Good Organiser

How good are you at organising things, be it at home or in college?

_____

_____

How do you keep your room? Is it a mess or spic and span?

_____

_____

_____

_____

How do you organise your college work schedules? Do you manage to complete your assignments on time or do you rush things at the last minute?

_____

_____

_____

_____

One good way of getting organised is using your cell phone to store important tasks that you must complete on a daily or weekly basis. Creating to-do lists is quite the rage today. Assign each day to complete whichever assignment or study one particular chapter. With proper achievable targets, you will find that the workload comes down considerably.

Organise your room

How?

★ Organise your cupboard.

★ Organise your desk or workstation.

★ Organise your college bag or satchel/briefcase.

★ File your papers, certificates, and applications.

★ Organise your computer as well.

To test your organizational skills, no place is better than home. Make sure you know where everything is so that you do not have to spend valuable time trying to locate things. Work life needs you to be terrifically organised. Your workstation must be neat as must your briefcase or handbag! A disorganised employee will get into the boss's bad books; so get organised. An organised person usually completes deadlines and is more reliable when it comes to meeting targets.

Good reasons to have good organisational skills

★ Being organised is essential to meet deadlines. Your work life entails daily targets. It is easier if you have specific targets to complete. You will also feel a sense of job satisfaction once you achieve those goals.

★ If you are organised you will not be as stressed out. Isn't it better if your bills, invoices, paper work, etc., are at your fingertips? It saves time and time is money. Once you start earning, you will need to get your finances in order too. So know your paperwork and be diligent about filing on a day-to-day basis.

★ Making your workstation clutter free makes it easier for you to locate things. People have a better impression about someone who is organised and usually organised people are entrusted with more challenging roles as they are seen as being more capable.

Good Time Manager

Are you a last minute person? This applies to the way you prepare for anything from an exam to a simple event such as going out in the evening.

I-can-do-it-at-the-last-minute is an attitude that many students resort to. It may work out. but it is far better to be well prepared. That's what you need to be at all times. If you are prepared in college, you will be better prepared for the interview. Of course, many things do happen at the last minute and sometimes people have no choice but to make sudden decisions. However, as far as possible, try to prepare yourself for the job hunt.

interviews. They won't be keen to hire someone who shows little preparedness.

Do you prepare in advance for a journey or project? How?

_____

_____

_____

There are many ways in which you can prepare in advance for any event – making to-do lists, creating itineraries or road maps on how to achieve your goals, etc. You can take help from any resources including people, magazines, books, and CDs.

You can tell others about it – when you tell people about what you plan to achieve you are committing to your goals.

If you have planned a journey, then take all steps necessary to make that event as comfortable as possible. The job hunt is a journey that being prepared can make much smoother and more enjoyable.

Time management = Discipline. Managing how you use your time helps you in every stage of your career and personal life. There is a management time buster called **Pareto Principle**
input of 20% from you to get an output of 80%. This helps you discard the everyday activities that you do that are an utter waste of time.

What are your time wasters?

Phone calls   Texting   Facebooking   _Chai-Pani_   Following instructions wrongly   Stress   Can't say No   Can't delegate work   Disorganised

_____

_____

_____

_____

Fresher Shoot

How do I juggle a part - time job and college work simultaneously?

The question is **how much**
can manage time usefully in class by being attentive. This way you can reduce learning time and spend more time on assignments and internships. **Wasting time at this stage of your life is probably the most stupid thing you could do.** Be clear about what you want to achieve in each semester. Also know what you want to achieve in the long term.

If you are juggling too many activities at once, step back for a minute. Are you doing justice to any of your roles? Don't take up too many projects at once. You may lose steam in the long run. This is where time management is so important. Set your own

can do it. Remember it takes a month to get into new habits. **So try for a month and see the change.**

Time Savers

After your BCA, then what? After your MCA, then what? A good job will be about as close as you can get to the answer. That's not good enough. Be about what you want. That way you save time.

Know

What text books and reference guides you must read.

How many assignments you must keep track of.

How many internships you can manage.

Part - time jobs you could apply for.

When you know the right books and the right sorts of internships that you must pitch for, you will be moving in the right direction. There's no point wasting your time on the wrong work. You have to invest your time correctly.

Also Know

Day - to - day study time.

Assignment time.

Semester examination preparation time.

Alternate examination course preparation time.

The idea is to work from small to big, keeping the big picture in mind. All the time you spend on your short-term goals should be compatible with the long-term goal you have in mind.

Time Tips at Work

The way to make big tasks achievable is by breaking up the workload into small

Don't postpone work. If you have a habit of postponing assignments, you will end – here pile-up of work is a crime!

Plan everything – even phone calls. Get to the point and sign off politely.

travelling is to travel light. The same rule applies to your surroundings – minimize everything, maximize results.

When you have an urgent project to complete, make sure you work without interruption.

Learn to delegate while on the job. When you are a fresher, observe how your seniors delegate tasks to you. Knowing how to delegate increases team spirit and helps work to be done on time. No results can be achieved alone.

Fresher Shoot

Should I work on weekends?

I'd say give yourself enough time to de-stress but work toward your personal goals daily, even during weekends. Allot time slots when you can work everyday. This gives you the stamina you need to handle work pressure.

Have you heard about the nail biting schedules of Korean students? When they are as young as grade two, they have a school cum study schedule that can go up to ten at night. When they come back from school, they rush off for tuitions till late at night. They never waste time.

Look at how hard students around you work for their Board Exams. Don't lose that momentum when you are in college.

However, don't live entirely by the calendar. That will drive you insane. Dates and schedules are not the be-all and end-all of life. Make a calendar to know what you must finish and not leave pending. But also leave time for yourself, friends, and family. The best employee knows when to work and when to have time for himself or herself. A balanced work schedule and personal life is what every individual aspires to achieve.

Fresher Shoot

I have enough time but I don't know where it goes. Help!

Managing time is a skill and sometimes technology that makes life easy can actually be a trap if you use it badly.

Use technology to:

★ Make checklists.

★ Remember important dates and appointments.

★ Post important notes and links.

➤ Avoid

★ Texting in class…what are you in college for? Text after the lecture is done.

★ Over-browsing on the Internet if you have not completed a task. Browsing every ten-fifteen minutes makes you lose on hours' worth of productivity.

★ Checking emails all day long – plan your Internet schedule. Unless your job requires it, don't keep answering emails all day long.

★ Forwarding jokes to friends – not a good idea if you have a lot of work on your hands.

★ Facebook when you are in office. It looks terribly unprofessional if you chat up with friends while at the work place, and it distracts you from the targets that you have to achieve.

Good Stress Manager

Many college students can get bugged by the pressure of their schedules. Students in professional colleges have seminars to conduct, work timetables to complete, projects to handle, examinations to cram for…how do they do it?

Many of them love what they do. That passion takes them forward.

For others, professional life is hard. "I don't even have a Sunday off," says a professional college student Veda. "Sometimes I'm drained. I get sick very often but that doesn't stop me from completing my work. Getting backlog is even worse."

Why do you get stressed out?

_____

_____

People get stressed out for various reasons:

      Personality disorders

      Family problems

      Relationship issues

      Financial tensions

      Addiction related issues

      Subject

What can you do about these problems? For personality and addiction issues, you can work on yourself independently or with the help of a friend, a mentor, or a counsellor. Some problems cannot be solved – if you have family problems, there is very little that you can do. If you dislike your subject or stream, you must develop interest in the subject. If you take your subject seriously, then commitment is an automatic side effect.

Going to a regular college can make you a little complacent. Every course has its dignity and if you dig deeper into any subject, there is a vast repository of knowledge that you can tap. If you like your subject, the stress levels come down automatically. **Learning more is the key to liking the subject more.**

There are so many reasons for stress that it is impossible to have any recipe to be stress - free. The only thing you can do is **learn how to handle the stress, without losing your sense of balance**. Problems come and go; you can either get stressed out about problems or live with them gracefully.

How do you handle college-related stress?

Am never stressed!   **Talk to my friends**   **Discuss with your family**

Handle it alone

Students have a variety of reasons to get stressed out. Problems could be peer pressure, relationship problems, exam phobia or tension, assignment overload, addiction problems, etc. Work on solving these problems **NOW** before they start to affect your personality. There are professionals nowadays who can guide you. Don't ever hesitate to ask for help if your problem is extreme, as it solves issues a little faster.

Stammering is an example of severe social anxiety that some students face. Says Gaurai, Head of Counselling India: "Stammering could be a symptom of anxiety. This can be cured with professional help."So don't live with a problem. **Solve it!**

How do you respond to stress?

There are people who have severe problems and deal with their work lives in a very professional manner. That's the kind of employee that you have to be. If you feel severely stressed out, no use shouting at your colleagues or friends. If in the future, a conversation with your boss stresses you out, you must be the one not to react. Just keep to yourself and collect your thoughts for a while. After a while, you'll come out of it and you can think of a more appropriate way to respond.

De-stress Tips

Breathe deeply when you are stressed out. When you are stressed out, your breathing becomes much tighter. When you inhale and exhale deeply, you will feel a weight is lifted off.

Write down what bothers you in your personal diary. Don't write in scraps of paper that people may read (another reason to get stressed out!) This really helps to get the stress physically out of your system.

Figure out the reason for the stress.

Are you overloaded with work?
Are you in a bad relationship?

Any health issues?
Any mental trauma that needs counselling?

Meet or at least talk to one or two close friends as often as you can.

Be more open to change.

Dedicate half an hour to the thing you love every day. It could be music or painting. 'Me-time' is a lifesaver.

Take help if you need it.

e. Computer Skills

Although computer literacy in India scores a dismal 6%, that's an area that I don't think most of you have to worry about at all. If you don't have computers at home or in the institution you study in, you can have a look and try the computers in any Internet centre in your vicinity. Today computer knowledge is a must as computers have become an essential part of the workplace.

What was once a dot com phenomenon is now an octopus spreading its tentacles in all spheres of life – conference calls, distance learning, online banking and bookings, call centres, and retail.

At a company level, well over 50% of the corporate work is done by way of emails to customers and clients; presentations for meetings, documentation for business letters, and performances charted out on excel sheets. The IT domain is huge and since it is so complex and vast in itself, all I'm talking about here is the fundamental need of basic computer know-how.

Binary Basics - are you able to

Switch on, switch off, keep on standby, and log off the computer?

Are you familiar with navigating the mouse to interact with screen icons?

Be familiar with the keyboard. Practise typing and try to get a reasonable speed of at least 40 words per minute.

> **The estimate goes that typing speed is around four times faster than your handwriting speed. You can calculate your own speed by using a mathematical equation.**
>
> **No of characters or letters including space in between/5 = No of words**
>
> **No of words/time = Words/second**
>
> **Words in a second x 60 = No of words typed in a minute**

Know how to create a sensible email id. Use an email id that sounds professional. The

sounding emails like loveydovey@hotmail.com.

See how computer literate you are. A computer literate student will know how to use the computer to create letters, spreadsheets, email, and media presentations. Tick against the skills you are sure about.

Using the Internet

Open browsers like Google Chrome, Mozilla, and Internet Explorer.

Use search engines like Google and search using key words.

Know the difference between url **www.xyz.com** and **e-mail xyz@gmail.com**.

Send **e-mail** and **attachments**.

Kanchana has typed a report and doesn't know how to send it as an attachment. She sends it in the body of the email and fails to get it formatted properly. First save a

► Word Processing Fundamentals (Microsoft Word)

- ☑ Save as doc file.
- ☑ Retrieve document.

MS Word knowledge is useful while creating a business report or letter. There are many practical applications that you should master like creation of tables, columns, insertion of pictures, adding page numbers, headers and footers, etc.

► Spreadsheet Use (Excel)

- ☑ Enter, edit, analyse, design, and store data.
- ☑ Perform arithmetic calculations.
- ☑ Sort data according to a given criteria.
- ☑ Create financial, mathematical, and statistical formulae.
- ☑ Create column headings, headers, footers, and page numbers.
- ☑ Create a graph or pie chart using data.

Excel is the most popular spreadsheet programme as it helps in financial analysis and number crunching; chart, graph, list and diagram creation; data access; and all the complicated data processing that you would prefer to avoid.

► PowerPoint Application

- ☑ Use colour, font, style, layout, and theme to present facts.
- ☑ Identify user interface elements to perform basic tasks.
- ☑ Add text and pictures to slides for effect.
- ☑ Save presentation to folder.

Fine-tune your skills according to the profession you are looking out for. If you are an accounting student, know the financial model that is required for conducting a PowerPoint. Your presentation must be persuasive and informative.

► Database Application

Knowing how to use database applications is a great way of using technology to organise material. Popular database applications include Microsoft Access.

Creating databases is part of corporate organization methodology. Organizing departmental records requires a systemic approach that programmes like Microsoft Access can provide.

- ☑ Store data and manipulate it.
- ☑ Analyze large quantities of data to create elaborate reports.
- ☑ Follow the instructions in the manual or the disc.
- ☑ Insert the disc into the installation drive and run it.

Communication: Verbal and Written Skills

WHAT IS COMMUNICATION?

College life is all about interaction. It's the time when you understand so many things about yourself like your dreams, your goals, and your personality traits. In school, you gathered skills. In college, you learn the best ways to incorporate those skills into your life. In other words, you learn about communication.

In colleges and schools, we are taught what communication means. It comes from the Latin *communis*, meaning share. Information is transferred between sender and receiver and back again through a feedback loop.

Communication becomes effective when there is no noise. Here noise means any kind of disturbance – be it really loud music during a presentation or the noise in someone's mind. These distractions stop communication from taking place. Ever noticed how after a lecture you sometimes feel that you heard nothing at all? This is because you were preoccupied by some other thoughts.

This is a kind of barrier to communication. What kind of barriers to communication do you face?

**Inability to follow   Cultural differences   Ego problems   Accent problems
Zero focus**

_____

_____

_____

Every step of the way you need very good communication skills to be liked, noticed, respected and retained. Says recruiter Anand Wadedakar (Teacher, Author, and Career

Consultant): "Communication skills make a lot of difference when it comes to getting a job. Along with this, freshers can make an impression with the strength of their academic and participation record in extra curricular activities. This reflects their personality and some abilities."

What Wadedakar is saying is that good communication skills are a number one necessity. Everything else is secondary.

If you are a good communicator, you will be more:

★ **Productive:** You will get more work done. If you can communicate your ideas well, people around you will be more supportive and you will achieve your goals quicker.

★ **Influential:** More people will take your opinions seriously and you will be listened to.

★ **Empathetic:** You will understand what people around you feel and this will make you communicate accordingly, very important when you are working in a team.

Communication is not just a word – it is life blood. If you do not know how to get your message across, it could mean a harder time landing a job and sustaining it. Every step of the way is an effort in communication. It is no use knowing how to communicate with everyone around you and not with yourself. Only if you communicate with yourself and know your values, potential, and aspirations well, can you make the right choices.

So ask yourself questions and find the answers in your own responses.

★ **Are you good at communicating with your peers in college?**

_____

_____

_____

_____

If you are then you have **people skills**, an essential component of work life. It's important to maintain positive relationships with people around you. It makes work life less stressful.

★ **Are you good at communicating with the faculty?**

_____

_____

If you are then you are good at **networking** and you already know how to manage the boss, an important skill that can help you get your promotion quicker!

★   **Has your resume been noticed?**

_____

_____

_____

If your answer is 'yes', you have **good presentation and writing skills**.

★   **Have you survived the interview?**

_____

_____

_____

If you have, then you have good **body language** and the **confidence to nail the job**.

So **communication is King.**

You must take useful feedback from your friends, family, lecturers, and employers. However, when you try to impress your friends and peer group, your family and bosses, are you really being influenced by their decisions?

Are you making your own decisions influenced by you?

_____

_____

This is your life and career. Your friends will have different tastes outside the classroom. Your parents speak from a perspective that matches their younger days. Are you going to play follow the leader or are you going to take charge and be your own leader?

First you have to know how to communicate with yourself. Ask yourself the right kind of questions first.

Each of the following students have problem areas or negatives. Remember how I told you that negatives can be a good thing if you are willing to work on them? Each negative affects your communication skills. Each negative can be corrected.

Varsha is a slow decision maker. As a result, she is hardly ever consulted in making important decisions. To gain better communication skills, she must learn to make quicker decisions so that she is trusted more and entrusted with more responsibility.

Navin does not have the motivation to succeed although he has the talent. To improve his communication skills he must work on his motivation levels by rewarding himself for every completed task he achieves.

worries Sandeep! English is a language that can be learned.

Although Anita speaks well, she has poor body language – slouched shoulders and supine posture. Having good communication skills is as much about **Non-Verbal Skills** as it is about verbal skills. We will discuss more about non-verbal skills in a later chapter.

How do I know that I'm a bad verbal communicator?

See if you have any of these qualities or habits:

Inattentive   Argumentative   Interruptive   Contradicting everyone   Using expressions repeatedly

always think only you are right. A good communicator is also a good listener. If you are inattentive, it means that you only listen to what you want to whenever you want to. This is a communication barrier that you have to rectify before you join work,

barriers and once you identify them, check yourself every time you get distracted or start arguing. This self-awareness automatically corrects you.

5-STEP IMMERSION COURSE

To improve your communication skills, you will have to go all out and take every opportunity to work on your Verbal and Non-Verbal Skills, along with your body language.

1. Attend Seminars

Conducting and attending presentations and seminars is one way of gaining more credits on your resume. A fresher has very little to write in the resume. Nowadays, recruiters judge college graduates based on much more than score cards.

Good reasons to attend seminars

A seminar is a perspective broadener. When you attend a seminar you listen to several speakers elaborating on the same subject. You get to assimilate different points of view and your knowledge base expands.

Listening to new speaking styles by several speakers from different parts of the country or town improves your **Listening Quotient** and makes you more attentive.

and understand the essence of the presentations? If you could, you have improved your attention span. This is something you will need a lot of when you join work, as you will be a sounding board for other people's ideas.

Seminars also expose you to different kinds of body language. You can watch several speakers and choose the presentation style and mannerisms that most suit you.

2. Conduct Seminars

Have you ever conducted a seminar? What did you learn in the process?

Microsoft PowerPoint   **Speaking skills**   **Preparation Time limit**   **Target audience**

_____

_____

_____

_____

Conducting a seminar is way different from just attending one. When you listen, you prepare yourself to conduct one. Even if your college doesn't give you the opportunity to make a presentation, you could take it up as an individual project. Make a seminar of any subject you are learning. Experiment with PowerPoint. The best way to gain computer

very taxing.

Good reasons to conduct a seminar

Making presentations is a common feature of the global workplace. It's better to gain the necessary computer skills now so that you become tech savvy. Employers are always on the look out for a tech savvy hand. So start practising early!

Making presentations helps you get involved and work with thoroughness. When you present a seminar, you do a lot of research. Each slide that you present needs hours of hard work and dedication. You have to get the perfect pictures, quotes, and information that will make your presentation interesting.

When you conduct a seminar, you understand what it means to communicate with a target audience. There are different kinds of audiences – for stage performances there is the audience who likes the song and dance routine. Then there is the specialist audience who likes only classical dance.

Before you prepare yourself for a seminar, you must know what kind of audience you are doing it for and present accordingly. A seminar for your class and a seminar for a specialist audience are very different.

3. Do Internships

Have you attended an internship programme? If so, where?

_____

_____

What did you gain from the experience?

_____

_____

Doing unpaid internships helps in learning career building skills. Some universities provide students with incentives to attend such programmes. If your college does not offer such options, you should consider taking up a part - time job or an internship to hone your skills.

Good reasons to do internships or part-time jobs

Doing internships gives practical hands-on knowledge. Textbook knowledge is very different from the way things work in the real world. For example, a journalism student should intern at newspaper houses and radio stations. There are so many things that a reporter has to perfect when it comes to interviewing, picture gathering, collecting quotes, page designing, and composing headlines. A journalism student must know how to write a story in different ways – the same event can be used as a news report, a feature, or an editorial.

If you are a good intern, you could build up on contacts. Today networking is the way to success. Always keep a good rapport with those you worked with during

your higher ups and what expectations they have from you. You learn about the importance of work ethic. Are you punctual? Can you meet deadlines? Can you handle work pressure? Different from exam pressure, isn't it?

4. Do volunteer work

Have you ever worked for a social cause? It could be a cause in your locality or for a grassroot organisation. If so, where did you work and for how long?

_____

_____

_____

Did you enjoy the experience? If so, why? If not, why?

_____

_____

_____

Social work is a great way of working on your people skills. If future employers know that you have experience working with people on a volunteer basis, it gives your resume an edge. It

of a cause and are willing to spend time on something non-

Good reasons to work as a volunteer

Working for a social cause can broaden your horizons and help build awareness. There are many areas you can specialize in. If you like working for children, there are various options like working towards getting kids educated or working against child labour. You can also work for the green or environmental cause, and for keeping your locality clean.

When you work for the upliftment of others, you rise. Remember the story I told you about how Baba Amte helped a leper in distress? This helped him realize his Emotional Quotient. Your Emotional Quotient or the way you handle people improves. Working as part of a team to alleviate any kind of distress can bring people together. You learn to deal with people like you whose minds are focused on making the world a better place. You also develop empathy; for instance if you have dedicated some time to helping spastic children, you understand the problems that those children face and the challenges their parents deal with. You develop a stronger mind to behave responsibly and with more kindness. This makes you a more reliable candidate when you go for an interview.

Volunteer work is a great way to make your resume stand out and look more attractive to a recruiter who is willing to give a fresher a chance. Social work timings are

a recruiter will have when she or he looks at your resume is "Here is a motivated candidate – someone who is motivated by something more than just money."

5. Assume Leadership Roles

Do you shy away from elections in college? Why? Choose from the options below or include your own reasons.

Not interested   **I'm not capable**   **No time**   **Poor communication skillss**

_____

_____

Standing for elections in college and working as part of a student body gives you exposure to the kind of politics that goes on in all walks of life. You will be a tougher person and more capable of handling responsible positions later on in your corporate life.

Good reasons to attempt securing leadership positions

★ *Starting early as a leader is a good idea.* Leadership skills help in many aspects of your job identity. You learn how to manage a crowd, assert yourself and make yourself heard, all good qualities for getting through a group discussion and securing a managerial post. A good manager is not bossy; a leader is someone who motivates, speaks well, and is knowledgeable. A good leader has positive body language – there is no room for any doubt when it comes to posture or eye contact if you plan to lead.

★ *Campaigning leads to enthusiasm.* Every time you canvas your party or yourself, you voice your convictions over and over again. This is a great way to practise oration – the art of speaking well, and helps when you do presentations, face the panel, and enter the boardroom.

★ *Being a leader is not about telling people what to do; it's about assuming responsibility for your actions.* A good leader is confident, not arrogant. Being part of any student body means you are given certain responsibilities and obligations you are expected to fulfill. By taking responsibility you are working towards a goal. Meeting those goals gives you the confidence to make decisions quicker and more efficiently.

Are you a leader? See if you have any of these qualities

**Visionary ideas   Optimistic, Influential, Positive, Intelligent   Likes challenges
Listener   Good team-builder**

Remember how the captain of the ship in the movie *Titanic* refused to get into the lifeboat when the ship was sinking? A captain never leaves his sinking ship. The same goes for a leader. Often people try to assert themselves by speaking in a loud voice, being manipulative, playing politics, and taking credit. A true leader is someone who is assertive and compassionate. She or he listens and makes decisions based on clear communication. A leader usually has some vision for the company or department she or he works in; a positive attitude is required to achieve these ideas.

There was a teacher who cared deeply for his students. However, he had no faith in them, as they were poor learners. So he punished them until they were able to produce reasonable copy. He was an excellent teacher but at the end of the day he was remembered as a strict teacher who tortured his students. If he were a leader, he would have been loved and respected. He under-estimated his students – that was where he went wrong. A leader must believe in his team.

Fix your Communication Skills

Verbal Skills

communication skills.

First we will examine Verbal Skills – "I have the skills" says Madhav, an aspiring engineer," but when I am asked to explain the work in detail, I am just too shy to speak in English. I feel my accent is not good enough."

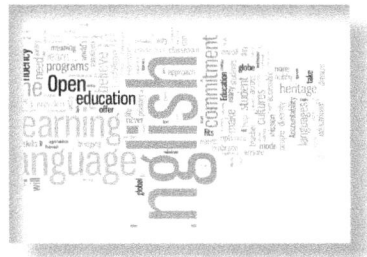

When you attend an interview, your accent and pronunciation say a lot, not just about

Perfect Pronunciation

There is no doubt about it. What you say and how you say it can make or break your chances of getting selected for the interview. There's a lot more to speaking than you

speak should be situation based – confronting an interviewer one-on-one requires a certain kind of tone and being a part of a group requires a different pitch. Besides speaking, listening is also an integral part of communication.

Speaking right is a combination of good pronunciation, good social skills, and good body language. It is also about knowing what to speak and when. It's always advisable to speak only what is necessary when you start out in your career. The reason: everything you say is judged and analyzed. It's not a place for your college-like rants. Communication at the corporate level is a tool you can use to reach success and something you can misuse to fail as well.

Phonological Awareness

Don't get put off by the word 'phonological'. Building phonological awareness is an integral part of becoming ready to work in the global world. Phonological awareness is all about knowing sound. Are the sounds you use in your language and the sounds used in English the same? What is different is the way a native speaker and you pronounce the same words. How should English be pronounced?

As we live in a global workplace and urban India is very cosmopolitan (a mix of people from all over the country), knowing English is necessary. He doesn't even know English. How will he get a good job? This is something we hear quite often. Remember that English is a language that can be learnt easily. So there is nothing to worry about. Knowing good English impresses the interviewer and so it is better to be a good speaker.

When a BPO recruiter talks to you, she or he may think on these lines:

Is your pronunciation good enough?

Will you be able to change your accent if required?

Do you have a sense of syntax or correct word order?

Are you comfortable speaking to the recruiter?

Are you polite? Do you conduct yourself well?

First, some pronunciation *gyaan.*

English is spoken differently from country to country. There are different kinds of English as trainees in BPOs will be aware of – British English, American English, Australian English, etc. All these are very different from the English known as Indian English. Each kind of English is again divided into various dialects. So even if you

It is the same with the different variations of English spoken in India. There are sixteen major languages spoken here. People from the North speak Sanskrit-based languages like Hindi, Gujarati, Marathi, Oriya, Assamese, etc. Down South, languages are Dravidian-based like Tamil, Malayalam, Telugu, and Kannada. Northerners and Southerners have distinctive pronunciation and grammatical errors when it comes to English. These mistakes are unique to them. Someone who speaks French or Greek makes different kinds of mistakes when it comes to English grammar and pronunciation.

An accent trainer teaches you how to speak English all over again.

> **Roberta Stanwood is the Director of Accent Training Resources (ATR) in**
>
>
> **want to improve their accent, they need help from a person who is training in**

In BPOs, you come across accent trainers who try to help you correct pronunciation problems. An *accent trainer* will :

★ Assess the sound system of each client during the first training session.

★ Compare their skills in British or American English with the sounds of their native language.

★ Then work on the sounds that have to be acquired or modified by providing drill sessions on those target sounds. "If a student finds it hard to differentiate between /w/ and /v/, I make them practice saying pairs of words called minimal pairs e.g., Vest-west, Vary-wary", says Stanwood.

★ Work on the same sound in different positions in the word. For example, /p/ in **put, apple, pump** all sound slightly different.

Accent trainers encourage you to read and listen.

Says Stanwood, "Practice makes the difference. Once you learn to discriminate the sound and differentiate it from the error sound, then you automatically start speaking correctly." So once you understand which sounds you are messing up, you can correct your errors automatically by listening to the correct sound and practising.

Fresher Shoot

Why should I try to change my accent?

If you make the same mistakes over and over again, better to learn, isn't it?

What's the point of knowing different kinds of English? Can foreigners speak our Indian languages?

Learning different kinds of accents is interesting. You can be a Brit in England and an Aussie in Australia! That's the advantage of being Indian.

Let them understand me.

They should. It doesn't work that way though. You have to be the one who has the advantage.

Pronouncing Vowels

In English there are **5 vowels in the alphabet – a, e, i, o, u**. You have learnt this in school and know that the **articles a/an** come before words that start with the vowel sound.

However, English has **22 vowel sounds**. Vowel sounds include diphthongs, a combination of two vowel sounds put together. E.g., Hair, Poor, Boy, Price, Stroll, Shout.

When you write these words in phonetic script, you find for example that the *ai* sound in hair is written as two vowel sounds. A common mistake that Indian speakers make is when it comes to pronouncing diphthongs correctly.

Try pronouncing

Word	Mispronounced
Said	sad/seid
Toy	tie
Coat	cot
Laugh	lof
Sell	sale
Vegetable	vegiteibl

Using Aspiration in RP

Indian speakers do not use aspiration – aspiration is a small puff of air that comes out of your mouth when you say the /p/, sound in a word like 'pebble'. When you say a word like *pani* (transcribe into Hindi), the /p/ sound or phoneme is not aspirated. No puff of air in *pani*.

Now try saying the words

Traffic

Chicken

King

In British English, aspiration before /p/, /t/, /ch/, and /k/ sounds is a must. There should be no aspiration, however, in a word like ghost.

How to say the th sound

Do you know that there are two kinds of 'th' sounds in English?

There	Three
Then	Thick

The	Thin
Their	Thought
Then	Thorn
Those	Thanks
That	Thyroid
Therefore	Teeth

Wet or Vet?

Another problem with Indian English is the /v/ (Hindi va) or the /w/ (Hindi has no equivalent)

Vet	Water
Van	When
Vacuum	Which
Voice	Wait

Pleasure and Pledge

Pleasure	Bridge
Measure	Judge
Treasure	Fudge

Sh or /s/?

Sometimes the 'sh' sound is mispronounced. Differentiate between the /s/ in sip and the 'sh' (Hindi equivalent) in ship.

Try saying

She sells seashells on the seashore.

Not

See sells sea sells on the sea sore.

'Istation' or 'station'?

Try saying Station. When you pronounce the sound /st/, don't add a vowel sound before it. It is not istation – it is **station**. Also don't add vowels between two consonants as in film (fil-um).

Now say:

String	Slow	Class	Tree	Glass
Stop	Free	Cream	Trunk	Grass
Steeple	Little	Pot	Money	Develop
Stuck	Luck	Power	Mother	Disaster
Star	Love	Piece	Move	Drown
Strange	Lust	Pack	Make	Drama
Sting	Like	Pack	Man	Den
Sports	Lack	Prove	Mask	Door

Stress in English

When a native English speaker speaks English, he stresses on certain words. European languages are stress timed.

Languages in India however depend on syllables – syllables are the different parts of a word. The word Dukan has two syllables – du and kan. The word banana has three syllables – ba-na-na. When you say Dukan, there is no stress on either syllable. In banana, the stress is on 'ba'.

Says Stanwood, "In terms of the rhythm and timing, Hindi (for example) is a syllable timed language and English is a stressed timed language. Word stress is often problematic for my Hindi speakers of American English. They need to understand what word stress is and take an inventory of words that they commonly use that have **Not so in English**."

You may have to understand a little more about where you should stress while you speak – one good way would be to watch the BBC where the presenters speak Received Pronunciation (RP). Also watch the CNN and see how American pronunciation diverges from the British.

Which accent?

different, so when you go to a company that deals with US clients, a British accent is not good enough!

What is intonation?

In the word intonation, you see the word tone. That is the hint. Tone is very important when you speak and makes all the difference during an interview.

Says Stanwood, "Intonation or use of pitch to convey meaning is problematic. **If you**

This is very important when your entire job depends on oral skills, especially when you spend most of your time on phone calls. Foreign clients are very sensitive to tone as the English they speak has an in-built rhythm that an Indian English speaker is not familiar with. The speaker is at an advantage if she or he knows this in advance.

For example, American English has:

A rising-falling tone for statements and Wh-questions.

Another tone for stating a series of items and for questions that require a choice.

Start taking note of different accents, tones, and rhythms. Read aloud every day. Observe yourself and if you honestly feel you need help with your English pronunciation, don't hesitate to take help from an expert!

Talking Tools

Having a good voice and good pronunciation is a good step forward. Another important Verbal Skill is making conversation. There are some people who don't have too many language skills but they manage to keep the conversation going.

Making conversation is a natural way of spending time but it is an art that has been studied and that can be acquired.

Fresher Shoot

What should I keep in mind before I start a conversation?

When you talk to someone, there are so many things that are taken into account

Age: Don't you speak differently with a child and with a senior? As your employer will be older than you, maintain a modicum of respect when you speak. Don't slur your words. No slang. No chewing gum. No texting and chatting on your cell when you are with someone elderly.

- ★ **Gender:** No need to be nervous of doing a handshake with a female employer. If she extends her hand, you follow suit. The same applies for female candidates being interviewed by men. If you are averse to handshakes, a Namaste will do. This works more in a traditional environment though, and would look out of place in a regular BPO!

- ★ **Experience:** When a recruiter sees you, you should come across as a person who can interact with a variety of people. Diffidence or shyness does not work in this scenario. Even if the people you are talking to are more experienced than you are, they will appreciate you more if you are responsive and friendly.

- ★ **Culture:** Different cultures have different expectations. You have to take cultural differences into account when you communicate with persons from diverse cultures. More on that when we discuss Corporate Etiquette later on in the book.

I'm pretty confident about my speaking skills but it's so weird to start a conversation with someone I'm meeting for the first time in my life. How to start a conversation?

Knowing how to initiate a conversation is the icebreaker. When you visit a job fair, you don't speak only when you are spoken to. Watch how professionals speak – they come across as very professional and refined. They speak about day to day things very casually. They are not *conscious* of themselves at all. That comes with practice.

Have you tried to introduce yourself in class at the beginning of the semester? How did you do it?

_____

_____

_____

Here is a typical introduction. *Hi, myself Shyam. From Lucknow.* Do you think this introduction will work? I don't. What's wrong with it then?

Well, for starters, you would say

I'm Shyam from Lucknow.

When you introduce yourself, you reveal a lot about yourself. On your first day in college, you want to make the best impression. Remember how the entire class turned towards you to listen to your voice, observe your body language, dress, and conversation skills? When you meet people for the first time in the corporate space, take it as an opportunity to make a good impression.

If you make a grammatical mistake at that crucial moment, you score poorly.

After you introduce yourself and discuss some pleasantries about the weather or a cricket match, then let the person you are talking to lead the conversation. You then take a cue from there and continue in that thread.

Language Tools

Knowing how to create conversation is an art in itself. Here are some tools you can use to make speaking easier.

Tags:

For a positive statement, use a negative question tag and vice versa.

When you say something like *This is a great movie, isn't it?* you are including someone else in the conversation.

Question types:

It's important to understand questions especially when you are being interviewed. There are two kinds of questions:

➤ Close-ended questions

★ These are questions that answer yes or no. Interviewers ask this to get specific information from you.

★ You must also be familiar with this sort of questioning pattern in your multiple choice question papers.

★ When you are trying to keep the conversation going, you do not keep asking yes and no questions as it becomes very tedious for the listener.

Here are some closed-ended questions.

★ *Did you pass this exam?*

★ *Are you on time?*

★ *Did you perform well in the Group Discussion?*

The answer to all these questions is a simple yes or no.

➤ Open-ended questions

★ These questions expect more general answers. Interviewers ask these questions so that they can understand more about your experience and personality.

★ The written equivalent is when you are asked to write an essay. Here you are asked to expand your views in a series of paragraphs.

How would you answer this open-ended question?

Tell us a bit about your achievements.

_____

_____

_____

_____

_____

_____

_____

_____

This is a confirmed interview question. To answer this, requires a lot of flair. You start chronologically backwards, telling the employers about where you are now and what you have done. To a question like this, you explain your resume in a detailed manner. It's how you package your answers that is important. You must answer this question with a lot of confidence.

➤ Besides Verbal Skills, another important skill is your Writing Ability.

How you write is linked to your research ability. What you write is linked to what you read and what you make of the world. It's easy to make out who reads by just reading a little bit of what they write.

How do you do your assignments?

Research at my library   Copy from a friend   Google most of the content

Don't do any of the above

A lecturer tried to make sense of a student's assignment once. The assignment was based on Japanese cartoons and the student had downloaded a whole bunch of pictures. There were website links and a lot of unnecessary content. The assignment ran up to 50 pages of unedited content. When the student was asked to talk about her topic, she could not say anything as all she had done was print out a whole bunch of material that she did not even bother to read.

Doing an assignment honestly is a learning tool. Merely googling the content is not enough; neither is copying from a guide or a friend. Whether you like it or not, copying is a standard practice in most colleges at all *Who takes assignments seriously Ma'am?* you may think.

Good idea if you do.

Good reasons to do your assignments well

★   *To understand* what you were asked to do. If you don't understand what you are supposed to do in your assignments, how are you going to understand what your boss asks you to do?

★   Every essay you are asked to write as part of your syllabus helps you in future composition, research, and sorting skills.

★   Writing essays educates you and also improves your grammar and punctuation. Every essay that you write deals with a specific topic. When you are asked to write about the Right to Information Bill, you will have to know everything about the origin of the bill and the benefits of its use. By the end of your project, your awareness of the bill will improve! When you write compositions, you will order your content into paragraphs and create meaningful sentences. This will improve your grammar.

Do you know that 30% of your time at the office will be writing oriented? So take your English lessons seriously if you don't already.

Most top-level corporate work involves letter writing on an almost daily basis. Writing is the bedrock of official communication. As the saying goes, good writing means good business. Effective writing is accurate, clear, and brief. The higher up the career ladder you climb, the more necessary it is to perfect your writing skills.

Benefits of writing

★ Writing well helps create a better resume and cover letter.

★ Writing helps organise your thoughts better. Remember, writing is a way of understanding the world around you.

★ The more you write, the more you get to proofread and correct your grammar. Better grammar means better English!

★ Writing is very exact unlike speech. If you write well, there are more chances that you will also be a better speaker as you will be able to present and organise your thoughts efficiently.

★ One advantage writing has over oral communication is that it can be revised. When it comes to oral skills, you have to be perfect in the first go. With writing you have the advantage of polishing your work.

Components of Business Writing

Business writing is very different from the kind of essay writing and compositions that you are used to. In offices, documentation helps to clarify, plan, record, and design. Good written communication skills in the corporate sphere involve the following aspects:

1. Planning and Research

How do you do research for your assignments or projects?

_____

_____

_____

Start developing a curious mind. Research material from books, and the Internet. Talk to people as well.

Whenever you start writing anything, be it a college assignment or a business report, you first have to be aware of the kind of format that you require. You then have to research adequately so that you will be able to do justice not just to the format but the subject as well. Many times this is where students falter the most.

If asked to do research on a particular theme, there is a tendency for many of you to download detailed notes from the Internet. The question is how do you convert these notes you have downloaded into something useful?

Use the principles of note making or mind map here. Start sorting out the material in terms of headings and sub-heads. Then collect information for the divisions you have made. Before you download material, scan through it and assess. Ask yourself *Is it useful?* This helps in the deletion process.

Also learn to acknowledge your sources. If you have used quotes or diagrams from a particular source, learn how to make a bibliography. Use the net as a source; the producer of the document is you.

2. Grammatical Know-how

Good grammar means practice. Go back to all your high school grammar. Be honest with yourself.

Can you write a simple sentence correctly with zero errors?

_____

_____

_____

If you can, can you write more structured documents with zero errors?

_____

_____

_____

Accurate copy should be correct in all aspects – subject-verb agreement, tense, and use of articles. We'll look at some of those aspects later on in this section.

3. Knowing How to Summarise

Do you remember the précis writing you did in school?

_____

_____

_____

When you write a summary, you make the article one-third of its original length. To do that, you focus on the central idea of the story. You can extend this idea of précis writing into understanding your study material. Instead of mugging up, you can summarize your text paragraph by paragraph. When you are through, you will have a clear idea about the gist of the lesson.

Corporate work involves drafting of long documents. Keeping the target audience

a summary of salient points. The body of the report will contain headings and sub-headings that are summaries of key points.

Good writing is nothing but being a good thought organiser.

4. Being Thorough

Do you read through your work in detail before submission?

_____

_____

If you are in a hurry to submit your work, then you end up providing a document that could have errors. You may have done all your research and created a good resume. However, if there are any grammatical errors in your work, then it is rejected. All your hard work will be wasted. Don't you scan your exam paper before submission? Apply the same rule in whatever documentation you submit, be it a report or an email.

Fresher Shoot

How do I know where to start to improve my writing skills?

List your writing strengths and weaknesses. You can choose from the words provided below.

Punctuation   Grammar   Sentence construction   Composition   Spelling Vocabulary

_____

_____

_____

Now you know which areas you have to work on.

Groom Your Grammar

Writing doesn't have to be such a boring subject. If you like English grammar exercises, then you will enjoy this part of the book. If you don't like grammar, remember one thing – grammar is a handy tool set when you aim to be an effective communicator.

What are the parts of speech?

_____

_____

If you've left the space above blank, you have a lot of brushing up to do.

Nouns

As you already know, nouns are naming words.

Your resume is full of naming words starting with your name, which is a proper noun, as is the place that you live in or your address.

Name:...

Address:..

Mobile Phone:...

Email ID: ....

What kind of job are you pitching for? All your Objectives are nouns.

Analyst	Content writer	Paediatrician	Teacher	Enterpreneur

Skills can also be nouns:

Time Management	Initiative	Leadership	Punctuality
Flexibility	Motivation	Management skills	Drive
Adaptability	Multi tasking	Creativity	
Research Skills	Dedication	Team Player	Research

Make your own noun skill table.

Verbs and Adverbs

A verb is an action word. Verbs are useful tools in the job hunt phase. Recruiters advertise jobs with a certain number of skill sets on the requirement list. It is up to you to turn those requirements into the right action words that will get you noticed.

sounds better than

Here the verb **trained** is a better substitute for the **noun trainer.**

an adjective, or even another adverb.

I trained students in algebra *well*.

Take a look at these job descriptions

> Develop new business to increase penetration in the market through existing and new accounts.

> Build strong customer relationships through effective account management and by providing right solutions to meet the customer's needs.

> Researching on varied topics using the Internet.

> Prepare and execute presentations.

> Okay to work in night shifts.

How many verbs/adverbs were you able to locate?

Create a Verb Table to build a strong resume. Here are some typical Job Verbs.

Accomplishment Verbs: These words show your achievements.

Achieve	Create	Manufacture	Conceptualise	Determine
Develop	Judge	Direct	Arranged	Mediate
Moderate	Participate	Present		

Banking and Finance Verbs: These words help you if you plan to enter the banking/

Audit	Accounted	Netted	Project	Create
Balance	Modify	Budget	Calculate	Compute
Estimate	Analyze	Tally	Maintain	Catalogue

Media Verbs:

Authored	Edit	Write	Translate	Interpret	Publicise
Draft	Perform	Interview	Design	Illustrate	Animate
Photograph					

Communication Verbs: These words are important to show your interpersonal and overall communication ability.

Negotiate	Consult	Referred	Joined	Address	Arbitrated
Articulate	Report	Convey	Correspond	Interact	Persuade
Clarify	Support	Motivate	Analyze	Collaborate	

Education Verbs: In the education field? Then these words demonstrate your potential.

Teach   Lecture   Coach   Prepare   Research   Facilitate   Explain   Guide   Evaluate

Management/HR/Sales Verbs: Useful terms in the field of Management and Human Resources.

Manage	Promote	Market	Appoint	Administer	Appraise
Sell	Provide	Hire	Execute	Organise	Purchase
Terminate	Inspect	Oversee			

Adverbs: This part of speech helps to describe how you performed the task. They are useful in resumes.

Accurately	Attentively	Efficiently	Intelligently	Responsibly
Successfully	Effectively			

Create your Verb Table

Pronoun

Pronouns replace nouns so that you won't have sentences like this:

Mohan lives in Shantinagar. Mohan wants to work in the accounts dept of a good company but Mohan has to pass his exams first!

Too much repetition of the proper noun spoils the flow of the passage.

Now see the same sentence with pronouns:

Mohan lives in Shantinagar. He wants to work in the account dept of a good company but he has to pass his exams first!

Adjective

Adjectives are the most important part of job description and resume vocabulary. Take these examples:

Productive self-starter
Strong team player

Multi-disciplinary approach

Comprehensive planner

Skillful negotiator

administrator

In-depth knowledge

Creative content creator

List of describing words to 'describe'

Brand you:

_____

_____

Your skills:

_____

_____

_____

The kind of team player you are:

_____

_____

_____

Your internship experience/volunteer work:

_____

_____

_____

Your weaknesses:

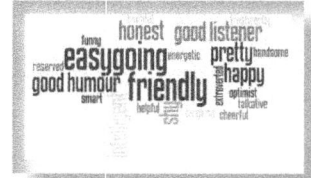

_____

_____

Your strengths:

_____

_____

_____

Preposition

This is a relationship word.

What experience do you have **in** this field?

What is your philosophy **towards** work?

We come across prepositions in phrases that we use all the time.

After the meeting

Before the test

For a month

By the office

Conjunction

Conjunctions connect words, phrases, or clauses. Avoid conjunctions as far as possible in resumes. Limit the use of 'and' and 'because'. When you want to list points, use bullet points rather than 'and'.

Interjections

These are exclamatory words like "Alas!" "God!" Obviously exclamations have no place in business communication.

Have a look at this resume:

There are more nouns and adjectives. More effective resumes would have more power verbs and adverbs.

Breaking the sentence down

Sentences are the building blocks of speech and the written word. Although students today are candid and fresh in their expression, their written skills suffer from lack of practice and reading. First we will understand the building blocks of sentences.

You must have studied that a sentence contains a **subject** and a **predicate.**

Vivek writes his resume.

Here **Vivek** is the **subject** and **writes his resume** is the **predicate.** To find the subject in the sentence, you ask the question to the verb.

Who writes?

Vivek writes.

So now how do you find the **subject** in this sentence?

There is one vacancy remaining.

The verb in this sentence is the word **is** (an auxiliary verb). Ask the question *What is?* The answer you get is vacancy. So *vacancy* is the simple subject.

How do you find the **verb** in this sentence?

Vivek has written his resume in an unsatisfactory way.

The sentence above has a verb phrase – *has written*. The verb in this case consists of more than one word.

Sentences are not always as simple as *Vivek writes his resume*. Take this one

Vivek writes and edits his resume.

Here a **compound predicate** is used.

Vivek and Shirin draft their letters.

Here a **compound subject** is used. **As two people are involved, the verb becomes**

singular. This is a very important rule in English. **Subject-Verb agreement** is one of the most important grammatical rules that you must follow and that can make your copy impressive. Commit mistakes there, and lots of doubts crop up about your English skills.

Do you know your Tenses?

Tense is important as it indicates the 'when' of the verb. Students often mix up tenses. When you attempt an answer, you write it in the present or the past tense. If the topic is about an incident that took place a long time ago, you will automatically use the past tense. If you are expressing an opinion, you will use the present tense.

In business writing, stick to simple present or simple past tense. Don't complicate your resume and cover letter with present perfect and past perfect tense.

Better to say *Collated information* than *Have helped Professors to collate information.*

Also avoid present continuous tense like *I am having the documents*. You should say *I have the documents*.

Use the correct present tense form of the verb placed in the bracket.

All grammar books have intense chapters on tense. You are advised to refer to essential grammar and revise.

Fresher Shoot

Use the correct tense of the verb in brackets

I ………my resume. (drafting)

They ………..the interview soon. (clearing)

I ………glad that I passed the test (be)

They………..joining as we speak. (be)

Either Meena or her friends …………….… to the job fair. (go/goes)

Key: am drafting, will clear, am, are, go

What we have to understand as students is the **structure** of the sentence.

Vivek writes.

Subject Verb

S   V

Here **Vivek writes** is an independent clause, a subject and predicate that can stand alone.

To this simple subject-verb, you can add a complement. The complement is the object and is part of the predicate. To understand the complement of the verb, you ask the question what after the verb.

Vivek writes a resume.

S   V   O

Here resume is the direct object.

Vivek writes me a resume.

S   V   IO   O

See how the meaning changes? In this sentence, Vivek writes a resume not for himself but for me – me is the indirect object.

Vivek *writes fast*.

Finish *by twelve*.

The freshers *crowded in the college auditorium*.

Here there is no complement. The questions give no answer.

Active and Passive Voice

Resumes and cover letters are usually framed using the active voice. Voice means how the subject and the verb are related to each other in the sentence. While writing in **Active** voice for your resume, you write about what you did.

I passed in First Division.

I scored 87%.

I worked as Marketing Trainee for a period of eight weeks in Gascal Company Ltd.

While writing your resume, most of the time, you drop the subject, in this case the pronoun.

Passed in First Division.

Scored 87%.

Worked as Marketing Trainee for a period of eight weeks in Gascal Company Ltd.

When you write in the **Passive** voice, you change the Subject Verb Object order. The

I was honoured for service skills.

Responsibilities included organizing events and distributing freebies.

While framing your resume you would rephrase the two sentences above, turning them into active voice.

Delivered excellent service.

The College Management rewarded me for my efforts.

Organised events and distributed freebies.

Hit it!

Turn Passive voice into Active by shifting the subject and object around.

Here's an example:

I was assigned the task of vouching of expenses to verify if all accounts were properly accounted.

Ans. Vouched expenses to verify if all accounts were properly accounted.

The thesis will be reviewed by the examiner.

Budget allotment will be discussed at the senior level.

The interview will be held at noon.

The essay has been written by a group of students.

Key:
The examiner will review the thesis.
They will discuss budget allotment at the senior level.
They will hold the interview at noon.
A group of students has written the essay.

Although writing resumes and cover letters requires knowledge of active voice, the passive voice is equally useful in most forms of business writing, particularly report writing.

Articles

Students often make mistakes with articles – a/an/the.

Never put the article 'the' before a proper noun – like The Pavitra Subramanium!

Hit it!

Fill in the appropriate article:

Anish distributed……… reports.

I want ……..brochure of that company.

I want…….brochure.

She has ………idea.

When does………… train arrive?

Key: the, a/a, the, a, an, the

Keep your articles in resumes to a minimum.

Trained staff sounds better than Trained the staff.

Avoid Dangling Participles

A participle is a verb that acts as adjective.

Present participles end in – *ing*   Past participles end in *ed, ne, t, d*

A participial phrase is a group of words that contains a participle and maybe a preposition.

Dancing in the hallway, she fell in love with him.

Here dancing in the hallway is a participial phrase belonging to the subject she.

When you use a dangling participle, your participial phrase doesn't have a subject. That is wrong usage. Here the subject is ambiguous and so the sentence is not accurate.

Writing the resume, my friends came over.

How would you correct the sentence? By adding the subject, of course.

While I was writing the resume, my friends came over.

Kinds of sentences

We saw the Subject Verb Object construction. That is called a **simple sentence**.

Vivek writes a resume.

Sheila applies for a job.

A **compound sentence** is a combination of two simple sentences.

Rajesh does his MBA in the mornings and teaches commerce in the evenings.

A **complex sentence** contains a main clause and a dependent clause.

Shirin applied for the job which she thought suited her credentials the most.

In resumes, stick to simple sentences.

> **Sentence Advice**
>
> **Write as many correct simple sentences as you can. If you can get the Subject Verb Object order right, it makes a lot of difference when you write letters or do self-intros.**

Personality of Sentences

A **declarative sentence** is a statement. These sentences are important when you write a cover letter.

We went for the walk-in last Tuesday.

Interrogative sentences always end in a question mark. These are the kind of sentences that you will face during an interview.

What is your expected salary?

An **imperative sentence** is a request or a command. In such a sentence no subject is mentioned though it is implied. When you speak to your recruiter, do not speak in the imperative.

Answer the question.

Come in.

Exclamatory sentences express surprise. Again, these sentences are best avoided in a formal situation.

What a difficult interview!

How simple was the group discussion!

So the best kind of sentences to use in a job-hunt situation would be declarative. Your employers will speak to you mostly in the interrogative and imperative.

Know the Person

In stories, you have something called a point of view. Sometimes the story is written by me, so it's in the **first person** or *I*.

The **second person** is *you*, the person who comes after I. This person is not used as much unless you are making a speech or writing a self-help book like I am right now.

The **third person** refers to *them*.

In a resume or a cover letter, you write in the first person. In a Group Discussion, you speak in the first person.

When you write a report, however, you use the third person.

Punctuation Matters

Most of the time, students are lax about punctuation. Unfortunately when you don't use the punctuation, your words get stuck in a word traffic jam. One word after the other, nothing makes sense at all. So when you cross check your documents, see if you have left out capital letters and full stops, commas and colons.

Fresher Shoot

When do you use a comma?

★   When you want to separate several items in a list.

I am required to *research, compose, and edit* the document.

★   When you want to separate a phrase or clause from the rest of the sentence.

After she interviewed for the job, she went for a long drive.

★   Sometimes you use commas before a conjunction.

They worked hard at the last minute, *yet* they flunked.

★   You use commas to connect the important parts of the sentence together. Annie who lives a few kilometers away joins me for violin class.

This sentence needs some work. Here Annie joins me for violin class is important. The adjectival clause can remain within commas.

Annie, *who lives a few kilometers away,* joins me for violin class.

Hit it!

Insert commas where relevant.

Mr. Viswanathan manager will arrive shortly.

You have created an adequate resume so you can start applying.

My interests are singing classical semi-classical jazz and opera.

The cover written which is on the top of the heap is the best one.

Key:

Mr. Viswanathan, manager, will arrive shortly.

You have created an adequate resume, so you can start applying.

My interests are singing classical and semi-classical music, jazz, and opera.

The cover letter, which is on the top of the heap, is the best one.

When do we use a semi - colon?

A semi-colon is almost like a full stop, but not quite. It separates two ideas that are closely related.

I composed the draft; she edited it.

He applied for the position in this company; however, it is doubtful whether he will get the break he desires.

When do we use a colon?

A colon indicates something is coming up: information, a list, a quotation.

and a smile.

Apostrophe

Now this is a tricky one. You use an apostrophe mostly to indicate the possessive, and the short form of **is** or **not**. You can also use it to indicate the plural of letters.

The girls' notes were useful. (Here girls is plural, hence the apostrophe after **s**)

The girl's notes were useful. (Here we talk about one girl, not many; so the apostrophe comes before *girl.*)

She's in a good mood.

It's past midnight and he's still on the job.

Don't slouch.

Mind your p's and q's.

Hit it!

Insert apostrophes in the right places

The accountants will talk to the managers on Tuesday.

The speakers talks were inspiring.

Key:

The accountants will talk to the managers on Tuesday.

The speakers' talks were inspiring.

When do you italicize?

Names of books, magazines, and journals are italicized.

Read *Outlook* and *Week* to update your current affairs' knowledge.

Spelling

about that.

drive, you learn road signs and routes. Spelling is the verbal road sign that makes better copy. So don't be careless when it comes to spelling.

No sms spelling please! Not when you are focusing on a regular job.

How many errors can you spot?

Befour she corrected her pronunciation, she was interupted.

He asked for an extention of time on the project.

The raize he belived he was privilaged to receive did not materialize. Had it ocured, he would have been saved much embaresment.

Go through your notebooks and answer papers. Spot your own spelling errors. That is the biggest eye-opener.

Capitalisation

All of you know that a sentence starts with a capital letter and that *Proper Nouns* always begin with a capital at the beginning of a sentence or at the end of them. How many of you follow that rule?

Hit it!
Capitalise

his interest in health education is serious.
we went to the ganges last may
has mr badrinath signed the documents due on wednesday?

Key:

His interest in health education is serious.
We went to the Ganges last May.
Has Mr. Badrinath signed the documents due on Wednesday?

What is Body Language?

A very important **Communication** Skill besides **Verbal** and **Written** is the **Non-Verbal**.

According to the **Mehrabian Rule**, **only 7%** of what you say is considered important during **a one to one presentation**. What attracts most attention is your body language!

Body language varies from culture to culture. What works in southern India may not work in Delhi. What works in the US may not work in Japan. Understanding the body language of the people you work with helps. Some of our expressions are not intentional. You could have a snooty nose and that could make you appear proud even if you are not. This fascinating science of non-verbal communication must be mastered.

Every move you make, every breath you take, you are being watched and judged. Body language is about how you use your eyes, head, facial expression, posture, hands, and space to convey information.

Every action of yours shows something about what you feel. Your emotions leak out into your gestures. This is why it is important not to carry around your feelings to the job interview or to work.

Your body language must be positive if you want to get good results.

Fresher Shoot

What does effective communication look like?

upper body pushed slightly forward. Watch your persuasive sales person sell a product – the upper torso pushed forward, the smiling face and the eye contact all make you want to consider the product even if you don't need it.

Most professionals are trained to adopt positive body language be it a customer service executive, a health care professional, or a teacher. Effective body language is a necessity in professions where you have to interact with people on a day - to - day basis.

Nowaday, everyone works on the computer or via phone. What's the need of good body language then?

I wouldn't be too sure about total absence of person to person contact. The face to face is still a part of work life unless you work on a telecommuting basis or as a freelancer. At some point you will have to interact with people in the office. Maybe you will have to do a presentation in your office or be a part of video conferencing (the trend nowadays where you can interact with people across the globe using face to face technologies). Face to face is part of corporate life. Even your entry into the workspace depends on the first challenge of your corporate career – the 'Interview'.

Read the Body

What kind of posture do you have?

Erect   Slouching   Average

A straight spine indicates confidence. Standing upright without slouching also makes you feel more confident. Tagore was right when he said to be the kind of person 'where the mind is without fear and the head held high.' Improved posture means improved self-respect.

If you slouch, then you don't appear very capable and can come across as weak. You can practise maintaining a good posture at home. Avoid the tendency to slouch, when you are at home watching TV. Make it a habit to straighten yourself and then you will automatically correct yourself if you are at an interview.

Posture is something you have to maintain throughout your career. It improves confidence levels drastically. Good posture is essential when you are working at your desk for long hours. A lousy posture can lead to many ailments.

Do you have too many strong facial expressions when you speak?

Not a good idea. Every expression on your face says something. The **furrowed forehead**, for instance, indicates a great deal of stress. When you speak to a recruiter you have to look as anxiety free as possible. Even if you feel nervous, you shouldn't show it!

Even small things like what you do with your **eyebrows** make strong statements and silently convey interest or disinterest. Arched eyebrows convey surprise. If you raise one eyebrow, you could be showing your doubt without actually expressing it.

Where you **touch yourself on your face** indicates a great deal about what you are thinking. You would think that your ears say nothing about you at all – touching your ear lobe during a conversation means that you do not want to hear the conversation any more. If your interviewer shows this sign, gear up to leave. If you touch your nose, it could mean that you are lying. Haven't you heard of the expression lying through his nose?

As far as possible keep your **tongue** where it belongs – in your mouth. Many times, you can have the *Oops*! moment when you are speaking to a crowd or to an interviewer. Don't stick your tongue out. It creates a bad impression.

Read the Face

Face it, your face reveals a lot. It has been proven that across all cultures, there are six expressions – joy, sadness, surprise, fear, contempt/disgust, and anger. Even before you speak or do verbal communication, you express your feelings on your face in a nano-second.

The festival of Holi is a good time to capture micro-expressions – if you are not used to being smeared with colour, you express your disinterest in the second before you are splattered with colour anyway! Watch out for that expression – the dislike and then the verbal 'No!'

Identify the Facial Gesture

1. Smiling, wrinkles around eyes, dilated pupils, raised cheeks

2. Wrinkled nose, lowered eyebrows, raised upper lip

3. Wide staring eyes, eyebrows drawn together and lowered

4. Eyebrows raised, wide eyes, tense lips

5. Mouth turned downwards, lowered eyebrows, raised eyebrows

6.   Wide eyes, raised eyebrows, lower jaw slightly dropped, lips parted

> **Key**
> 1. **Joy**
> 2. **Disgust**
> 3. **Anger**
> 4. **Fear**
> 5. **Sadness**
> 6. **Surprise**

Read Eyes

Do you make eye contact when you speak to someone?

Sometimes   Always   Never

_____

_____

Do you make eye contact when you speak to several people in a room?

Sometimes   Always   Never

_____

_____

Looking at people is one way of getting their attention. The best way of being forgotten is to look away. Your eyes are the window to what your intentions are.

> **The Eye Files**
>
> When you look at a person, you convey your interest in the person and your willingness to listen. Sometimes **shyness** can cause you to maintain **zero eye contact**
> eye contact translates as impoliteness, dishonesty, insecurity, embarrassment, total lack of cooperative tendencies, anger, arrogance, and even lack of interest.
>
> Eye contact tells someone so much about you – didn't you see how the eyes indicate all human emotions be it joy, anger, hostility, boredom, affection, or suspicion? Do you know that your pupils dilate when you are very happy? This happens without your knowledge.

> **Staring** is not a good way of keeping eye contact. There is an incident when a teenager was caught staring at a boy once. The boy became extremely uncomfortable and asked her if she was okay. Staring too long could mean many things like rudeness, aggression, superiority, and disrespect. In this case, however, the girl apologized – 'Just started wearing contact lenses,' she told the boy. So some gestures could be the result of some kind of physical discomfort – don't forget that.
>
> **Darting**
> defensive, or even deceitful.
>
> **Blinking** too much and **rubbing your eyes** a lot shows that you are bored or trying to withhold information.

As you go for more and more interviews, you may not like the feedback that you get about yourself. Take all negative feedback in a positive spirit. Looking away is not the solution. Look at the person head on and acknowledge or disagree directly. The direct approach is always better and your eyes are equipped to speak volumes.

Handshake - Hows

What kind of handshake do you have?

Firm and friendly   Hard and forceful   Soft and gentle

_____

_____

The handshake is an important part of the corporate life – master it soon.

"As an employer, one thing that tells me a lot about the person is the handshake." – a common recruiter sentiment.

Fresher Shoot

Is there any prescribed way to do the handshake?

> When you walk into a room, don't walk in with your hand extended. Walk up to the recruiter, make eye contact and see if your recruiter is interested in shaking hands. Then and only then do you make the handshake.

> If you score well on the right handshake, you have more chances of making that

> Don't forget handshake etiquette – in some cultures handshakes are not popular.

What do you do with your hands when you have to speak before a crowd?

Keep your hands on the side

Gesticulate or move your hands furiously

Wring your hands tightly

Keep your hands on your hips

Every action is weighed and measured when you are being interviewed. Fidgety hands are a sign of discomfort and boredom. While speaking, try not to make too many gestures. While standing, keep your hands to your side if you want to look like you are in control. A bad idea would be putting your hand on one hip as it makes you look aggressive.

When you speak before an audience, do you:

Stand constantly in one place?   Move around the room continuously?   Put your body weight on one hip?

Stance indicates confidence levels. Try to use space appropriately (this is called Proxemics). You shouldn't stand like a soldier to attention during a presentation. You shouldn't run around the room either.

Fresher Shoot

How should you sit before an interviewer?

With crossed legs   Leaning forward   Leaning backwards

It's not only how you stand that's important but how you sit as well. Being far too tense or far too comfortable is not advisable.

The way you lean your body or **body orientation** conveys a lot about your level of interest in the person you are talking to.

★ When you lean forward, you indicate that you are interested in what the other person is saying. You could lean forward and take notes in your class. Your lecturer would then think you are attentive, which is the case. But when you lean forward make sure that your arms are not folded and hands are not hidden – this could make you look more hostile than interested.

★ Leaning backward is preferable in an interview. This makes you look more in control. Of course, you must not lean too far back and appear casual and contemplative like you are the boss. If you lean backward and cross your hands, you come across as disinterested.

If you are suddenly angry with the interviewer's question, would you:

Look away   Shout back   Change the topic   Agree or disagree with the interviewer

_____

_____

As freshers you sometimes carry emotions on your sleeve. This means that you show your emotion. Well in the real world, emotions have to be put on hold. It is better not to act on emotions as it can lead to hasty decisions. Haste makes waste, and sudden anger, if shown, can make the job interview ugly. If an interviewer's attitude upsets you, remember that interviews are designed to build up the pressure. If the insult is too much to bear, then quietly state your issues and leave. No making a scene when you do not intend to work there.

Where will you place your briefcase or certificates when you attend an interview?

On your lap   On the table   On the floor

_____

_____

Safest bet is beside your chair. Putting your bag on the desk is not the right thing to do as you are impinging on the employer's space. Putting all your belongings on your lap is a sure giveaway of insecurity.

When you face new people in the crowd for the first time, do you:

Attempt to start a conversation   Wait for the other person to speak first   Ignore the person

_____

_____

If you are a nervous sort of person, starting a conversation is a good way of getting over stress. Ignoring people during the job-hunt phase hardly does you any good.

Fresher Shoot

If I am in a room full of strangers, what kind of gestures should I have?

Don't be nervous. Read the context of the occasion – are you in an interview room or at a wedding party? Act according to the occasion. Take a cue from the body language of people around you.

How will someone understand if my smile is real or fake?

The real smile lies not in your lips, raised cheeks, or the depth of your dimples. Where does your smile start - in your eyes! Real happiness is in your pupils. – It is very hard to fake happiness. That is why posing for a camera feels so unnatural – real joy cannot be seen on the face unless it is there in your heart. So when you go for an interview, go with confidence and enthusiasm. It will show in your eyes.

Different gestures and expressions mean different things. How do we read so many gestures together? It's confusing.

Now that is a good question.

One good way to understand body language is to put it in **context**. A man raises his eyebrows and talks freely to a woman at a beach party. Now this behaviour is quite normal. If the same man speaks freely to a woman in the office with raised eyebrows looking often at her in the course of the day, then the man is trying to connect with the woman. He wants her attention.

A woman is on holiday – she is bored and stretches herself often. She yawns a great deal. If she does this in the office during the day, it looks like she is disinterested in her line of work. Repeated display of boredom at your workplace can cost you your job.

So a person displays different gestures at different times of day, in private and public. Do you behave the same way in your home and in a public place? Notice how you automatically change according to the expectations of people around you – you do it unconsciously.

Another way to understand gestures is by reading **groups of gestures**. A group of words in the correct order (or syntax) makes sentences. These sentences combine to create paragraphs which in turn combine to form essays or a novel. Gestures combine in the same way to give you a **body syntax**.

A young girl who had been harassed by eve teasers refuses to tell her mother that she is not fine. When she speaks, she shudders involuntarily and looks away. Her eyebrows are knitted and she looks worried. Even though her verbal communication says that she is fine, her mother reads her body language differently. Her body syntax and verbal syntax are not in sync. Her mother adds her gestures together and knows that her daughter is hiding something.

So how can I improve my body language?

Be very **observant**.

★   **When you travel:** When you are travelling by bus or train, waiting at a bus station or restaurant, watch people without staring.

★   **When you watch TV:** Watch TV on mute – character actors in serials exaggerate their non-verbal gestures. When you watch programmes in different languages you can observe how body language changes across cultures. An American has a different body language from an Indian. There are differences within cultures as well and between those who live in cities and others who come from villages.

★   **When emotions run high:** Assess your own non - verbal skills and learn to read the gestures of those around you. Watch a person communicate when she or he is angry or aggressive. You will see how every verbal communication is accompanied by a subtle non-verbal gesture that gives away more of the truth.

★   **When you are at work:** Watch your employers. Study their mannerisms. This gives you a clue on how to behave and what is expected of you.

★   **When you are inspired:** Watch the body language of leaders you admire. Listen to the sound of their voices and the posture they adopt. You can easily learn by observation who is a real leader and who is a fake.

See how much your body language says about who you are and how you feel?

4

Making Sense of Corporate Life

So many skills make you a desirable candidate – verbal and written skills; research ability; the way you manage, time, stress, and your surroundings; the way you interpret or make sense of the people and situations around you.

The corporate world is way different from college. Communication rules are the same everywhere but in the corporate world you need the three C's: Be **Clear**, **Concise,** and **Credible**.

Communication is also about understanding Context and Presentation. The interview is not about you but what someone else viz. the interviewer thinks of you. You must put yourself in someone else's shoes.

What will the interviewer think when she or he sees you?

What will your audience say when they hear your presentation? Thinking in someone else's shoes is the key to improving your own presentation skills.

What is the value of your verbal and non-verbal communication skills? Are you able to create an impression every time you talk?

Then you have to think as your self.

What do you want? The interview is about the interviewer but it is also about you, the person you are investing in. Think of the long term – *your long term*. Don't keep

years. This sound track should play in your head if you want to make the right decision.

Fresher Shoot

Will I be able to adjust to corporate life?

Of course you will if you follow the golden rule. The golden rule when it comes to understanding corporate life is:

Check. Recheck. Double Check. Cross Check.

You are new to the corporate world. You will have endless doubts and queries. So ask.

Ask your colleagues questions. If the answers are not clear enough, ask the higher-ups. Keep asking until your doubts get clarified. There is no other way to learn on the job. This is why you have to be polite at all times. You never know who will help you understand the job well.

Corporate Speak

Corporate communication is all about being polite, firm and clear. Use a strong tone – not too aggressive as a full stop and not too doubtful as in a question mark. Listen to the speakers and take a cue from them. Watch body language.

Are you shy? Yes or no?

_____

If you are, your colleagues may think you are too superior or too inferior. Do you want them to judge you that way?

Do you have the habit of interrupting everyone when they speak?

_____

_____

This is a negative way of getting attention. Frame questions and ask at an appropriate time. Plan out your questions so that you give the impression of a mature individual.

Do you give free advice?

_____

_____

Keep your advice to yourself. The corporate world is full of people from different walks of life and they have different solutions to their issues. You may not always have the right solution. Use corporate life as an opportunity to learn about new solutions rather than distribute your freebies when no one asks for it.

Do you comment on someone's looks or manner of dressing?

_____

_____

No need. This is not college. People come to work and earn a living. No need to remark on their dress, figure, attitude, culture, etc. No need of making deprecating remarks or flattering statements. First treat all your colleagues with respect and save your remarks for a time when you become good friends.

Do you talk loudly?

_____

_____

Control your volume. No employer appreciates an employee who speaks without modulating his or her voice.

Are you a positive speaker?

_____

_____

If you speak with self – confidence and lack of doubt, you will be appreciated more. Have you ever heard a politician speak in a defeated tone? That's the easiest way to lose votes.

Some Speaking Tips

★ Stick to formal talk in the office and the boardroom.

★ Say **Hello** (instead of **Hi** or **Hey**) and **Please excuse me** when you are in the middle of a conversation and have to attend a phone call or attend some personal business.

★ Never speak when you are chewing food.

★ Introduce the older person/client/senior first.

★ Speak in grammatically correct sentences.

★ When you leave thank your client, no exclamatory Bye!

★ Speak in a measured tone – don't get too excited or too dull while speaking.

★ Avoid too many gestures – maintain poise.

Leadership Skills

We already saw how important leadership is when it comes to running a team. In corporate life, you will have to play the leader more often than you would like to. Being a leader means:

★ Taking responsibility.

★ Knowing how to delegate without feeling ashamed about it.

★ Encouraging your team and motivating as many people as you can.

★ **Do you continuously doubt yourself and your talents?**

★ **Do you feel superior to the people in your team?**

★ **Do you let others know when you are anxious?**

★ **Are you worried about making it to the top?**

If your answers to these questions are YES, then you have to stop doubting and start affirming your positives. No one is superior or inferior – these are all perceptions that we have of ourselves and each other. If you are the team leader, you are expected to share responsibility for success or failure. Your mood reflects on the team – if you are worried all the time, your team cannot function as a whole.

There is a saying that a leader is born, not made. This may or may not be true. Nowadays leaders are being made – a leader is someone who is in control of all aspects of his or her life. This does not mean that bad things never happen to a leader – it only means that good leaders do not let their troubles interfere with their work.

In fact good leaders become the goal and they motivate everyone around them to follow their example. Gandhi was such a man. He had a set of common goals that he lived by and the following that he received arose from his commitment.

Leaders also think differently – they call a crisis an *opportunity* and a road block a *challenge.* This is the kind of person that a corporate player should aim to be.

4 tips for being a good leader

★ Have a goal that you can communicate.

★ Be a good team builder.

★ Walk the talk and do it with the team.

★ Be a good listener and motivator.

Some of you must have watched the Times of India Lead India Campaign when RK Misra made the big win. Why is he a leader? He *walks the talk* – he believes in the projects he is involved with and works passionately to realize his goals. A leader is a doer and a listener.

Many times we mistake bullies to be leaders – but people who criticize and belittle others lack the central quality that a good leader must have. A good leader dreams big and works hard. When there is work to be done, you don't waste time.

When you join a company for the first time, you will be part of a team. A good team is the result of the open mindedness and positive attitude of the team leader and all members on board.

How do you know if you are in a good team?

★   People will be open. They will be honest but not judgmental and highly critical.

★   Each member will know the exact nature of his or her role. Most conflicts occur when there is no clarity about what you have to do.

★   Disagreement is accepted and solutions will be worked upon.

★   The goal is the same for the team leader and members of the team.

★   Everyone gets a chance to contribute. People with talent are not snubbed.

Negotiation Skills

Are you good at talking your way out of a problem? Explain with an example.

_____

_____

Problems are part of life. How you deal with the problems is what gives your life character.

A mother and daughter fought all the time. They fought about sharing chores and they fought about priorities. They fought so much that one day a neighbor who was fed up of the noise came up to them and asked them: When are you two getting divorced?

The mother and daughter realized at that moment that they were behaving childishly, sticking to their own egos and thinking that the one who won the who-shouts-louder-contest would be superior. They decided to come to a compromise. They valued the relationship that they had. They both had to win and fighting was making their problems bigger than they really were.

If both sides have to win, both sides have to sit at the table and communicate.

How hard is it for you to make a compromise?

_____

_____

All offices are made of individuals. Most of the time there will be conflicts of interest – with your colleagues, with your boss, with your subordinates. Not everyone is the same and different people have different ways of thinking and expressing themselves. It is hard to compromise if you are not an open person. Compromise is confused with losing. Compromise can be turned into a win – win situation if you can understand what motivates the other side. The idea is to steer the dialogue in everyone's favour, not just your own.

Negotiation is not only about conflict management. If you are able to negotiate a deal for your company, you have an opportunity to make more profits for the company and that can help you get promoted or get a bonus.

Negotiating is all about timing your talk. **When you say what makes a big difference in the outcome of a discussion.**

Negotiate and how! Think in terms of a chess game.

★   Be clear about where you stand.

★   What should your next move be?

★   What will the other side's next move be?

★   What could your future course of action be and what about theirs?

★   Are you willing to be checkmated or do you know the right time to back out?

★   One more thing – like the game and remember it is a game. Any more serious than that and you could lose.

When you negotiate you learn to put yourself in the other side's shoes. In the corporate sphere, you have to work smart and word hard. Negotiation is a complex skill that will take years to perfect. Right now you speak what's on your mind but when you negotiate in a corporate atmosphere, you are persuading people to move things to your favour and as per the company's expectations. You will have to learn from observation and experience.

Customer Relationship Management Skills

Whatever profession you get into, be it the BPO sector or retail, you will have to deal with customers or clients on a round the clock basis. Unlike your time in college, you are accountable for your behaviour with your customers. In a BPO centre, your calls are recorded. Besides having the required accent, you also need to adjust your EQ or Emotional Quotient.

Are you good at handling people whether they are polite or impolite?

_____

_____

Customers come in all shapes and sizes. The key to being a successful employee is treating your customers right. How do you do that? You listen and communicate the company norms with clarity. There are as many kinds of customers as there are people. There is more on customer etiquette in a subsequent chapter.

Be direct with your customers. If they are unhappy or agitated, do not reflect their behaviour in your verbal and non-verbal conduct. Be polite at all times.

Take the case of the employee who is hired specifically to fire under-performers from the company. This is not an easy job. The employees who are fired hurl abuses and sometimes they are very upset. The only thing to be done is let them say what they have to say and go on with your job.

When you deal with customers, you have to be very professional. Don't let your emotions run too high. Just do your job and be as ethical as possible.

Fresher Shoot

Suppose I'm new on the job and my customer complains. How do I handle it?

★ Whether you are new or not, customers will complain. The key is not to take it personally and try to understand the reasons for the customer's anxiety.

★ Ask the customers a lot of open-ended questions so that the customer can explain what's troubling him or her. This also gives you time to think of a solution and it gives the customer an opportunity to express disappointment.

★ Explain to them what you can and cannot do. This way you streamline their expectations from you.

★ Be as courteous and cooperative as possible and speak with a smile on your face, even if you are on the phone.

Business Writing Skills

► The Professional Writer

Don't get worried about the word business communication. It's actually a simpler form of writing – not as detailed as the essay writing you did in school. Business writing is more about being very concise and getting into the précis writing frame of mind than the expansive essay mind.

Be concise: Writing concisely is an art that you must master.

This letter is with regard to the fact of the matter that I am interested in the study of phonetics and would like to pursue the opportunity of working in your institute in the capacity of an intern.

This sentence is long and very dull. Let's chop off whatever is irrelevant or of no use.

I am interested in phonetics and am excited to work as an intern at your institute.

Now isn't that more fun to read! Remove all those clichés and redundant expressions and write simple sentences, sentences that you can read and understand quickly.

Be clear: Writing well means that you are able to convey relevant information in a way that can be understood. Why were you made to write so many essays in high school? Besides essays helping you to improve your punctuation, grammar, spelling, and vocabulary, writing about a theme develops your organizational skills.

Putting a group of sentences on a page does not make your copy "good English".

Good language skills = unity of presentation

If you are asked to write a letter, create a presentation or lecture on a podium, you are primarily asked to expand upon a single theme.

How do you do that? When you write you use paragraphs, or blocks of sentences. Each paragraph deals with one aspect or idea of the overall theme. There must be some logical progression of your ideas. The copy should flow naturally.

I'll give you an example. If you are asked to write about a topic like "job hunt":

★ First, you talk about the job hunt process and how it can be easy if you are prepared.

★ Talk about knowing the media – where do you find that job?

★ How do you narrow down your search?

★ How do you understand a job advert?

★　How do you create your resume and cover letter?

★　The big day - the interview!

So the central premise of the proposed topic runs through the entire essay.

Once you decide on the overall flow of the essay, you work on the essay at a micro level. Each paragraph will contain a topic sentence. This is the primary sentence in the paragraph around which the rest of the paragraphs revolve. A paragraph typically contains three to eight sentences.

Here's an excerpt paragraph from this book:

English is spoken differently from country to country. There are different kinds of English as trainees in BPOs will be aware of – British English, American English, Australian English, etc. All these are very different from the English known as Indian English. Each kind of English is again divided into various dialects. So even if you know BBC English (the UK Standard Received Pronunciation), you will find it difficult to follow Scottish English at first.

The topic sentence indicates that I'm speaking about different kinds of English. The rest of the paragraph is an extension of that idea. You can place the topic sentence at the beginning or the middle of the paragraph. Examples and details add body to your paragraph.

How do you order your paragraphs?

Well, that depends on how creative you are and what kind of material you have.

★　You can move from the general to the particular. This means that if the topic is climate change, you can start talking about climate change and then go deeper and deeper into its hazardous effects at the local level.

★　You can move from particular to general. This means you can start your argument with a particular instance of climate change and then expand upon it.

★　You can tackle the pros and the cons; this helps a great deal when you are preparing reports and trying to come up with recommendations.

★　Another way of ordering paragraphs is by going step by step. This is ideal when you are writing a theorem or a scientific article or fact finding in a report.

Mind Map the Road Map

A brilliant way of creatively understanding material and creating a document is by using the good old hand-drawn mind map.

★ To plan and organise ideas.

★ To compose any kind of document, even something as simple as an email, a deceptively easy document but one that really requires a great amount of skill and thought put into it.

A mind map looks like a tiny brain (the central idea) connected by many branching ideas.

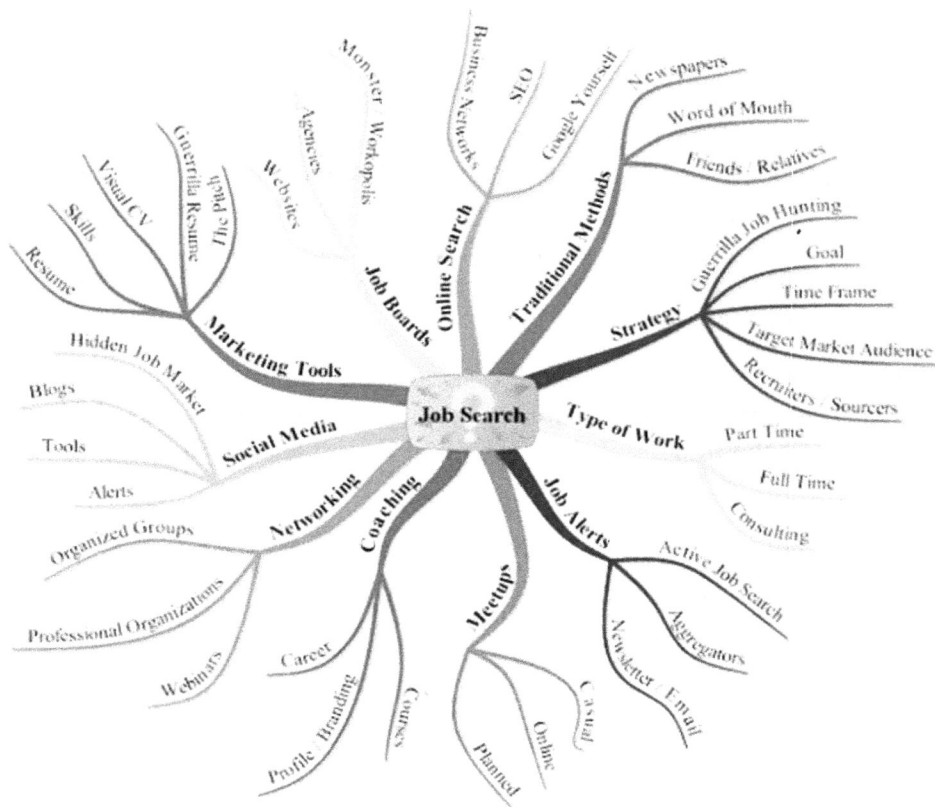

Benefits of Mind Mapping

★ This is a good way of organizing your thoughts. Each branch and its ideas can be expanded into a paragraph.

★ When you map out your points, you automatically remember them. It is a better way of memorizing than the usual mugging up.

★ Mind maps give you clarity. When you create one, you automatically organise information.

★ Mind maps are great for presentations, creating, reports and even for group discussions when you need to debate pros and cons.

Business Writing Checklist

All matters of composition or all the business writing you will ever do will have a basic checklist:

★ Whether it is an email, a report, or a cover letter, your communication is addressed to **someone**.

★ Every communication you write out will have a **subject line**, telling the reader what it is about.

★ You will be dealing with any one or some of these objectives – **request or provide information, persuade, explain, evaluate, or recommend.**

★ After you have communicated your intent, you have to **sign off**.

★ Before you send out any document, even if you have a deadline and even if you are a good writer, do a **grammar check and a spell check**.

★ **Revise the entire document and check whether your content is clear**, each paragraph conveying the message appropriately.

★ If you are in doubt about some aspect of the documentation process, don't hesitate to **ask**.

► **Write an Email Right**

Email ID

★ First you must have your own email id. For the purpose of the job hunt, make a professional sounding email id – the best email is your own first name and last name. All of you know how to open an internet browser, right? Once you open Internet Explorer or Google Chrome, go to Gmail, Yahoo, Rediff or the website where you create your email id. Then create your own username and make sure that you remember the password or write it down in a safe place.

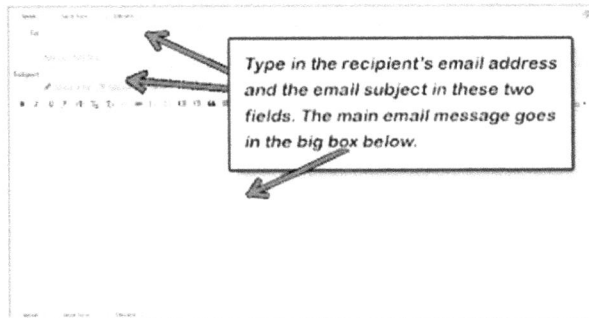

> Type in the recipient's email address and the email subject in these two fields. The main email message goes in the big box below.

Compose

Once you sign in, you can compose your email.

★ In the **To** section, write the person's or recipient's email id, not name.

★ Fill in the subject line with the intention of your letter. Do not leave it blank! If you want information, type **Info Required**. If you have been asked to send out an email and provide feedback, then you type **Feedback as requested**. If you are applying for a job, then type **Application for post of** …………………...

★ Be clear when you write. State the intent of your email in the subject line and elaborate on it in the body of the email.

★ Introduce yourself in the first paragraph the way you would while writing a cover letter.

I' am writing with reference to your post on naukri.com for the post of _____.

★ The body of the letter will expand your subject line. Before you write the email, decide how many paragraphs you need and what each paragraph should be about.

★ Remember to sign off with a *Regards,* and your name below.

Email Language Tips

★ Write to the point. Be business like. Just state the obvious and sign off. That's how professional writing is.

★ Never write sms language like thr, u, w8.

★ No emoticons like :)

★ Use capital letters at the beginning of the sentence and for Proper Nouns in a sentence. Close sentences with a full stop.

★ Do a spell check and check all sentences for Subject-Verb agreement.

★ Check the tone of your language. Written language has a tone as well. The tone you must adopt is one of politeness.

Have a look at this email:

Your letter could also be elaborate like a cover letter.

To: designdot.org

From: xxxx@gmail.com

Subject: Application for post of Corporate Communication Executive

Dear Ms Rashmi,

I am writing in response to the ad posted on naukri.com for the post of a corporation communication executive (Ref No: 1243).

Please accept my attached resume and cover letter as an application for this position. My skills and experience meet your requirements.

While I was studying at Anne's College, I had the opportunity to work as an intern with Cactus Media House. During this brief stint, I was involved in writing press releases and pitching stories to the media. I have excellent verbal and writing skills. While in college, I was selected at the University level for a debate on the corruption menace and I qualified second.

In addition to graduating with honours, I have also worked part time as a sales representative with Haroun Pinto Ltd. During this stint, I have improved my communication skills and learnt more about networking, so crucial in today's work culture.

I am eager to learn more about the post and look forward to hearing from you.

Thank you.

Yours sincerely,

Gita

Report Writing

Writing a report is an essential part of your future corporate life.

What is a report? A statement of precise, unbiased, and accurate factual information. Like all business communication, a report has a neutral professional tone. All the figures and facts are presented in an empirical or scientific style.

A report consists of:

- ★ Title page
- ★ Table of contents
- ★ Introduction
- ★ Summary
- ★ Detailed findings
- ★ Conclusion
- ★ Recommendations

Let's go into each section in a little detail.

Title Page

- ★ Title
- ★ Addressed to
- ★ From
- ★ Date

First you need to make a working title. The title usually conveys the **purpose of your report**. Then you must mention who you are creating this document for. You also mention your name and the date on this page.

Contents Page

This is optional. If the report is brief, then it can be avoided. For a longer report, this page functions as an Index.

Introduction

- ★ Who asked you to compose this report? To whom are you reporting?
- ★ When were you asked to submit it?
- ★ Terms of reference (Aims of your project)
- ★ Scope of your report (How you will go about it/Methodology used)

Summary

This is the backbone of your report. It is easier to write this section of the report once you have finished composing the rest of the report. This is a very important part of the document, so it must be written with a great deal of attention. Here you summarize:

★   Important findings from your investigations

★   The conclusions you have reached

★   Recommendations

Detailed Findings

This is where all your hard work finds it way. Here you can use jargon or technical language related to the industry you are talking about. Diagrams are also presented in this section. The information is divided into several sections each separated by an appropriate sub-heading.

Conclusion

This includes what you have understood after your investigation or study. This is based on past or present events, so use the appropriate tense. Keep this paragraph as simple as possible.

Recommendations

If you have been authorized to provide recommendations, this is your chance. Recommendations refer to the future course of action. The action plan you provide should be based on your findings and the conclusion you have drawn. List recommendations in order of importance.

Appendix

The appendix contains any data that is relevant to the reader. The appendix is proof of the research you have put in to arrive at the conclusions you put forward in your report. Appendix could contain:

★   Other reports, memos, letters, questionnaires

★   Statistical or comparative information, maps, charts

★   Flowcharts

References

Reference is different from the Appendix. This shows the books or journals you have referred to. Alternatively, you could use footnotes.

Best to refer to a previous report of the company you are in to get a feel of the in-house

Report Do's

Style: Be clear. write in simple sentences and active voice.

Source: Make sure that you refer to the right websites and collect the correct material. A report with false material can put the author in very bad light.

Tone: Reports are based only on facts and **not opinion**. All possibilities of a situation should be explored, not only the positive ones. So the tone must be **Objective** and **Business like** – no describing words like *great, boring, uninteresting*, etc.

Graphics: Diagrammatic representation in the form of bar graphs, pie charts, bar

graphics in the body of the report. A paragraph of explanation can be followed by the appropriate diagram.

Report Don'ts

No copying: Do not cut and paste from old reports you have referred to. Use previous reports as guidelines, just to help you with the formatting.

No carelessness: Don't make grammar and spelling mistakes in the copy. This

Sample Report

> **Global Etiquette – Proposed Immersion Course for Employees of XYZ Company**
>
> As part of additional soft skill training, Dr. Shivmani has dealt with eighteen employees at XYZ company on a one-to-one basis. The four hour process has yielded assessment details of what kind of skills each employee stands to gain from a global etiquette programme. Based on this, a customized course will be created.

> **Executive Summary**
>
> Of the eighteen employees, only two, namely Mr. Harsha Murthy and Ms. Vasudha
>
> a global scale. The rest need to dedicate a great deal more of time and effort to improve basic introductory skills, business writing, and interaction etiquette.
>
> **Recommendations**
>
> The proposed training programme will consist of a detailed presentation on global etiquette norms and a short class on simple business writing etiquette.
>
> further training if required.
>
> **Dr. Shivmani**

Business Letter

still exist in case you are under the impression that emails have pushed letters into extinction.

Letter Writing Basics

The letter is **addressed to someone**. Usually a business letter is composed on a page with a **letter head**. The letter head is like the From Address. It includes the name of the company, the address, email, phone, and fax numbers.

Nowadays the **date** and the **To address** (to whomsoever you are addressing) appear at the left side of the page.

As in all communications, the business letter contains a **salutation**.

Dear Sir/Sirs

Dear Madam

Like in an email, a business letter also contains a **subject line**.

The body of the letter begins with an **introduction** to your intent. Like in a report, you **summarize the purpose** of your letter, **elaborate it in the subsequent paragraphs** and then at the **end of your letter emphasize on the information you require or that you wish to provide.**

★ You sign off saying **Regards,** no apostrophe on Yours and sign your name below.

Fresher Shoot

You talked about the four Basic Skills – Comprehension, Study, Participatory, and Management Skills. You devoted an entire chapter to Communication Skills (Verbal, Written, and Non-Verbal) and then devoted a chapter to Corporate communication necessities like Corporate Speak, Business Writing, Leadership, and Negotiation Skills.

Is practical experience the only way to get these skills?

An example will answer your question. A woman went to driving school and mastered the theoretical aspects of driving. You could quiz her about the engine or carburetor, and she would answer instantly. However, she took much longer than average to get her license. The reason is that theoretical knowledge is useless without practical knowledge. Driving a car in theory and driving a car in real time are like doing two different things.

So theoretical knowledge is not enough. What you need is hard core practical experience. Even if you are a first ranker, you will find your first day at any job difficult. You may say, "I know my subject inside out but I don't know how far I will succeed on the ground." Reason? Books are a wealth of information but reality is very different. Books are like a map – they tell you the exact nature of things but does a map look like the real world? It's just a marker – important but very different from the real thing.

So gain as much practical experience as you can and you see how your soft skills and life skills automatically improve. With experience you become more confident and you find it easier to communicate your ideas. Your inhibitions and hesitation also disappear. If you have some work experience before your interview, you will not be half as intimidated by the interview process.

How will I juggle college and work to gain all these skills?

Deepak doubles as a student by day and a call centre employee by night. How does he juggle his roles? "It's hard. I need a lot of focus in class which is hard when I have had a strenuous night at the call centre", he says.

You don't always have to go out of college to get the kind of experience that counts. It's all about participating in college as much as you can and keeping your eyes and ears open for more confidence-building activities.

Opt for internships – think how much fun it will be to be a part of something new and that pays in experience. Experience is one's biggest asset.

5

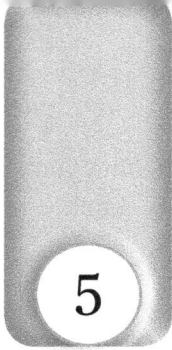

You: Personal Branding

Have you noticed how important branding has become? Companies use successful celebrities and athletes to endorse their products. Why? Because successful people sell. A lot of effort goes into branding a product – there has to be a good logo, a good message, an impressive packaging overall. Nowadays, a concept called **personal branding** is in vogue –
from your unique potential. Do you know that online branding is a phenomenon in itself? That means you have to do a lot of networking, interact on blogs and forums, make your voice heard even in cyberspace.

When you were in school, you may have been taught not to blow your own trumpet. This means you were told not to boast too much about your achievements. Today, however, that advice does not hold as much. To be known, your presence must be

So how do you turn yourself into a brand? That's what we have been talking about from the beginning of the book. Every effort that you make to improve your self-

branding. A lot of focus is being made on how the product is packed. How you present yourself is as important as what your personality really is. You cannot be perfect of course, but you can give the impression that given an opportunity you will become the ideal employee.

A brand is unique and so are you. That is a lot to have in common.

Which is your favourite brand? Why do you identify with it?

_____

_____

_____

There are so many brands out there – be it hospitality, fashion, or transport. Each brand carries with it a certain set of features and values. It is these brands that give companies a life of their own. Maybe you like how cool the product is or you like a distinct feature like its design or usability.

What makes you different from the rest of your peers? What is your brand USP?

_____

_____

_____

Each brand has a distinctive quality. Apple is famous for its sleek design, Nokia for its durability. As an aspiring job seeker, you have to find out what makes you tick. That gives you more clarity about your goals and the potential within you.

Dan Shwabel is Managing Partner at Millenial Branding and the international best-selling author of personal branding book Me 2.0. He is an expert on personal branding and is the branding guru for the new generation. He has these things to say on what personal branding means in this day and age.

★ *Brand yourself for the career you want, not the job you have.*

Even if you get a job in a call centre, and you have plans to work as a designer later on, you should position yourself to achieve those goals. Even if you are going to do the night shift in XYZ company, are you getting the time to focus on the latest aspects of design? Are you creating a designer portfolio simultaneously?

★ *Get as many internships as you can in college so that you can figure out what you don't want to do when you graduate.*

There is no substitute for being enterprising. Working in various companies gives you the exposure you need to tackle the job hunt with confidence. There is no room any more for inexperienced candidates. Accumulate as much learning as you can during your graduation years. That way you can narrow down your interest and make the right choices. It makes the job hunt much easier if you know where you want to go in advance.

★ *Network as much as possible, both online and offline, because people do the hiring.*

Sharpen your verbal skills to the maximum. Confidence is a requisite if you want to chat with ease to potential employers. It's not just the face to face any more; the world operates on internet etiquette. You have to start making an impression in person and on cyberspace as well.

★ *Get your own website (yourfullname.com), make it creative, and put it on your resume and everywhere else.*

This piece of advice works especially well for freshers who have ideas of turning to entrepreneurship or want to work in the media space. Having a website of your own makes you look professional. It is expensive of course; the next best thing would be to make a profile on linkedin.com or create your own blog. There you have to post real details about yourself – your real name and achievements.

★ *Get business cards, even if you don't have a job, so you can market yourself because you never know who you will meet and where you will meet them.*

Imagine yourself exchanging a business card when you go for a walk-in. It's so much more professional than scribbling your contact details on a scrap piece of paper!

★ *Get to know yourself, your strengths and your passions so you can avoid jobs that aren't the right fit.*

You are a lucky generation. Never before in the history of civilization has so much importance been given to the individual. You have so many resources at your disposal and so many opportunities to choose from. No need to make sacrifices when it comes to your career. Choose what you love and the company automatically chooses you.

Getting prepared for the corporate world requires a complete self-branding exercise. Every individual who comes for an interview is prepared. You cannot fall behind. Branding yourself involves changing how people perceive you and how you perceive yourself. Your resume and cover letter are written presentations of your life history and experience. Your personal branding statement is your cover letter objective. The way you groom yourself for the big day indicates how much effort you put into creating a better look. Self-branding is not just about looking good and selling yourself with the right words; it's also about increasing your credibility. In this section, we look at the different ways we present ourselves – when you draft your resume and cover letter, when you groom yourselves to impress, and when you present your world view.

Your Look

Fresher Panic Button: I am not sure about my appearance.

These days you have to be sure about your appearance and the good news is that you can. Looking good has never been more important. It is essential to be neat and well dressed at all times, particularly when you are planning to get a job or once you are formally employed. Haven't you heard the phrase "It's all in the grooming?"

Fresher Shoot

How can someone judge you based on what you wear? That's unfair.

Don't you put all your experience and work into a narrow folder called your portfolio? This determines the kind of work that you do. When you dress well, you showcase your taste, the care you put into choosing your attire, and your seriousness about the interview.

Grooming makes you feel good about yourself and this makes you more confident. You can dress effectively and hide any perceived defects. Nobody is perfect. Well dressed people know how to dress in a way to look more attractive or in way that will flatter their body type. You can also shop appropriately within an adequate budget if you know exactly what kind of clothes suit you and make you look smart. People will appreciate you if you have spent a little time making yourself look more presentable. To put in that effort, read on!

Just like you select a good A4 Bond paper to print your cover letter and resume and find a neat envelope to keep it in, you have to present yourself well.

When you finally get the call to go for the interview, you should not be under prepared. It is very important to look 'today' or be suited for the times. You have to be contemporary and also look yourself. No use wearing stiletto heels or the Rado watch, if you can't pull it off.

The bottom line is anyone can look good nowadays with a little bit of investment. With the right clothes and haircut, you look smart. No need of worrying about your weight or height as by wearing the right fit, the right colour coordination and the right accessories, you can market yourself easily.

Young men, don't skip this section. Today grooming is everyone's number one priority.

Do you know how to dress well? What kind of clothes do you wear?

_____

_____

Looking at your wardrobe gives you a clue about what kinds of clothes you need. College attire will not work for office – what you wear to college is mostly casual wear. You'll have to completely revamp your dressing style. Take some time to create a decent wardrobe as you don't want to buy formal wear the day before the interview. It's not just clothes but shoes and accessories that need changing.

Do you have an adequate wardrobe or do you need to do some basic interview shopping? Where do you shop?

_____

_____

_____

Compare your shopping venues with your friends' options. Ask your shopping savvy friends where you can get the most reasonable clothes and shoes. Sometimes you can get exclusive outfits for a good price, if only you know the right place. Like with creating your resume, creating a presentable you also requires a lot of time and effort!

Grooming is based on many factors. Mention your personals in the space provided.

Your body type

Thin   Average   Overweight

_____

Your height

Average   Short   Very tall

_____

Your skin type

Babita Jaishankar, image consultant, provides grooming tips. Jaishankar is a certified skin and colour analyst. She has worked in the U.S and India helping various clients with makeovers. She is launching her own company, Wardrobe Solutions (WSol) with the credo that a dynamic personal and professional image can be created without giving up personal comfort.

_____

Grooming tips with Babita

Grooming tips for women

It's essential that you appear professional, capable, and confident without going overboard.

★   Western Wear

The classic is a charcoal, black, or navy suit (preferably in all season wool or linen) with a single pop of colour like a scarf or a silk blouse that matches your skin type. Skirted suits are more acceptable for interviews than pant suits.

★ Indian Wear

☑ Stick to clean cut and well - fitted (never tight) silk kurtis.

☑ Avoid heavy embellishments and sequins.

☑ Saree in tussar or raw silk is also an elegant option.

Body Type: Thin

★ The material used for the kurta, suit, and shirts should be textured like sweater fabric, khadi silk, raw silk, or tweed.

★ Always remember to colour contrast the top and the bottom.

★ You can layer your clothing by wearing:

☑ a smart shirt inside your blazer/suit jacket

☑ shirt with a cardigan

☑ layers of tops in different colours to give an illusion of a fuller body

☑ horizontal stripes or a printed yoke on the kurti

★ You can wear

☑ a bold belt

☑ big pockets and cuff on the trousers

Body Type: Overweight

★ Use vertical detailing or lines to gain height and slenderize.

★ If opting for a suit skirt, opt for a skirt that is longer in drapable and soft fabrics (small prints/plain chiffons/crepes).

★ Use shoulder pads (not the ones that protrude out) or slightly puffed kurti sleeves to balance the lower body fullness.

★ Use some detailing on the outfit near to the face, so that the face is the focal point.

★ Trousers and skirts should be tapered slightly towards to bottom (not the skinny fit style).

Body Type: Short

★ Use of prints should be in moderation – on the upper half of the outfit so as to let your face be the focal point.

★ Opt for 'V' necks in kurti/shirts/tops.

★ Use monochromatic colours.

Body Type: Tall

★ Use horizontal details (a horizontal yoke kurta in a different colour).

★ Wear wide lapels for the suit.

★ Wear top and bottom in different colours.

★ Choose flared skirts.

Grooming tips for men

Men look good in white or blue shirts paired with navy or khaki slacks. A plain necktie defines their office dress code best. Shirt sleeves can be rolled up and neckties removed to "dress down" quickly for social occasions or just for comfort in the summer months.

★ **Body Type: The Average Guy**

Average-sized men by definition don't stand out in a crowd. The clothing has to do it for them.

★ Don't put in too much colour and strong patterns, unless it matches your personality and you are headed for a party!

★ Take advantage of a body that wears most things well. Try different cuts of suit jackets and more unusual combinations like vested suits or even vests without the suit.

★ Ties, belts, pocket squares work well on average guys but remember **for interviews stick to conservative dressing – suits and blazers please.**

Body Type: Big Guy

★ A generous fit is the key to all clothing for big men. Do not try to squeeze into tight-fitting clothing. It will be uncomfortable for you and not ideal to look at!

★ Larger men should instead seek out fabrics with a good, clean drape and wear their jackets and trousers slightly loose.

★ Wear dark colours for a slim effect.

★ A slight taper at the waist of a jacket helps draw the eye up towards the face rather than keeping it down on the chest – **so wear tapered jackets.**

★ Trousers should be worn high on the natural waist, so that they drape clean over the belly rather than squeezing tightly beneath it. Keep the waistband of the trousers from bunching unattractively and **no pleats** on the trousers.

Fresher Shoot

Dressing is important as is the kind of make-up you wear.

Are there any good hair day tips?

Men: You can never go wrong with keeping your hair short. Long hair for men doesn't always work during the first interview. Maintain your hair – shampoo it, no need for too much gel. As for facial hair, the clean shaven look is neat. If you have a moustache or beard, keep it trimmed.

Women: Wear your hair down to balance the masculinity of the suit you wear for an interview. To give a healthy gloss to your hair, use serum and spray on your hair. You can't afford to have a bad hair day on your interview day. Keeping your hair in place is the best way to prevent yourself from fiddling with it, something that makes a very bad impression on your interviewer.

Is personal hygiene so important?

Absolutely.

Men: Your teeth should be clean, no nicotine stains please – use mouth freshener for unpleasant odours. Bathing everyday is a habit you should stick with. Clip your nails short. Every little thing counts.

Women: Basic hygiene is a must. Wax to remove excess hair on arms and legs. Use deodorant in moderation. Thread eyebrows for a neat look. Check for cracked heels and wear shoes accordingly.

Is make-up a must? I'm happier to be a plain Jane.

Yes make-up is a must but keep make-up and jewellery simple. More than fashion, make-up gives a fresh and confident look. This is good during interviews, particularly walk-ins where you have to wait a long while for your turn.

You should take care of your body – more than deck it up with make-up.

Should I manicure my nails?

Buff, not polish, your nails. In case you want to show off your nails, use a neutral pink. No hennaed hands to work.

Bindi rules?

Stick to wearing a small bindi if you must – overelaborate ones are not required in the corporate space.

How do I decide which colour suits me?

You'll have to look at your skin, hair, and eye colour. Look at the mirror and ask yourself *Am I wearing the colour or is the colour wearing me*? Try to avoid too much of a contrast. **No loud colours** for an interview please.

Men: Wear light shirts and dark trousers. Colour coordinate ties.

What kind of accessories are must-haves during interviews?

A good watch, a belt, and well – kept shoes or sandals. No dangling and flashy jewellery as they can be quite distracting.

Recommended shoes for men and women? (For office wear and interviews)

Men: Dress shoes preferably one pair in tan (as they can be worn with differently coloured trousers) and one in black.

Women: Closed sandals or shoes with kitten heels. Second best, a closed front and sling back sandals with kitten heels. Keep in mind that you may have to climb stairs or stand for a long time during a presentation. The shoes need to be well maintained ones. Keep your work shoes separate from your usual wear.

Is it okay to use perfume when you go for an interview?

Nothing too strong. It is good to smell nice, but too much of perfume or cologne doesn't sell and can distract the employer.

What about nose and ear piercings?

The usual ear piercings for women works but too much of piercings may put the employer off as what they are looking for is something more conservative.

Have I missed anything?

Don't forget to dry clean your clothes for the best effect. Starch and iron saris as crumpled clothes give a very bad impression.

Dress for success and success will follow!

Your Voice

Good pronunciation must be accompanied by a good voice. Your voice reflects your personality and confidence level.

Fresher Shoot

How can we change our voice? It is inborn.

There are a lot of inborn traits that we can improve and your voice is one of them. Voice improvement is an art and a science. A good voice is pleasing to hear. It is a proper balance of oral and nasal. Your voice should be just loud enough – never too loud, never too low.

Sometimes your confidence levels can affect the quality of your voice. What is the use of having good English speaking skills if you lack the confidence to use your voice well?

★   **What kind of voice do you have? Choose the option that best fits.**

Confident   Hoarse   Soft   Weak   Melodious   Dull   Enthusiastic

_____

_____

Some students have very weak voices owing to lack of confidence. With continuous practice, you will notice how your voice can become much more confident and assertive. For this you have to take every opportunity that comes your way to speak and be heard.

★   **How loud are you?**

Inaudible (difficult to hear you)   Very loud   Clear

_____

_____

This is a problem area for many students as they don't want to assert themselves. Your voice defines who you are, so don't be ashamed of speaking up.

Have you watched how some mothers have a lot of control over their children? "She doesn't even hit the child once but the child listens to her," people say. The real secret is that she knows how to use her voice effectively. Teaching is one profession where effective voice modulation is an asset.

Watch how people behave with you when you speak in a weak tone and when you speak in a more assertive manner. There is a difference.

★   **What is your speaking pace?**

Very fast   Average   Very slow

_____

_____

Speaking fast gives away that you are nervous. It's as though you want to say everything as quickly as possible and leave the room! If you are too slow a speaker, you cannot engage the interviewer or the audience. You lose their attention very soon, not a good thing during an interview.

★   **What pitch do you speak in?**

Shrill   Monotonous   Gentle   Varied

_____

_____

If your voice is a monotone or flat, you come across as a boring person. If you want to interest people, you have to raise and lower your tone continuously. If you are too shrill, you put people off.

★   **Define your voice quality.**

Nasal   Flat   Clear   Enthusiastic

_____

_____

Your voice quality can change the entire mood of your environment. Always try to create a positive vibe around you. Watch how positive people interact with others. What kind of voice quality do popular people have? What draws you to them? Listen and learn.

★   **Define your articulation.**

Mumble-jumble   Crisp   Clear

_____

_____

Articulation is the way you pronounce words. It's not just what you say that makes a difference. It's how you say it. If you hurriedly mumble an answer looking away, you show disrespect, lack of interest, and lack of knowledge. Why do you want to come across as such a person? Be clear and others will be clear with you.

★ **Define your voice quotient.**

Emotionless   Unfriendly   Natural

_____

_____

Be as natural as possible. Sometimes when you go for an interview, you could be surprised by the way you spoke. Says Nita, a B.com student, "I was just not myself. It was as though someone else was in my body – the way I spoke, the way I held myself, all these things were different from who I really am." Why is that? It happens because fear really spoils the way you hold yourself together, it takes something away from you, that thing that makes you special, that makes you 'you'. Don't let it get the better of you.

★ **When you speak do you pause?**

_____

_____

Remember how your favourite teacher paused at all the right places to make the lesson interesting? Pausing is an essential part of speaking. When you make the right pauses at the right places, the listener becomes more interested in what you say and will wait for you to say more. It is nice to have an interviewer interested in your ideas, right?

★ **Give examples of the times when you sound tense/calm/shrill/strained.**

Tense

_____

_____

Calm

_____

_____

Shrill

_____

_____

Strained

_____

_____

Understanding the situations which agitate or calm you helps you modulate your voice accordingly. If being in a stressful situation affects your voice or articulation skills, then you have to work on the way you handle stress.

Voice matters. There are voice coaches out there who fix all kinds of problems that crop up. Voice coaches help you improve your existing voice. They teach you when to slow down, pause, when to emphasize, and when to raise your voice. They also provide professional help to cure problems like stammering.

Voice Facts

★ A good voice requires good body posture.

★ Proper breathing influences voice quality.

★ Having a good voice can make up for any articulation errors.

★ Do you notice that your throat muscles get constricted when you are extremely tense? Sometimes even swallowing becomes difficult when you are tense.

★ Exercise releases stress and that can give your voice a lot more throw.

Warm - up your Voice

★ Prepare your voice by drinking warm water before the big interview. Drinking water helps you calm down. Always carry water to your walk-ins and interviews.

★ Get into the habit of listening to your voice by reading passages to yourself as part of your daily pre-interview practice routine. Reading to yourself is the best way to learn, understand, as well as identify your weak areas when it comes to the way you pronounce words and assess the pace of your speech. You unconsciously tap into a good resource of grammar know-how when you continuously read works by good authors.

Your Perspective

General knowledge about GK

What is your attitude towards learning in general? Your attitude decides your success.

★ **Are you confident and motivated enough to plunge in and learn?**

_____

_____

_____

Broaden your horizons. Know things and get interested in knowing things. Don't think that you can get on in the world without some general knowledge. An innovative and knowledgeable person always has more chances of getting noticed by the right people. Also get the scores you need to make the cut!

What have you learnt today?

_____

_____

Every day make it a habit to learn something new. A fact, an anecdote, a puzzle, anything of this sort can make you a great conversationalist. It's also a good way of updating yourself. Follow the trends in the industry you are pitching for on a day - to - day basis, not at the last minute.

What have you learnt the last week?

_____

_____

_____

If you are a knowledge seeker, then it would be a good idea to catalogue or note down what you learn. Some students read many books but if you ask them a year later what they read, they become speechless. A lot of knowledge is stored in your brain but knowing where exactly the information comes from helps you during interviews. Rachael, a student in her final year, remembers how she got stuck when an interviewer asked her the name of her favourite author. "I wasn't scared but the name just slipped away." Noting down the things you know, the people you meet, the dates to remember makes it easier for you to remember when you need to.

What have you learnt the last semester?

_____

_____

_____

_____

_____

Lose the habit of leaving behind everything you learnt in the previous semester. Make a mental note of things you should remember from a job perspective.

Didn't you learn how to use mobiles maybe in the last five years? Can't you send a hundred texts a day? These are all skills you have accumulated over the past years – skills you learnt so quickly because you had to keep up with your friends. The same goes for academic and communication skills. If you want to keep up, learning fast is the only choice you have. Keeping up requires confidence and confidence is the result of a lot of hard work!

★　**What do you think of your GK quotient?**

_____

_____

_____

Most of you have the jitters when you are asked about your general knowledge. GK is not just about knowing the name of the tallest mountain or the longest river. It would be interesting to know those things as well but you can expand your GK by focusing on your interests; that's a good way to start the process. Knowing about your favourite topic in depth helps during interviews, particularly if you are asked to speak about your interests. If you say that you love books, and you are unable to state straight away the name of the book you are reading, the author, and some details about the book, then the interviewer decides that either you don't read books at all or that you are too nervous to speak about it.

★　**What kind of GK do you have: Sports, Fashion, Political, Movies?**

_____

_____

_____

_____

If you have an interest in a theme like car racing, then you automatically know about racers from different parts of the world, the different racing tracks they drive in, details about the venues, banners that sponsor these initiatives, etc. Every interest you have is a minefield of information in itself. If you like fashion, you learn about so many different cultures and the kind of preferences they have; the history of dress is the history of human civilization.

What you should do is sharpen your area of interest. That's how experts become experts; it's because of how much hard work they do to understand a particular subject. When you love something so much, you don't feel that you are working hard at all!

However, employers are looking for people with more than niche interests. So while you may have in-depth knowledge about cars and have a limited working knowledge of world affairs, you may not get the job as you are not well-rounded enough.

★   **Do you read the paper every day?**

_____

_____

_____

Most of the time you'll say, *No I didn't read the paper today.* Scanning through the headlines and listening to the news and debates is essential on a day - to - day basis. You have to be well-informed to make your own decisions and not be easily swayed by mass sentiment. For that, it is necessary to read the editorial page. Slowly, you will start developing your own point of view. During a group discussion, this kind of view point helps a great deal. If you read editorials everyday, you understand that every issue has two sides. You also come across so many issues that are relevant at present. This gives you a lot of information that you can use to prove your point and impress.

★   **An interview question to watch out for is "Give us the top ten headlines of this month." Can you answer that one?**

_____

_____

_____

_____

_____

_____

_____

_____

_____

_____

_____

All you have to do is to know the top two local stories, top two regional stories, top two global stories, top two entertainment stories, and top two sports stories. Now you have your ten!

★ **What sources of GK do you like the most?**

_____

_____

_____

_____

Believe it or not, books, newspapers, and the Internet (including websites, blogs, and online books) are not the only sources of GK. Watching TV is a great way of enhancing your general knowledge too. Watch period movies and documentaries. Watch the local, national, and international news.

Watch debates during prime time and you have an anchor arguing out issues with a select group of panelists. By watching professionals speak, you can learn many aspects of language like pronunciation, tone, how to express ideas, and how to carry yourself.

Take the Swachh Bharat phenomenon. How many channels have discussed the various aspects of cleanliness and the lack of it in India? There are so many opinions that are voiced in our democracy. If you are eloquent, meaning if you can speak well, you can present your view and persuade as well.

Watching BBC gives you exposure to good English. You also understand world events. Many students think that there is no need to understand the rest of the world. They say they are patriotic and thereby India-centric. In a global world where if the markets crash in the US, the Indian stock market becomes cautious, this attitude is wrong.

Besides TV, quiz games and face - to - face discussions also work as great GK builders.

Fresher Shoot

Everything is available on Google. Why should I have GK then?

That's a relevant question. Google is a tool. It's a means to an end, not the end itself. A simple example will illustrate the fact. If you are asked to do an assignment, googling all the content doesn't help. You have to selectively Google. Then you have to select what parts are relevant to your assignment, understand those and rewrite.

Having general knowledge is key for starters like you as you don't have much in terms of experience. What you do have is your personality. An employer is looking for a well-rounded personality – the kind of person who can interact with people from all walks of life. If you are working in a global company, you will meet people from across the globe. It helps if you have some knowledge about their culture and the current affairs of those countries. Making conversation becomes much easier. You can't Google your way through a conversation, can you?

How can I memorize so many GK facts all of a sudden?

This is when googling can actually become a problem – you have too much information at your disposal. Stick to some general knowledge books that are out in the market. Become thorough with that information. The more books you refer to the more information that will crop up. Remember you are not doing a thesis. You should know **what to read** and **how quickly you can read them.**

Reading the paper everyday gives you a lot of information about the latest trends. Don't read the paper randomly; it's when you read on a daily basis that you understand the continuity of world events and your knowledge becomes more thorough. Preferably don't memorize all of a sudden. Keep accumulating knowledge about the world that you live in. You may live on 6th Cross, but your view should be more than a sixth cross view – it has to be a world view.

What kind of GK am I expected to have for an interview/GD?

You need to know what is happening right now. You need a point of view or an opinion about current affairs, particularly in your own state and country. It helps to have a wider knowledge of the world, especially when you are pitching to join a more global kind of workplace.

Bettering your GK quotient is about doing the self-packaging a little better. There are two kinds of candidates – one with a comfortable working knowledge of the world and the other completely clueless about the world she or he lives in.

Having good GK helps as we live in a global world. Everything is so interconnected. To make sense of things, we need to have a basic knowledge of the problems that plague our society and the world at large. We need to know the kinds of scientific changes that are happening as we speak. Why? Only if you understand the world can you become a part of it. Only if you understand how things work can you be part of a system like corporate culture.

How can I create a reading habit now? It's too late.

Reading books changes the way you think about the world. There are so many authors out there who have interesting perspectives. It's never too late!

First ask yourself these reading - related questions and then we can decide how to fix your reading habit issues.

How many books which are not on your syllabus do you read every month?

_____

_____

It's not just syllabus that you read but books outside your syllabus that make you develop a better world view. Says Reshma, a B. Com student, "I don't get the time to read after all my assignments." If you are motivated enough Reshma, what you said is not an excuse at all.

Most students say that they have so much course work to read that they don't have the time to read general fiction like stories, thrillers, romances, and mysteries, let alone non-fiction which is factual.

Words are everywhere and whether you are aware of it or not, you are using language all the time. When you talk, when you text, when you shop and bargain, when you read. You are influenced by movies, movies are made out of scripts, and scripts are made out of words. The bottom line is everything you do has words involved.

There are corporate managers who manage to read in between their busy schedules. The question is do you really want to read books and improve your knowledge base?

★ **Do you read Indian writers more than foreign ones? Which authors do you love?**

_____

_____

_____

You should read in as many languages as you can. It is an opportunity. Do you know that different languages cover different aspects of the personality? So the more languages you know, the more of an all-rounded person you become. It is imperative that you read English language books as well, as reading automatically prepares you for writing better. By the college level, you should have read full-fledged novels. Saying that you read The Harry Potter's series only is not going to get you anywhere.

★ **Do you complete the books you start?**

_____

_____

_____

Start finishing what you started. Reading is like any other task. Complete the novel and you will get a better idea about what the author intended to say. Completion is an important part of the corporate world work culture.

★ **Do you buy books or borrow them?**

_____

_____

_____

Try to get a continuous stream of books coming in either from your library or second - hand book stores. Invest in reading as it changes your world view and dramatically improves your sense of who you are and where you want to go.

Reading books changes the way you think about the world. There are so many authors out there who have interesting perspectives. Try to soak in as many ideas as you can!

Knowing what happens around you is a must. This is a global world and what happens in one part of the world influences people in other parts. This is called the butterfly effect. When you read the paper and watch the news, you get the world pulse. Don't miss it.

Books are not the only informative source – magazines are equally important. Some trade magazines expand your knowledge base about issues, opinions, and products. Reading internet articles is a good idea; you will stay up to date and get bytes of information that are useful from the point of view of interview. Reading builds vocabulary, debating skills for GD, writing skills, and GK. It makes you tolerant of varying points of view. Better start reading now during your college years than later!

Fresher Shoot

What about my IQ levels? How do I know my Quotient?

Take Intelligence Quotient (IQ), personality, and career tests online. Nowadays you don't have to wait to be interviewed to understand your potential. If you really want to know how you score on a variety of assessment tests, all you have to do is go online and find out. Libraries also have books on their shelves that deal with various assessment tests. Browse them.

Each kind of assessment test covers a different aspect of your personality. An IQ test tells you more about your verbal, mathematical, logical, and analytical skills. A personality test could tell you about your social skills – whether you are an introvert or an extrovert. This helps you when you pitch for a job. If you want to be a DJ, you should have a high X factor. An introvert could function brilliantly as a research assistant or an editor.

You shouldn't limit your job options to your kind of personality. However, it is good to start off in an area where you are comfortable and then gradually hone skills to fit in different areas.

Career tests are designed to match your preferences to the kind of job that would work for you. This is a useful tool for students who are confused about how they can capitalize on the core subject they have opted for.

TYPES OF KNOWLEDGE

There are two kinds of knowledge:

Quick knowledge: This is the knowledge that Gen Y wants. It's easy to get – read a few quiz books, follow the top news stories, and read a few political magazines. Do all this two weeks before your competitive exams, at most start general knowledge acquisition a month beforehand.

However, why do you have to wait two weeks before the campus interview to dig out papers and solve puzzles? Even though last minute learning is very effective for some, it is more effective if you have put in as many hours before that.

You can improve your overall skills before that. Learning is a process. Where many students go wrong is that they get very result-oriented. This spoils the whole learning experience. It's like going on a two - day visit to a forest reserve and then saying that you are a lover of nature. What can you understand about nature in two days if you have lived in an apartment all your life?

You have three to five years as an undergraduate. Do you utilize that time to the maximum? If you haven't already, then no harm starting now.

All your life knowledge: This knowledge is knowledge on a daily basis. It's knowledge that you collect from all kinds of sources with a lot of interest. This kind of knowledge may not be specific but it is useful as it helps when you are making conversation or trying to impress your employer. It also helps to have some general knowledge when you are being assessed for your writing skills.

Which kind of knowledge should you seek? Both. Quick knowledge is target specific. All your life knowledge is what sets you apart from others. Keep learning and your mind keeps expanding.

At the end of the day, whom do you respect? A well-learned and well-rounded person, of course. One negative of today's education system is that you are encouraged to be very good at just one set of subjects, at the expense of others. It pays to have good knowledge of not just academics but history, current affairs, and the arts. Being knowledgeable makes the interview a pleasure; no need to fear if you have knowledge, is there?

Your Presentation

Doing a presentation is an opportunity not to miss. Convincing an audience using technology is such a confidence booster. Students go through the rigours of presentation for various reasons including training and assessment.

Most students are familiar with the idea of using the visual media to speed up the learning curve; it's not enough just knowing about it though. Many colleges do not provide students with the opportunity to create their own slides, so these students have to learn on their own.

Presentations are essential boardroom tools. Having a hands-on approach with technology makes you more equipped to face corporate life where being tech-savvy is the biggest advantage yet.

What kind of problems do presentations bring up? These are what some students had to say.

★ **I have stage fright, so doing a presentation is scary.**

If you worry about how you will perform on stage, you suffer from performance anxiety. The fear of anxiety can make you more nervous and spoil the entire presentation. Think of all the effort you put in to make the slides visually appealing. You don't want to spoil it by getting cold feet!

★ **How will I organise so much material into a space of twelve slides?**

If you are worried about how to get your act together, you suffer from something called process anxiety. This means you feel you don't have what it takes to create a fantastic product that your audience will love. Well, this is just the beginning of your journey. You can't get nervous even before you begin! Paying attention to the process is important. Each slide requires a lot of attention and focus. No time for jitters!

★ **I only learn from my presentation; I don't care about the other presentations.**

That is true especially the first time round when you put all your effort into one presentation. The more presentations you do and the more you watch other presentations, the more information you subconsciously pick up. Remember no experience is wasted if you are alert. You learn a lot about communication skills when you observe your peers and your experienced seniors make their presentations. Even participation as audience is a valuable experience that will help you in the long run.

★ **I hate group presentations! I end up doing everything or nothing at all.**

This attitude has to change. Taking leadership automatically gives you more opportunities in your career. If you let the other person do all the work, you stand to gain little. If you ask yourself what you gained after that half hour presentation your group slogged over, and say you gained nothing, it means you have a long way to go when it comes to personality development. Forget the blame game – she did this, he did this, and I did more. What is important is what the experience of putting together a certain number of slides taught you. There are so many benefits in making your presentation that they far outweigh the negatives.

Questions you ask yourself before you start preparation for your presentation:

★ What is my theme and how much research does it require?

★ How do I organise my material?

★ What idea comes first in my presentation?

★ How does that help to get the audience interested?

★ When do I use slides?

★ When do I use humour, quotes, or anecdotes to get my point across?

★ How do I conclude my talk?

Name the speakers whom you most admire. The person you admire could be a celebrity, a politician, an activist, or a writer. What makes them stand out?

_____

_____

_____

_____

_____

What will you do to emulate this role model in terms of improving your presentation skills?

_____

_____

_____

_____

If you are too embarrassed to take feedback from a friend, look in a mirror or video cam your own rehearsal. Watching yourself is the best clue you can get about what others see as well. Compare your talk to the talks of those you admire. Where have you gone wrong?

I highly recommend that you log onto http://www.ted.com, an informative website from where you can access scores of presentations from senior professionals in various fields. Each speaker is an achiever. Study their body language, speaking style, and slide presentation technique. Always observe the best and you will reach the top. Look where there are stars, down there is dirt.

Presentations: An oral checklist

- ☑ Know the topic. You can't walk into a room without any kind of preparation and expect yourself to speak volumes. Even experienced speakers read up on their subject before they speak to an audience. Knowledge is king.

- ☑ Know your audience. Speak in a style that they can understand. Simplify difficult terms if required.

- ☑ Know when it's your turn to speak and be at the venue on time. That way you can prepare yourself and avoid any sudden confusion.

Know about the venue, do a mock rehearsal. Sometimes surprises are not a good thing!

Know the motive of your talk. Is it to inform, persuade, entertain, or commemorate? This will help you form the tone of your talk.

Presentation body language

Make eye contact while speaking. One place you can look at is the space just above everyone's head. That gives the impression that you are paying attention to the audience in its entirety.

No fast pace while you talk. If you rush while speaking, the audience thinks that you are nervous and you won't get the attention you desire.

No fake smiling please. Try to be as comfortable as possible.

Don't show your nervousness. It's nobody else's business. If you are tense, breathe deeply and have occasional sips of water. That will calm you down.

When you do a presentation or a lecture and move on the stage:

Stepping forward indicates that you are at an important point.

Stepping backward means that you want to take a rest.

Lateral or side to side means that you are going to the next topic.

▬Recap▬

Will your skills – take an effort to make Brand You better.

Polish basic skills like Comprehension, Participation, Study, and Management.

Polish verbal, written, and non-verbal skills.

Polish Corporate skills that help you negotiate your way through corporate life.

SECTION 4
THE JOB HUNT

Preparation
Job Market
Reading your Job Ad
Your Portfolio
      Resume
      Cover Letter
Your Attitude
Job Hunt Prelims
      Becoming the Right Fit
      Preparing for the Interview
      Interview Rounds (Written test and GD)
      Doing the Teleconference
The Interview
      Your Interview Quotient
      Kinds of Questions
      Stock Questions

1

Preparation

How does a soldier prepare himself for war? He knows his mission and his country's mission. He feels at one with his cause and that of the country. His intellect and body

Preparing for a job hunt is the same –
eye on success and a mind ready to fail and pick itself up again. Be a samurai!

Have you uploaded your resume on a job site?

_____

_____

on the net, make sure it is your best. The reason is that today there is far too much competition and a jittery global economy. A good updated resume makes you stand out and allows more opportunities to come your way.

Have you ever visited a job fair? What did you do there?

_____

_____

_____

If you haven't, it's high time you started getting out there and looking at how the world of jobs operates. Don't think that someone will offer you a job on a silver platter. Gone are the days when a teacher will recommend you and praise you for your efforts. School is over and done with. Once you are at the degree level, each for his or her own. If you make the effort, you get the opportunity. Otherwise, no matter how good you are, you will be left behind.

> **Recruiter speak: Jaya Narayan, Freelance Human Resources professional, behavioral trainer, assessor, and writer.**

> Companies recruit just 10% freshers. The freshers who make it are extremely positive and they have taken a lot of initiative during their academic and project time span.

Job Market – Where the jobs are

year of Computer Science.

So where are the opportunities?

can just go in person to companies where you are interested to work and ask about

as you might have to face an on-the-spot interview. Better though to scout these

1. Media

Jobs show up in newspapers and job portals on the internet. Start subscribing to a newspaper that has a career page. Career pages usually appear on a weekly basis.

Which newspapers do you read? Do they have career pages?

_____

_____

_____

_____

This is why reading the newspaper is so important. It keeps you in the know about everything – current affairs, international events, sports, and of course the job market. If you compromise on reading the newspaper and say that you read once in a while, you are just missing out on opportunities. No need to do that, is there?

Which job sites have you uploaded your resume on to or at least heard about?

_____

_____

_____

Six Authentic Job Portals:

Naukri - www.naukri.com

Monster Jobs - www.monsterindia.com

Times Jobs - www.timesjobs.com

Click Jobs - www.clickjobs.com

Jobs Ahead - www.jobsahead.com

You can never underestimate the importance of social media networking in today's day and age. Be very computer savvy and know how to navigate job sites effectively to find out the job that suits you best. Nowadays there are more job listings and recruitment opportunities on social networking sites like Linkedin and Facebook than you can find in the print media.

Most of you have a Facebook id by now. Be consistent about how you use your name on all social networking websites. Stick to your first name and last name or whatever name you have used in your college records. Your social media profile reflects your interests and hobbies as well. Make sure that your online profile and your resume profile match. Also, before applying for your job, tweak your online profile a little. Be careful about the kind of pictures, links, and comments you place. All these reflect on your character and will influence the employer's decision to hire you.

2. Walk-ins

Many offices have walk-in interviews. Those are the places for freshers to start. Walk-ins are advertised regularly in newspapers. There are specific sites that advertise walk-ins as well.

Fresher Shoot

How can I prepare for a walk - in?

Pretty much the way you prepare for any other interview. Some things you can pay attention to include punctuality and alertness. No point saying that there will be so many applicants and timing makes no difference. Walk-in ads specify the time and venue. Be there on time and make sure you have had a heavy meal as there will be many other applicants and you will have to wait.

What do I do during a walk-in? How will I not get so bored that my interview turns dull?

Use the time in the queue to get to know some of the other applicants and observe the

How can I stand out in the crowd?

a little practice and effort. Other highlights that help you stand out are etiquette or manners, your resume, and a little bit of grooming.

Do walk-ins and interviews have different rules?

slot. The difference is that you are not contacted during a walk-in. You just go and take a chance.

The rules are the same. Be prepared and arrive on time. With a head start, you could

a while, interviewer fatigue creeps up or the interviewer gets tired, and your chances come down.

Walk-in Checklist

Two copies of a well - drafted resume.

Look in the mirror, check for your watch, cell phone, etc.

3. Recruitment Consultants

The job hunt is not just about doing it alone – either by scouting the media or attending a walk-in. You can get people to help as well. There are many recruitment consultants

like telecalling, sales and marketing, hospitality and retail.

Fresher Shoot

Should I give my resume to the recruiter?

Of course. The recruiter will ask you to submit your resume. It is your job to specify your job preferences, so that you get a job that fits your credentials. A good recruiter could also help you to make your resume more effective.

How should I behave with recruiters?

Be courteous. Behave politely and maintain a professional relationship. Keep yourself constantly updated about any developments on your resume. Call every two weeks even if they don't call you. They have thousands of CVs to deal with – don't expect them to give you a ring!

What should I prepare for before approaching a recruiting agency?

Make a recruitment consultant checklist first.

★ Be selective when you are looking for recruiters and don't shoot out your resume to every recruiter you come across. Recruiters are specialists; so you must make a list of recruiters who specialize in your area of interest and ideally contact two or three agencies.

★ You should inform your recruiters that you are sending your resume to other agencies as well.

★ You must be clear with the recruiter about the kind of job that you are pitching for, your salary expectations, and when you will be able to present yourself for interviews.

★ You have to take initiative on your part as well. Depending entirely on recruiters is never a good idea. However, if you find the right consultant, then you will get a job in no time.

Recruiter speak: Neelabh Shukla, GM at CareerNet Consulting

Retail is the most fresher - friendly sector and banking the least. The qualities I look for in a candidate are communication, aptitude, and a willingness to learn.

4. Job Fair

A job fair is not a walk-in although you could end up getting interviewed. Also known as career expos, job fairs are a great place for employers and prospective employees to interact. The company gets to meet as many potential employees as possible on a single day. A job fair is pretty much like a job supermarket. If you have your list

Remember that a company will have its list of requirements as well.

When you go to a job fair, you get to 'see' companies, go through brochures, and submit resumes. What makes a job fair so attractive is that you can 'walk in' with your resume and 'walk out' with a job!

There are private job fairs where individual companies or consultants zero in on future employees. Commercial job fairs are more carnival-like with sponsors and advertisers. Campus - sponsored job fairs are the best bet for students.

Job fairs prepare you for interviews in the future. When you visit, consider it as a kind of mock interview preparation. Carry a couple of resume copies with you.

All the same interview rules apply. Before you go, do some basic company research of the companies that will set shop there. If the career fair has its focus on the BPO industry,

companies you would like to apply to. Your decision could be based on factors like commuting distance, salary expectations, and possible career growth.

Take a look at a job fair ad:

Most of the essentials like the venue, the date on which the expo is held, registration dates, whom to contact, which companies to expect, and the

industry space that is being slated are outlined in the ad.

What you haven't been told is how much preparedness you need to nail the job expo. You will need to do your homework on the companies they have mentioned. That means you will have to understand the USP of those companies, the kind of roles on offer, and how your skills connect to those roles. We will go into the details of company research in a subsequent chapter.

Consider whether you have the soft skills, verbal aptitude, and job requirements needed to apply for the post. If you do, then plan to introduce yourself to the recruiters you are banking on.

Job Fair Checklist

★ At a job fair, be alert. Don't walk around casually. While you explore the venues, keep mental checks of where you want to apply.

★ Collect any written material pertaining to the company before you attempt a face - to - face interview. Any casual meeting with an employer is a potential interview, so you should know what you are about to say.

★ Talk to people around you and gather as much information as you can. Don't stay away from people or avoid eye contact as that gets you nowhere.

★ Dress formally as you would for an interview. You have to put a lot of thought into your wardrobe even if this a job fair. Always be ready as you never know when an opportunity will come your way!

★ Get a feel of job fairs while you are in college. Regularly visiting job fairs makes you familiar with the whole idea of what being a professional means. You also learn the ropes of handling interviews later on.

★ Always carry your resume, certificates, and any letters of recommendation in case you get noticed.

★ If you have been successful in introducing yourself and have been able to convey your interest in working with a particular company, they may ask you to provide your resume.

★ You could ask for a business card if you think the meeting was positive. Send an email to the employer you talked to thanking him for his valuable time and information provided. It pays to be nice!

5. Campus recruitment

Recruiters come on campus and pick out the brightest and the best! Placement interviews can be challenging. Companies pose several rounds to test students. The best part about campus interviews is that students from any stream can qualify if they pass the tests. Since freshers don't have company experience, they are tested in various areas like:

Aptitude: Aptitude tests deal with basic math skills, logic, verbal abilities, and comprehension. This is where everything you have understood in your syllabus can be used.

Group discussion: How good are your speaking skills when you are in a group? Group Discussion is a test of personality and confidence. It also tests your verbal and non-verbal skills.

Interviews: You could be quizzed in various areas like your core subject, interpersonal skill quotient, and technical know-how. Ice breaker sessions could be conducted to see how much stress you can handle. Your ability to work as a proactive part of a team is also tested. Technical interviews are primarily for engineering and IT students, questions being mostly project based. The HR interview is more about how you see yourself in relation to the hiring company.

When you have clarity about which companies are attending, do your company research. Check the details of the company. Know if it is a publicly listed company. Know what industry the company is in. Carry your resume and certificates. Be prepared for the real interview.

The best ingredient you need for a campus interview is energy. You can't give an impression of being disinterested as that could kill your chances of being selected.

If job fairs are being conducted in colleges other than your own, go have a look at what an interview feels like.

Fresher Shoot

How can I crack the Campus Recruitment Tests?

What is your response to tests in general? Did you attempt the tests in Section 1? Do you prepare or postpone all preparation? Why?

_____

_____

If you are positive about taking tests, then make the most of this opportunity that comes on campus. If test taking is an issue, work on your focus on a day - to - day basis. A major reason that students fail or do poorly in subjects is because they don't spend enough of their valuable time with the subject. If you interact with your books daily, are you telling me that you will not be able to retain anything? I won't buy it.

Find out what area you are strong in – verbal, mathematics, logic, or analytics. How will you work on strengthening your weak areas?

_____

_____

_____

_____

Like I told you earlier, identify an appropriate study method, be it visual, auditory, or kinesthetic. Apply the method to get over the barriers that have come before you. If you are very good at mathematics, you may want to make your verbal skills better. Nowadays, a jack of all trades is far more appreciated. If you are good in a little bit of everything, you will be more suitable for the corporate life of multi-tasking.

To crack the test, be prepared. Find out what kinds of tests the concerned companies provide. There could be questions in circulation on the internet and various other books available. Your seniors could also help you out in those areas.

Do a whole lot of brain teasers...you know the sort of books by maths whiz Shakuntala Devi, CAT guides, and GRE question banks. There are books on verbal aptitude and company - centric examination papers that are doing the rounds. Some students have posted several important book names and papers on the internet. That is a good reference area. Network with other students who have cracked the exams. Reach out and you will get help!

Like in the case of a job fair, know about the list of companies that will visit the campus. Do a background check on:

★   Company history

★   Jobs available

Find out about the recruitment process beforehand. Each company will have a slightly different recruitment model.

Reading your Job Ad

Doesn't your employer check your credentials and understand where you are coming from before he employs you? Your skills sets are matched with company requirements. You should do the same thing before you apply. Don't blindly apply for a role. Haste makes waste, remember?

Be thorough with the advertised role. It's like going to a trial room to make sure your dress is the right fit. If you feel comfortable about the dress go for the purchase or try again. The same principle applies in job-hunting.

If you try to land any job you come across, without being thorough about the requirements, then the interview is more likely to be a failure.

To be thorough about company requirements, you can start out with the job ad you are looking at. Do you understand the job completely? Are you familiar with all the key words or important words used in the ad? Take some time to go through a few job ads in the paper or the internet. Knowing how to read your job ad is the first step to getting interviewed.

But that's easy! You'll tell me. It's no big deal. Well, it is easy but many freshers are in a hurry to land themselves a position that they don't do their homework well enough and that can delay the process of getting a job much more. The best way to read a job opportunity is to be attentive and take enough time to understand the relevant details completely. A job advert speaks about job specifics the same way your resume speaks about you.

Reading a job ad is not like reading a magazine. You need to do focused reading. Do you have a pen and paper by your side? This is important if you want to note down anything relevant. Start getting organised. What do you see?

A job ad reveals a lot about the kind of company you are applying for and the kind of profile you are pitching for. Understanding a job ad is part of your research on the job. These are some things you should look out for in an ad whether it is posted online or in the newspaper.

★ Did you identify the job title? This is the first thing that stands out in a job ad. It indicates what the requirement or vacancy is for. The name of the role is important when you send your resume application.

★ What is the job description? What kind of responsibilities does the post offer? Do you have the credentials to apply? Sometimes the skills you have will not match the requirement word for word. If the requirement is for a content editor and you have experience writing on a freelance basis, you can apply as writing and editing are content-related skill sets.

★ What is the EXP or experience required to apply for the post? Do you qualify? Some companies mention that they are on the lookout for freshers. If the requirement is for a candidate with minimum one year experience and you have a reasonable amount of experience as an intern, you could apply. If any experience above one year is required, wait for your resume to show the experience before you apply.

★ Where is the job located? Is it practical for you to apply? If the job is situated at a distance and you still want to apply, you have to be sure about accommodation arrangements and expenses you are willing to incur for this job. You may be quizzed about why you chose to apply for this particular post despite the commuting time, so be prepared with a relevant answer.

★ Is the vacancy for full time, part time, or a contract job? If it is a full time job, be prepared for the company timings. No point negotiating for flexi-timings when such an option does not exist. A contract job requires completion of task within a particular period and you are not considered a permanent employee of the company. A part time job requires you to spend only specific allotted time in the company.

★ Is there a trainee programme? Freshers usually have a skill sharpening programme. In the induction programme, they are trained to meet the requirements of the job. A common example is accent training in BPOs.

★ What is the closing date for application forms or resumes to be sent? Send your application on time. If your resume is not posted on schedule, don't expect a response. In the corporate world, time is money, so be punctual.

★ How do you respond to the ad – via email or telephone? Sometimes your resume or CV must be posted online or through regular postal services. Follow instructions to the tee, otherwise chances are that your application will be rejected.

Fresher Shoot

How do I understand company ad jargon?

Here are some terms that you find in job ads:

★ **Organization skills:** Remember how you assessed your own organization skills earlier? All job ads look for candidates with this skill. A good organiser can meet deadlines or company targets efficiently on a day - to - day basis. While you are being interviewed, you should provide clear examples of how you have succeeded in meeting deadlines. Project details should be covered in your resume and your ability to meet targets could go into your cover letter. In a company where teamwork is essential, organization skills means you are comfortable working in groups. It all comes down to good communication or soft skills with a goal to achieve targets.

★ **Multi-tasking:** This is a commonly seen requirement. Can you answer fifty calls, send seventy emails, and create a financial report in one day? Well of course not. At the fresher level these targets seem undoable but this is what some jobs look like at a more senior level. It sounds difficult but doing several things at a time is becoming an essential part of corporate life. To juggle roles like this you need clarity about the nature of each task. You also need excellent time management skills to handle a set of deadlines.

★ **Proficiency:** Every company looks for a candidate who is proficient or who excels in his or her work. If you plan to apply for any post, you must be proficient in your core subject and your subject knowledge must be up to date.

★ **Attention to detail:** Every job must be clearly understood from start to finish. Job ads specify that they require candidates who can contribute to quality control.

★ **Dynamic vs Mature:** A company could be looking for 'dynamic' candidates, meaning that it is willing to engage young and energetic people. A company with a more 'mature' ethos will be interested in people with more experience. These kinds of adjectives give you a clue about the kind of company you are applying to. As far as possible, a company's values must reflect your values. That makes the transition from college to work much easier.

★ **Salary matters:** Many ads on job portals outline salary packages. Expected CTC is Cost to Company or the remuneration package. Some jobs work on a commission basis. They provide what is called OTE or On Target Earnings.

Sometimes a potential employer could ask you what Gross Salary you are looking for. Gross is the amount you earn before deductions, and Nett is the income you receive after all deductions are made.

If salary is competitive, it means that salary is based on industry standards. If you are asked to mention expected CTC, you should have a well-thought out answer. Your salary expectations must be based on information you have got via networking. Ask your friends or seniors what the job role you are applying for usually pays. Usually salary details can be found out on a word - of - mouth basis. Make sure that you never undersell yourself – that means you should avoid working for less pay. Also don't oversell or ask for too much, as that way you may lose out on the interview.

Recruiter speak: Anand Wadedakar, Faculty/Author/Career Consultant/ Information Researcher

Having high expectations about salaries is a trend among students these days. The

earners after post graduation.

What freshers forget is that every candidate is different from the other.

When one is starting one's career, salary expectation should not be high. The focus should be on what has been learned during post graduation/graduation. The candidate

the best person for the job.

I have seen that a candidate having very sound knowledge gets a relatively higher salary than a normal fresher. After all, employers want work from candidates, and candidates should always remember that high salary is a factor that follows if you have a sound foundation and gain the experience to foolproof it.

Take a look at the job ad below. Whenever you read an ad, mark out the job title, job description, CTC, etc. Mark out the required skill sets and tally it with your own achievements.

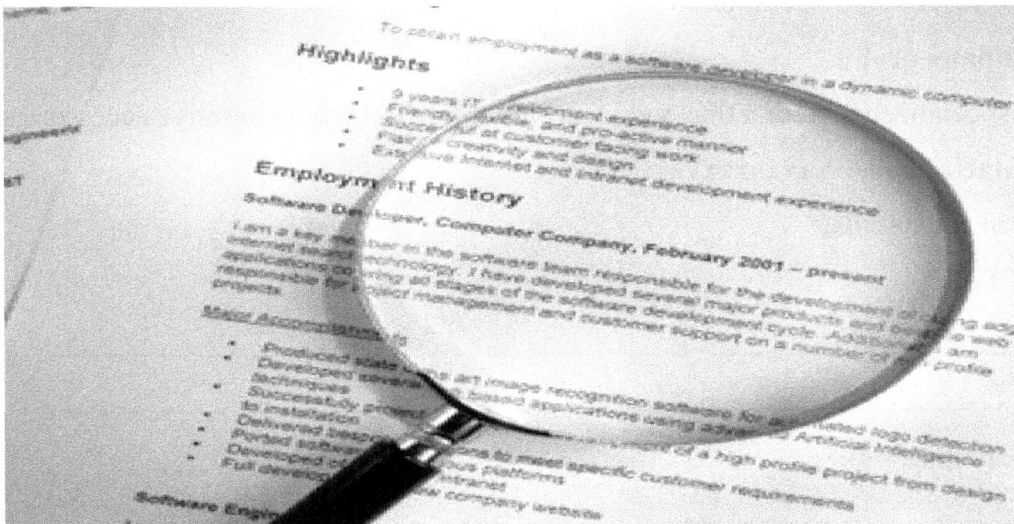

Know your job advert

Experience: 0 - 2 Years

Location: Bangalore

Compensation: Rs. 6500 to 12500

Education: UG - B.Com, BBM

Industry Type: Finance

Role: Accountant

Posted Date: 20 Sep

Job Description

★　Tally and accounting basics (Computer skills required).

★　Good knowledge of income tax, sales tax, and service tax regulations.

★　Making daily payments, raising invoices, tracking the payments, filing returns, bank reconciliations.

Desired Candidate Profile

Education: Graduates

Salary: Rs.10,000 per month.

Company profile

We specialize in Automation and Distribution of Hi-Tech automotive accessories.

Contact details: Xxxxxxxxxxxxxxx

Fill in the details:

Job Title

_____

_____

Company Details

_____

_____

Job Description

_____

Required Skill Sets

_____

_____

_____

When to apply

_____

_____

_____

CTC

_____

_____

Interpreting the ad

★ From this job profile, it is evident that a fresher commerce student can apply, though the job title is not clear.

★ You are expected to call the concerned contact.

★ Your skill sets have to do with accounting, taxation, and tally processing. Experience is required.

★ Having done a part time stint will be useful.

★ Salary will depend on how you present yourself; if you are impressive and your knowledge base is strong you can expect a higher range salary.

★ You need good communication skills and you must show your interviewers that you are able to speak fluently and that you are confident.

Freshers required for marketing/sales

Experience: 0 – 2 Years

Location: Nagpur

Compensation: Rs. 1,00,000-1,25,000

SALARY + WEEKLY INCENTIVES

Education: UG - Any Graduate - Any Specialization PG - MBA/PGDM - Marketing

Industry Type: Media/Dotcom/ Entertainment

Role: Client Servicing Exec.

Functional Area: Marketing, Advertising, MR, PR

Posted Date: 21 Dec

Job Description

★　Up-selling the existing clients

★　Servicing the existing clients and generating revenue

★　Attracting new clients

★　Responsible for client retention and relationship building

★　Job may involve traveling to different locations

Desired Candidate Profile

★　Candidate should have good communication skills

★　Candidates having direct sales experience are welcomed

★　Strong analytical and interpersonal skills

★　Able to build credible relationships with influencing ability

Company Profile

IndiaMegamind Ltd is India's largest B2B marketplace, and world's 6th largest company operating in this domain. It was established in 1990 and accredited with ISO 9001:2000 certification. It has over 2000 employees with a network of 50 offices across India.

Contact Details

Company Name: Megamind Ltd

Website: http://megamindindia.com

Executive Name: Gopi Visvanath

Address: Not Mentioned

Telephone: Xxxxxxxxxxx

Reference ID: xxxxxxxxx @megamind.com

Now fill in the details as per the job ad:

Job Title

_____

_____

Company Details

_____

_____

Job Description

_____

_____

_____

_____

Required Skill Sets

_____

_____

_____

_____

When to apply

_____

_____

_____

_____

CTC

_____

_____

Interpreting the ad:

★ The requirement is very clear. A client servicing executive canvases products for his company and acts as a representative of the company and its products. In other words, this is a job for a sales person.

★ You will need your own vehicle as traveling will be a regular part of the job.

★ You will need good interpersonal or person to person skills so that you can effectively engage your customer and sell your merchandise.

★ The analytical skills mentioned refer to your ability to gauge where the product is likely to sell.

★ Details about the company reveal that this is a company with a good reputation. A good company history is a plus. If you are retained there, there are benefits. Also, if you have to shift base, you can apply with the same company in any other branch across the country.

Your Portfolio

A career portfolio is what you carry to the office when you are being interviewed. It's a file that contains everything that you have achieved – your certificates, your qualifications, skill sets, your resume, and cover letter. You can also upload your portfolio online on sites like Linkedin.

Parts of the portfolio:

★ Resume

★ Cover letter

★ Illustration of your work

★ Research, publications, reports

Letters of recommendation

Resume

What is a resume? A summary of Brand You. A resume carries all your details – your educational background, skills, and achievements. It's called a Curriculum Vitae or CV in the UK, Resume in the U.S., and bio-data in India. The advantage of the resume is that it is your chance to showcase yourself as positively as possible. The

place.

A resume helps you nail the interview; getting the job is the next step. Framing a good resume also helps you to get an opportunity to do an internship, get admission into a better university, or receive a scholarship.

Kinds of Resume

Normally, a resume is written in reverse chronological order. This means your

work experience.

A functional CV works well for freshers like you. In this kind of resume you can

A hybrid resume is a mix of reverse chronological order and functional type.

This is what an experienced candidate's resume may look like. You'll see many like these on the internet.

Objective

Executive position where I can utilize my communication and project management skills proven by 10 years of successful entrepreneurship.

Motivated business professional with a successful 10-year track record of

- ★ Effectively deal with confidential records.
- ★ Produce accurate reports.
- ★ Thrive in deadline-driven environments.
- ★ Excellent team-building skills.

Skills Summary

- ☑ Project Management
- ☑ Report Preparation
- ☑ Written Correspondence
- ☑ General Office Skills   \
- ☑ Computer Savvy
- ☑ Customer Service
- ☑ Scheduling
- ☑ Marketing and Sales
- ☑ Accounting
- ☑ Front-office Operations
- ☑ Professional Presentations

Professional Experience

Communication: Reports/Presentations/Technology

- ★ Prepare complex reports for reputed organizations.
- ★ Author professional correspondence to customers and vendors.
- ★ Conduct small-group sessions on entrepreneurial methodologies.
- ★ Rapidly learn and master varied computer programs; recently completed Microsoft Office Suite certificate course.

Detail Mastery and Organization

- ★ Manage all aspects of day-to-day operations as multi-site owner of ABC Ltd.:
  - ☑ Facility rental/maintenance.

- ☑ Finances: accounts payable/receivable, invoicing, insurance billing, budgeting.

- ☑ Supervision of a total of eighteen employees.

- ☑ Compliance with all industry requirements.

Employment History

XYZ Ltd, 1995 to Present

Education

XXX COLLEGE–XXX

What does this resume contain that your resume will not contain?

Experience, of course. A professional resume contains experience that will impress the employer and make him or her feel that you have the necessary skills for the job. Since you probably don't have much experience, understand the basics of resume creation.

As a fresher then what do you fill your resume with?

Parts of the resume

- ★ The objective clearly states what you wish to achieve and where you want to go. Many resumes contain brief objectives but it is better to position yourself clearly, and go in for a 2 – 3 line opening that will get the employer's attention.

- ★ Qualifications are your bread and butter. At this stage of your life, this is what comes on the resume first. Highest qualification first. The qualifications you list must have some connection with the target job if you are specifically applying to a job advert. If you have a diploma in catering and you are applying for job as programmer, no need to mention this diploma as it doesn't serve your purpose and distracts the employer when he/she goes through your resume.

- ★ Work experience can come in second. If you have plenty of internship experience, it will make a positive impression. When you go for an interview carry the certificates that prove you have worked in these places or have qualified for the respective positions.

- ★ Awards you received in academics and achievements you have made such as publication, recognition, etc. can be stated here. No need to be modest!

- ★ Volunteer work you were involved in puts you in good stead. If you have been involved in initiatives that help the greater good, you come across as a better team player and a more reliable human being.

Your resume showcases your

★ Skills-What you have learned

★ Worth-What you have contributed

★ Role-Responsibilities you have assumed

★ Potential-Why you are better than the others

★ Problem solving ability – The skills you have that can be an asset to the company

Now let's look at the resume part by part.

1. Contact Details:

Put down your contact details like this:

Emanuel X

2nd cross, Flyover Road, XXXX-yyyyyy

emanuelx@gmail.com   mobile no: xxxxxxxxxx

Now write down your details:

Name (First Name /Last Name)

_____

Address

_____

_____

Email

_____

Phone no

_____

2. Objective:

All resumes contain an objective. This is your motive. Although this a short section of two to three lines or even a single phrase, it makes or breaks your chances of being interviewed. A well-written objective showcases your skills and your fit in the company. If your objective is interesting, your resume may be noticed.

The objective should be:

★ Concise

★ Specific

★ Well-edited

★ Should contain key words

★ Target oriented: It must match the requirements in the job profile (if you are applying for the job).

★ Flexible: Depending on the job you are applying for the objective should change.

Here are some examples:

★ Position in a venture capitalist firm where I can use my business study credentials and entrepreneurship bent of mind to be a part of ventures from the grassroots up.

★ A position at XYZ institute where I can maximize my training experience, programme development skills, and analytical abilities.

★ Obtain a position in ABC Ltd where I can maximize my customer-service skills in a challenging environment to achieve corporate goals.

★ Seek a position as Office Secretary where my computer skills and organizational abilities can be fully utilized.

★ Obtain a human resources management position where I can effectively utilize my academic credentials and contribute toward effective staff recruitment.

★ To secure a position that will lead to a lasting working relationship in the field of accounting or book-keeping.

Now frame your objective:

_____

_____

_____

3. Educational Qualifications:

First you will have to collect all your documents from Matriculation onwards. Make a list of all your percentages.

★ Tenth

Name of School	Year of passing	Percentage/Grade Scored

★ Twelfth/PU

Name of School/College	Year of passing	Percentage Scored

★ Degree

Name of College & University	Year of passing	Percentage Scored

★ Post Graduation

Name of College & University	Year of passing	Percentage Scored

★ Other

Name of College & University	Year of Passing	Percentage Scored

Make a list of all the courses you may have done.

★ Personality Development

★ Computer

★ Creative

★ Academic

Make a list of all the seminars you have attended.

★ _____

★ _____

★ _____

★ _____

By doing this exercise, you learn a lot about how you have progressed throughout your academic years.

Now for framing your academic qualifications into resume format:

★ BCA from Charan Singh University (CCSU), Meerut in 2008 (Secured xx%)

★ Diploma from Government Polytechnic, Rajkot in 2010 (Secured xx%)

Now write your qualifications down:

_____

_____

_____

4. Work/Internship Experience

This part of your resume is very important as it showcases your work and the reasons the company would have to employ you. You start with your most recent experience first and go backwards. For employment details, you mention date, job title, company, responsibilities, and achievements. Mentioning achievements is appreciated more as this gives the employer some idea about your competency for the job.

You can work on this part of your resume straight away. Make a list of part time jobs/internships you have done.

Latest Experience

Date (specify the time frame)

Job Title

_____

Company

_____

Responsibilities you had on the job:

★   _____

★   _____

★   _____

Your achievements on the job, if any:

★   _____

★   _____

★   _____

Date (specify the time frame)

Previous Experience

_____

Job Title

_____

Company

_____

Responsibilities you had on the job:

★   _____

★   _____

★   _____

Achievements on the job, if any:

★   _____

★   _____

★ _____

5. Achievements

Listing your achievements is a great way of showing the employer that you have already achieved success in your own way. First be familiar with your own victories. Make a list of all competitions you have won honours in at the:

College level

_____

_____

_____

School level

_____

_____

_____

Other extracurricular activities you have won recognition for

_____

_____

_____

Training certificates in any extracurricular/computer-based/academic discipline

_____

_____

_____

_____

Now based on your analysis, write down three or more prominent achievements you have made:

_____

_____

_____

6. Interests

Here too you must state interests that will make your employers excited about having you work for their company. Never say you love sleeping, even though it may be closer to the truth. If you want to apply for the post of editor, it would be nice to say that you like reading. If you want to apply for a teaching job, no point in mentioning that you have animation skills!

What are your interests? Link them as closely as possible to the job you are pitching for.

_____

_____

_____

7. Personal Details

Some employers need to know about the marital status of their employees as part of company policy. List any essential details if necessary.

Now you are ready to create your own resume.

Layout Tips

★ Once you've written your CV, you can present it. Formats are easy to choose from as there are so many available online to guide you.

★ Centre your contact details at the top of the page or align it to the left hand side. Make sure there is enough margin.

★ Use a uniform font throughout, preferably Times New Roman or Arial.

★ Keep headings of a uniform font size say 14, sub-heads at 12, and the rest of the resume at 10 point.

★ No clutter please. Choose a layout that is pleasing to the eye.

★ Don't underline headings.

★ Use bullet points for detailed lists.

★ Don't print on both sides of the paper.

★ No colour in the resume!

★ Don't fold your resume – put it in an envelope.

Just like you get a makeover done, your resume can get a makeover too. If you are not

resume as far as possible. When you write down your experience and details, you are doing a dress rehearsal for your interview.

When you are involved in the process of drafting, you automatically memorize

unnecessary pauses and doubts.

This is a sample resume of a student who has some internship experience and wants to get into the accounting profession. Have a look at it and identify any problem areas.

Divya Ramachandran

XXX

Mobile: xxxxxx email: xxxxxx

Objective

Seeking entry level position as accounts professional with growth-oriented company

Education

| 2006-2009 | Bachelor of Commerce | XXXXX University |
| 2006 | Higher Secondary | XXXX School |

Experience

Internship

    ABC ltd, Chennai, April 2007 – June 2007

MIS support for the Accounts Dept

    XYZ Company, Jan 2008 – October 2008

Stores Person

Prepared Store Ledger on a daily/weekly basis

    XXX Company, Jan 2009-June 2009

Skills Acquired

Expertise in general accounting, finance

Computer literate, familiar with various databases

Comfortable working as part of a team

Hobbies

Athletic interests in swimming, long distance running, and biking

---

This resume is quite lifeless and needs some spunk. Says Jaya Narayan, Executive Coach, "This is a very run of the mill profile. I wouldn't be motivated enough to shortlist this one. Divya should present her achievements and competencies. She should demonstrate any leadership skills she has and mention a unique hobby that makes her stand out. She should have at least 3 – 4 powerful adjectives that are sought after in the industry she is pitching to be a part of."

What Divya needs to do is a personal evaluation. Remember the personal stock taking we did in Section II?

Divya identifies her skill sets.

Listening   Public Speaking   Speaking on the telephone   Motivating   Resolving conflicts

Organizing   Training   MS Word   Xcel   Photoshop   Sophisticated computer skills

Writing letters, emails, reports   Accounting   Budgeting   Analysing data

Since Divya is confident about her skills while conversing and listening on the telephone, she can emphasize that she has good oral communication skills and provide some kind of experience in her resume to validate that.

Being computer savvy is a qualification that will benefit Divya. She hasn't mentioned clearly in her resume what computer skills she has and it would be a wise move for her to do so.

Divya is interested in accounts, so she is an ideal candidate for an accounting - based job. She has already mentioned this in her objective. She has to convey a little more enthusiasm though if she is to come across as a confident individual who is ready for a company job.

into an introductory sentence that is especially useful when she writes her cover letter.

I'm a commerce graduate with accounting experience. I have the communication skills that would make me a good team player. My analytical and computer skills could be put to good use in your company.

Divya's resume would be interesting if it is a functional resume. As she does not have enough experience, she can categorize her experience based on the skills she has accumulated during her internships. Here is her reworked resume.

Divya Ramachandran

XXX

Mobile: xxxxxx email: xxxxxx

Objective

Secure a position in the Finance and Accounts domain of a growing company where

knowledge and analytical skills.

Education

2006-2009	Bachelor of Commerce	xx%	XXXXX University
2006	Higher Secondary	Grade/Percentage	XXXX School

Skills and Experience

Organizational Skills

At XYZ Company (Jan 2008 – October 2008), worked as a stores person. Preparing the store ledger on a weekly basis has honed my organizational skills. Familiarity with operating various databases was an asset for this job.

Communication Skills

Worked with XXX Hotel (October 2008 – February 2009) as a telephone receptionist. Learnt the importance of perfect oral communication skills, effective grooming, and customer service.

Accounting Skills

Management trainee at ABC Ltd (Chennai, April 2007 – June 2007) and worked as

MIS support for the Accounts department. Gained knowledge of the various facets of accounting in a practical capacity.

Learnt company etiquette, the value of team work, and the priority of meeting deadlines.

Computer Skills

I am familiar with word processing, spread sheets, and database software to produce, record, and analyze information.

Achievements

★   Qualified at the national level in long distance running.

★   Participated in the Sunshine Marathon four subsequent times.

★   Avid biker – attempted two triathlons over the past two years.

Now have a look at Rajiv's resume.

Rajiv Deora

XXXXXX

Mobile: xxxxxx email: xxxxxx

Objective

Secure a position as sales representative at a high end BPO where I can utilize my communication skills and improve my learning curve.

Education

Awaiting B.Com results

Technical Skills

Microsoft Certified Professional

MCSE in Windows 2003 Server

CCNA

Work Experience

Working as CSR in outbound process in XXXXXXXX company

What's missing? Let's rework the resume a little bit and see if it looks better.

Rajiv Deora

XXX

(Mobile) xxxxxx (email)xxxxxx

Objective

Secure a position as sales representative at a high end BPO where I can utilize my communication skills and improve my learning curve.

Work Experience

Currently working as CSR in outbound process in XXX company. Here I have imbibed the value of being part of a process that allows companies to meet ethical, legal, commercial, and public standards.

Responsibilities:

★ Perform billing and invoicing related tasks

★ Respond to purchase inquiries

★ Coordinate promotion events

Skills

★ Work independently and efficiently to meet deadlines

★ Able to promptly answer sales and billing related email and phone calls

★ Self motivated, detail-oriented, and organised

★ Creative thinking abilities

★ Proficient with various software applications

★ Excellent communication (oral and written), interpersonal, organizational, and presentation skills

★ Typing proficiency: 40-60 wpm

Technical Skills

★ Microsoft Certified Professional

★ MCSE in Windows 2003 Server

★ CCNA

Education

★ Awaiting B.Com results from XXX University (2008 – 2011)

★ Passed with Honours from XXX School (xx%)

Achievements

★ Vice President of XXXX College Board

★ Represented XXX University at the National Level in the Annual Debating Competition sponsored by XXX company

★ Published several features and interviews in College Magazine (2009, 2010)

★ Served as Head Boy in XXX School

See how a little bit of tweaking has made Rajiv's resume far more comprehensive? Most freshers write very brief objectives. Even if they do internships, often there is very little clarity about the role.

From now on, make a list of task related responsibilities on a daily basis. Keep a diary and list your own version of the job report.

★ What responsibilities were you asked to assume on the job/project?

★ How well did you perform those responsibilities?

★ What kind of feedback did you get from your superiors?

★ What kind of skill sets (nouns and action verbs – refer to the list we made in Section III) can you now mention in your resume?

★ What makes your contribution different from others?

★ Any recommendations from your bosses?

★ You have achieved targets – do you have any certificates or written statements to prove it? Do you have any figures to prove it like Increased sales by 10% compared to the rest of the team?

★ What was your role in helping the company attain its mission statement?

Writing a resume is a continuous process. It is the result of observing your own duties and updated skills. No more sleep walking! Start knowing what you are learning and how that can help you in the future.

Warning!

No fake credentials please. However poor your scores may be, there is a lot to be said about integrity. Fake degree certificates and recommendations will just make you look bad and jeopardize your future for good.

Also don't blow your achievements out of proportion. Stick to the correct facts and figures. Only state the facts – your work should speak for itself without you boasting about it.

► Your Cover Letter

Most of the time students get their resumes written for them. Most resumes end up looking very similar and standardized. The cover letter is where you can bring out your individuality and personality to the maximum. We know by now the format of a regular business letter. This is the format you use for a cover letter as well.

So you provide:

Your contact information (name, postal address, phone numbers, email).

Divya

XXX-XXX

Mobile:xxxxx, Landline:xxxxxxxx

divyaramachandran@xyz.com

You don't have to mention email when you type your id, the same way you don't type postal address when you write your address.

To remove the hyperlink from the email id you have typed in, right click and click on 'Remove the hyperlink' option.

Parts of a Cover Letter

★ Date

★ Salutation: Dear Sir/ Madam

★ Body of the letter divided into paragraphs

★ Signing off

★ Signature

There are several kinds of cover letters. Here are two kinds depending on whom you are sending your letter to – the employer or the headhunter.

A solicited cover letter is a letter in response to a job opening. This is the letter you send to the employer. The body of a targeted letter looks like this:

★ **Paragraph 1**

Summarize yourself. Who are you and where did you see this job opportunity? Why do you want to work in XXX company? When you mention the reasons, you already catch the recruiter's eye. It means you have researched the company and done the necessary homework about the company before sending the letter.

★ **Paragraph 2**

Here you explain 'Brand You' in relation to the kind of post you are applying for. How does your work/trainee/volunteer experience and your academic performance help you to apply for this job? This is the paragraph where you will match the job requirements in the job ad with your skill sets.

★ **Paragraph 3**

In this paragraph you can highlight your skills and achievements. You could write it in full sentences or condense it into bullet points. Most important achievement must be mentioned first.

★ **Paragraph 4**

Here you mention how you can be reached and when you will be available for the interview. This paragraph is optional.

When you write a letter to a **headhunter** or for a job portal, you make slight variations.

★ **Paragraph 1**

Summarize yourself. Who are you and what kind of job opportunity are you on the lookout for?

★ **Paragraph 2**

Here you explain 'Brand You' in relation to the kind of skill sets you have accumulated. Explain why you think you can be an asset to the company.

★ **Paragraph 3**

In this paragraph, highlight your skills and achievements. You could write it in full sentences or condense it into bullet points. Most important achievement must be mentioned first.

★ **Paragraph 4**

Mention any requirements you have on your part with regard to location and willingness to work in shifts, etc. Also mention how you can be reached and when you will be available for the interview.

Cover Letter Do's

★ A resume and cover letter should use the same kind of paper, font and line spacing.

★ The tone should be formal and polite.

★ Paragraphing is essential. Full sentences should be written unlike in a resume.

★ Stick to one page format.

★ Grammar check and spell check are essential.

★ Check the date: make sure it is recent, otherwise it looks like you are re-using your letter.

★ Cover letter is an introduction to your resume, not an extension of your resume.

Cover Letter Don'ts

★ Don't cut and paste your resume points into your cover letter. If you do, it becomes too repetitive and boring.

★ Don't cut and paste job descriptions into the cover letter. Match your skill sets to the requirements. This doesn't mean you mention all the skill sets required in your cover letter. You have to customize it. If oral communication skills are required, show your skills by mentioning your experience as a telephone operator or a BPO executive.

★ Do not write in slang!

★ Don't oversell yourself. If you write about your accomplishments, be sure you can substantiate these claims during the face - to - face interview.

★ Don't undersell either. If you are afraid to highlight your achievements, recruiters will not understand your true worth and consequently you will not receive the kind of salary you deserve.

★ Fit the letter into one side of a page – long letters will not be read.

Now write your own cover letter here:

_____

_____

_____

_____

_____

_____

_____

_____

_____

_____

_____

_____

_____

Your Attitude

► Fear Fighting Tactics

You are now ready for the job market. You've polished your skills and groomed yourself. You have written your resume and created your cover letter. You are ready to go! But there's one more thing you have to fix – your attitude.

A positive attitude and a broad smile that is heartfelt can help you in the most difficult interview. Of course it is difficult to smile when you are scared. You saw how fake body language can be read – an interviewer can make out if you are afraid in a matter of three seconds. So you will have to root out the fear from your system.

The biggest problem that students face during an interview would be nervousness. Most of the time, students forget everything at the time of the interview. They know their facts and all the do's and don'ts of interviews, but just knowing about the benefits of positive body language and eye contact is not good enough. Being able to express yourself with clarity and correctness improves confidence hundred fold and helps the student get recruited instead of rejected!

Having the X factor when it comes to getting a good job means saying goodbye to nervousness, a common panic button for all students.

This story could help you get over your fear – there was a young man who trembled with fear as he walked through a dark forest one night. There were shadows everywhere and spooky sounds of bats and strange insects. Suddenly he saw a snake. He fainted on the spot, so paralyzed was he by his fear. In the morning, the man became conscious. He saw a group of men stood around him. They gave him some water and then asked him what happened. The man explained that he saw a snake and that he was lucky that he had not been bitten.

One of the men in the group was an elderly man with a silver beard and grey eyes. He walked around and picked up a rope from the soil – "Isn't this your snake?" he asked.

When we are afraid, we see what we are afraid of. We make decisions based on delusions. Only a clear mind can give you a clear solution.

Fresher Shoot

I am a good student but I am not confident. I'm shy.

Academic scores are your ticket to making the resume cut. Without good grades, you have little chance of getting noticed in your field of interest. Being confident is equally important. Today soft skills are as important as academic scores. Work on your communication skills. Collect the right amount of writing and speaking skills.

Being confident doesn't mean being oversmart or arrogant. If you are being interviewed, you must not talk back to the interviewer and feel proud of yourself for your smartness. That just comes across as rude.

Once you understand how to communicate in formal (corporate/office) and informal (casual) situations, you are already half way on the road to success.

Many celebrities and writers have been reported to suffer from social anxiety, another word for shyness. If you are shy, though it is painful, it is not necessarily a problem. People have overcome it by making the effort. You can't wait for someone to pull you out of shyness; you have to learn to live with it and at the same time be efficient in spite of it.

Bollywood actor Hrithik Roshan has mentioned in some interviews that he was a shy child. Anyone can be shy. Shyness can be positive as well, as it sparks off the ambition to grow and can actually be a great motivator. If you feel you can't speak well, you will put more pressure on yourself to deliver. Pressure is the best learning tool, especially if you are the one who is putting pressure on yourself.

Getting over fear is the first step that you need to take before the job hunt, as confidence is a quality that every employer looks out for. Without confidence how will you talk to clients from different parts of the world, be trusted with financial details, type out memos and effective business letters, and conduct meaningful telephone conversations? How will you do something as simple as walk into a room with your resume and as complicated as have a four course meal while discussing business with your clients at a five star hotel? For every aspect of corporate life you need confidence with a capital C. No short cuts there.

Getting through nervousness with Gaurai

Gaurai Uddanwadikar, Head of Counseling India, speaks to hundreds of clients on a regular basis and she agrees that nervousness is a genuine problem.

She explains that "what you call a case of nerves is another way of saying Social Anxiety. When you stammer, it is social anxiety at an extreme level."

Gaurai believes that nervousness is common and that it can be tackled. "Nervousness can be due to multiple issues – sometimes it's health-related, sometimes it's body image issues. But it can be overcome. It is a slow process but if you are patient you can change."

For instance, if you have a thyroid issue you can become nervous. So nervousness can be medically corrected.

There are many students nowadays who are obsessed with their body image. Particularly among women, there is a continuous concern that you have to be the right body type. Advertisements and movies only make the obsession worse. If you are unsure about your body image, you could become nervous. The same goes with skin complexion – does being fair give one extra confidence? What do you think?

Why are you nervous? Is it your appearance, poor communication skills, or any insecurity at home? Is there any other reason?

_____

_____

_____

Knowing why you suffer from nervousness is the only way to cure it. It is not a life-long problem. There are quiet people who are not shy. There are extremely talkative people who are filled with fear. First identify the reason. If your shyness is so severe, you may need professional or medical help. If your fears have to do with your appearance, there are ways to look good. If your fears have to do with communication skill problems, go back to Section 2 and revise your communication skills!

Has anyone made fun of you or belittled you in any way? Why?

_____

_____

_____

_____

Sometimes there is a memory of a presentation that you messed up or a poorly written essay by you that the teacher read out in the class. Sometimes your friends laugh at your accent or mannerisms. Many times in life people goof up. That is okay. If you are perfect, well there is nothing to learn. Even the job that you are looking for has so many lessons for you. If you take criticism constructively, you can actually turn the tables around and learn something useful. Have you heard of a term called petty tyrant? This term refers to all the bullies you come across in your life at one point or the other. Believe it or not, the petty tyrants who have made you sad are the people who have taught you the biggest lessons. If someone has made of fun of you, take it in good spirit and don't let that stop you from wanting to excel.

Are there too many expectations from you at home or in the educational institution you studied in? Do you have high expectations of yourself? Why?

_____

_____

_____

_____

Maybe you are a good student and your parents have very high expectations of you. Maybe you do not want to disappoint your parents and you get depressed by the thought of your future. We all know what happened to the character Joy Lobo in the Bollywood movie *3 Idiots*. Be realistic about your expectations.

Sometimes you can fail – failure becomes failure when you hang your head down and think that this is the end of the world and I've had enough. Every successful person has gone through the darkness of failure.

Having too many expectations of yourself can make you too frightened to act and thereby fail. Behind every achievement there are many baby steps. A step - by - step approach is more systematic and less intimidating or scary.

Step - by - Step formula to rid yourself of fear

Face it. Acknowledge the problem. I am shy and I want to change.

Prepare to desensitize yourself. This means start coming out of your shell.

safe place.

House	Grocery store	Fancy super-markets/Malls	Public gatherings	Public places

The table above shows a steady moving outward. If you have extreme shyness, you

Language problem   I'm not good enough   I hate malls

_____

_____

If the answer is I hate malls, it means you are not willing to admit that something

surroundings. They make friends everywhere.

Do you hate going to weddings? Why?

Weddings are boring   Too many people   Feel out of place

_____

_____

All these excuses indicate that you are not ready to face people. This is okay. The more you expose yourself to these kinds of events, the more you will learn to deal with it.

Pointers to make the most of public places and gatherings

- ☑ Remember people's names.

- ☑ Make a note of how they look, what they do, and where they live.

- ☑ Get interested in others and you will find the whole experience of meeting people more productive!

- ☑ Don't worry about yourself too much. Participate!

- ☑ Be curious. Don't be nosy!

The phone is a great tool to practise your speaking skills. Since it is not face - to - face, the phone provides an opportunity to practice confidence building.

- ★ Answer the phone. Don't be too brief. Ask who is on the line and the reason for the call.

- ★ Make enquiries. Call the beauty parlour and fix an appointment. Call the gym instructor and ask about the services provided at the gym. Is there an annual membership? Is there a quarterly one? How much does it cost? What are the timings?

- ★ Ask, ask, ask. Use every opportunity you have to listen to the sound of your voice and get information.

You can use college or the institution you are studying in as an opportunity to tackle any phobia or fear you face. How?

- ★ In college, volunteer to read. Listen to the sound of your voice in English class. Reading helps you improve the throw of your voice, pronunciation, tone, and pitch, all themes we dealt with in Section 2.

- ★ Say the answer if you are asked. Don't keep it to yourself. What is the use of knowledge if it is hidden inside you?

- ★ Read your essay if your lecturer praises you for it and asks you to read it. Don't sit down and say I won't or I can't. Your words are your own – respect your words and say them out loud.

- ★ Clear your doubts. Some lecturers may not encourage you to. So ask questions in classes where you are encouraged to. Ask and persist till you get the answer.

These are some pointers that you can use. List your fears here and write down what method you could use to tackle them.

Fears	Getting over it

Dealing with overconfidence: I have an attitude. I don't need any fixing.

Says Ranvir, a final year student, "Why should I be nervous about an interview? The office needs me, right?"

While on one end of the spectrum, there are extremely shy candidates, on the other end, there are extremely confident students like Ranvir who are sure that jobs need them. While confidence is entirely good, you have to be capable as well to sustain where that confidence can get you.

Overconfidence is something that employers don't really like. Recruiters believe that the biggest problem with freshers today is that they are far too confident and don't have the experience to back it up with. Too much humility doesn't work either. The bottom line is if you put on an act, the employer sees through you. So be reasonably confident but don't stretch it by thinking that the company needs you. It works both ways. You need the company and the company needs you.

When has overconfidence back fired or had a negative effect in your life?

_____

_____

Too much of confidence can never be a bad thing. However, at an interview you are not expected to be extremely casual, as though you have come to have a cup of coffee with the interviewers. An over confident person may be judged as someone who takes decisions without thinking the details through. That could be dangerous at a company level when decision making will be your core focus area as you climb up the ladder.

It is true that spirituality teaches you that you are already a perfect being. However, that perfection is the result of a lot of introspection or looking inward. The name of the game is get better and keep getting better! So companies reinvent themselves, systems are redesigned, change is continuous. Although you may have the attitude that works for the present environment, that attitude cannot help you in the long run because growth is about change.

If you are happy with your lot and think you don't need anything but a super cool attitude, you won't be able to survive that long in any industry. Ask any successful person what made them successful and they will not say words like destiny or coolness quotient. They will say hard work.

Interview attitude spoilers or Demons

Fear: We saw how shyness can be a barrier to your career prospects. This is an obstacle in you that you have to work on. I'm not saying become a loud person one fine morning. I'm saying learn to live with your shyness in such a way that it is no longer a barrier. History has shown that introverts can be a powerful influence on society - so channel your fear so that you can succeed because of your quietness. Quiet people tend to be more focused on tasks and less distracted by needless activities. What you need to do is focus more on being assertive.

Facing fear during the interview

★ Be prepared for the interview. Carry your portfolio. What can be scary is arriving at the interview without any of your credentials. Know what you are carrying with you so that you can show it when required.

★ Be groomed. Follow the grooming tips I've given you. Dress formally and presentably. If you look smart, you feel smart.

★ Be punctual. If you arrive on time, you get enough time to relax and be seated calmly.

★ Be aware. Observe other candidates who have attended the interview. Smile at the receptionist. See if the office atmosphere suits your expectations.

★ Be hydrated or drink lots of water. Avoid too many beverages like coffee, tea, and soft - drinks. The caffeine in these can make you a bit jumpy. Drinking water decreases your nervousness immediately.

★ Be calm. It's not easy to be calm when you are frightened but it is possible. Take a few deep breaths. Belly out when you breathe in, and belly in when you breathe out. You can breathe deeply without other candidates even noticing.

★ Be dignified. Even if you are nervous, sit straight and avoid touching your face or hair. Your body language in the reception area should not show that you are afraid. By adopting a dignified stance, you will feel more in control.

Arrogance: Today freshers have a know - it - all attitude. To a certain extent they know much more than a fresher would have known thirty years ago. However, when you honestly examine the knowledge base that you have, you see a lot of cracks everywhere. When you say, don't-tell-me-what-to-do, it comes across as arrogant, as knowledge comes from anywhere and you must be attentive to it. Learn all the time and take good advice from whoever gives it.

During an interview, arguing with the interviewer comes across as arrogant. When you are in the employer's office, you must understand his or her terms first. Unless you are a genius, there is no excuse for ego problems.

Self pity: Wipe it out. *I'm not good enough. I did not get good marks as the University was careless. I never had a good rapport with my lecturers. The course was not my cup of tea.* No employer wants to hear your sob stories. Your problems are your own. Take ownership and be responsible for the decisions you have made.

Casual attitude: Overconfidence can lead to casual behaviour, another thing recruiters don't appreciate. When you go for an interview, you are not in college. You are a potential employee, someone who can be of service to a company. You have to be professional in your attitude and body language – be a pro and the pro employs you!

Job Hunt Prelims

► Becoming the Right Fit

So far, we have dealt with the preparation for the job hunt.

What have you learnt? You have taken stock of yourself, charted out your objectives, understood the fundamental nature of the job hunt, and have your resume and cover letter ready. You are well-groomed and armed with communication skills – oral and written. You know your daily headlines. You have a smile on your lips and an organised folder. You are ready to go but where to? It's time to start applying.

Fresher Shoot

How do I know if I'm ready for the interview process?

You know what the job hunt is about. You want to get the employer interested in your talent. If you can answer the questions, "Why should you be hired? What makes you so important to the company and what can you contribute to its growth?" you are on the right track.

You won't be able to answer those questions right now as you need a little more preparation. Keep in mind that at the end of the day working for a company is all about giving your best for the benefit of the company. It's not about you but about balancing what you want with what your employer expects.

A job hunt is not something that you can get into in a day. It's a possible six month hunt for acing a thirty minute interview session.

I'm ready to start applying – now what?

The minute you decide that you are ready to work, you will have to start doing your homework. Getting a job could take some time – it could be as easy as getting hired via a campus interview and as difficult as waiting for six months to a year after several interviews. If you have the clarity of the kind of job profile that you are suited for, it could take longer. No hurry! It is always better to work in an organization that you have great respect for. If you have the means to wait for a good offer, by all means wait. However, when you are a fresher, consider that it is also useful to accumulate as much experience on your resume as possible. Don't be too choosy when you start out.

Are you confident to sell your brand now?

_____

_____

_____

If you still feel embarrassed about selling your brand, then you have to rethink. Since the educated population of the world has increased, more and more eligible candidates have entered the workforce. In any field from IT to the arts, there is so much talent that unfortunately only the person who shouts loudest is heard. In a free market economy, competitiveness is part of the survival technique.

Don't you post your views on Facebook? Don't you text chain messages to your friends? Every time you reach out using these kinds of social networks, you are promoting your brand. Brand equals to how popular you are. You can extend the same philosophy into your job hunt process. The more people like 'Brand You', the more chances you have of getting employed.

Are you willing to change to sell 'Brand You'?

_____

_____

_____

If you don't like to change, then remember that you have no choice. It's no use having a resume that you can't show off. The resume is just a piece of paper until you give it some value addition with the strength of your personality. For every different job interview you go to, you will have to change your answers a little as well. The same goes when you speak to several interviewers on a panel interview. Each interviewer will have a different point of view – so you will have to take all of that into account when you answer. One answer doesn't fit all.

Fresher Shoot

What does the employer want?

Once you start out on the job hunt remember that the interviewer is also a person with strong likes and dislikes, a person just like you. Just as you are trying to sell 'Brand You', the employer also has a key agenda and responsibility of selecting the best candidate for the job. The interviewer has researched you and come to certain conclusions about you based on your resume, your presence or absence in the social networking space, your objective, etc.

What kind of qualities do I need to get the employer's attention?

The employer looks for certain traits in you like responsibility, integrity, adaptability, positive personality, and ethical goals. Let's examine these traits one by one.

Responsibility: It's one thing to take on work in a smiling manner and another thing to get it completed on schedule. Willingness to work must be combined with results. If you are unable to meet your deadlines most of the time, the employer will judge you to be someone who does not value the job. Delay on your part means delay for the company – so responsibility is a must, be it in relation to punctuality, deadline completion, or providing information about new schedules.

How responsible are you? Look at instances in your resume where responsibilities you have taken are highlighted.

_____

_____

Integrity: All employers are on the look-out for employees who are sincere and honest in their dealings. Your body language says a lot about your motives. Employers don't need people with fake certificates. They are looking for people who execute their tasks in a straight forward way. As employees represent the company's integrity, it makes more sense to hire people who can deal with customers with utmost integrity.

How honest are you? Answer this question as honestly as possible.

_____

_____

Are your certificates real? Is the experience you have cited genuine? Employers can see through most dishonest attempts. You might think that the days of honesty are long gone and that the smartest hand makes the most money. That's really a choice that you have to make. Dishonesty has its share of problems as well.

Adaptability: The corporate sphere keeps changing. Your office space keeps changing. If you are rigid and uptight, you will find it hard to adjust to new work schedules, new colleagues, new cultures, and new bosses. The beauty of work life is that there is so much activity and change going on. Employers look for people who are able to handle fast-paced changes without too much fuss.

How comfortable are you with change? Does the idea of campus to corporate scare you?

_____

_____

Positive Attitude: It's no secret that employers look for people who give out a positive vibe. Being positive adds weight to your brand value. A positive employee is happy to be productive and makes the workplace experience more pleasant. That doesn't mean you have to be jumping around like a kangaroo, just that being happy will make your work smoother and team work much easier.

Do you think you can be positive at the work place? Can you show your positive side during the interview, even when you are under reasonable amount of stress?

_____

_____

Work Ethic: A good work ethic is proportional to the amount of work you put in and how quickly you can deliver. When at the company, finish your work. Achieve company targets. Prioritize your targets. Work ethic is about doing your best for the company – if you inculcate this quality, it will serve you in good stead later on when you are trying to achieve your own goals. Being disciplined and motivated for the company gives you the preparation you require to work toward future goals.

Did you work hard enough at college? Are you inspired by your own work ethic or do you think there is room for improvement?

_____

_____

Besides these traits, what does an interviewer really look for?

Many things like:

★   What kind of internship and part time experience or volunteer work experience does the candidate have to make him or her suitable?

★   What does the candidate know about the industry and particularly the company?

★   What are the competencies she or he has to do the role in question?

★   How well does the candidate communicate to the interviewer? The interviewer will assess what is said and how it is said.

★   How motivated is the candidate? Motivated, intelligent candidates impress employers with their feel-good attitude.

★   How does the candidate behave when under pressure?

★   What kind of social skills does the candidate have? Is the candidate ready to change for the company?

★   How good is the candidate's overall packaging – oral presentation and body language?

Do you have a positive, enthusiastic approach? Do you sound and look confident about handling the job? How intelligent are your answers to questions?

You will also be judged based on your questions to the interviewer and your general energy level. The more senior the position you interview for, the more difficult the line of questioning may be. So freshers should have little to worry about except for the basics.

What you should know at this point is your subject. We talked about improving your perspective by reading trade journals, business weeklies, and newspapers. If you are an Economics student, know the latest trends in the Indian economy and the global economy; be up to date on latest industry news and which companies to watch out for. If you are looking for a copywriter's post, know the best tag lines and catchy phrases, the senior copywriters who are well-known in the industry, the best ad campaigns to date, etc. What you know makes you more appealing to the person who interviews you.

What do you have to offer? If you don't know, then find out. What you have to offer is what the company should be looking for.

What's the difference between competencies and transferable skills?

Competencies are specific skills needed to perform the job. These skills are mentioned in the job advert.

Transferable skills are all the skills you have accumulated throughout your learning life in school and college, during projects and internships, and while cultivating hobbies. Every experience is an opportunity to learn. If you can identify what you have gained, then you know your transferable skills. Examples of transferable skills include all the verbs you tabulated in your verb table – remember editing, writing, research, auditing, accounting, coordinating, etc.

➤ Preparing for the Interview

An interview is a test of nerves. If you are prepared, then interviews are actually a great way of expanding your personality and feeling good about yourself.

What is the first thing you do after you see the job advert and decide to apply?

_____

_____

_____

Yes, you should rephrase your cover letter and rewrite your resume objective but the first thing you should really be doing is researching the company.

Renuka is a student in her final year of graduation. Her credentials are impressive. She has good scores, sound syllabus knowledge, and a pleasant demeanour. She doesn't get the job though. Why? She failed to answer one question – Tell me something about this company. Renuka went blank. She hadn't done her homework there and thought that she could get away with it. The employer simply said, "The least you could have done is learn a bit about the company you are applying to join, isn't it?"

Another question that you could get on the same lines is whether you had an opportunity to look at the company website. If you shrug your shoulders or try to evade the question, be sure that the job in question will not be yours. Reason – it shows that you haven't put in that extra effort to be prepared.

Knowing about the company gives you an advantage over candidates who have not done their homework. It also makes you more confident when your interviewer asks you the crucial question.

Fresher Shoot

When should I start doing company research?

You should do company research when you are identifying potential companies to apply to. You will do research before a job fair or a campus placement session.

When you apply for a specific job, you should research the company and the post you are applying for so that you can create a tailor - made resume and cover letter.

That's not all – if your resume is shortlisted and you get the interview call, then you should do a complete research of the company so that you can give the interviewer the impression that you are prepared for the post.

What information are you looking for when researching the company?

★ The financial position of the company and whether the company is profitable.

★ Who is on the board of Directors?

★ Organizational structure of the company.

★ Who might interview you (that gives you a head start to face the interviewer)?

★ How many years the company has been operational for and some history of the company.

★ The products and services provided by the company.

★ Locations of the company brands.

★ Whether the company priorities match your own.

★ Whether the job title and requirements match your competencies.

★ Advancement opportunities at the company or whether you have an opportunity to grow there.

Research the Industry

It is not enough to research the company you are applying to. You must also understand:

★ The nature of the industry you wish to be a part of.

★ The key competitors in the industry.

Fresher Shoot

I want to apply to the best companies in the country. How do I zero in on options that suit my qualifications?

Thank God for the internet! Run a search on best companies, List of top 10 companies, Forbes 500 List, etc. Then go to individual websites of the listed companies to find out if a vacancy for your qualification is available.

Locating Information

Renuka went back home a bit upset but determined to find out more about the company where she had applied. She googled the company name and its location. They had a website after all! She went through the Company Mission and Vision Statement. She then went back to Google and found the latest industry news about the company she had applied for in the News Section. It just took her a couple of minutes to find out the information she needed – she decided that it would be the first thing she would do the next time she got a chance to be interviewed.

News about the company you apply for can show up in many places – newspapers, television, and social networking sites like Facebook, Linkedin, etc. Official information about company details can be found via the internet. Information from these sources gives you a clearer and more reliable picture of what kind of company you will be applying to. It is easy to get information about listed companies or companies listed in the stock exchange:

★ Listed companies (companies listed in the stock exchange). Go to http://www.sebi.gov.in/ (Securities and Exchange Board of India or stock exchange site).

★ A limited amount of information about unlisted companies can be obtained from the ROC (Registrar of companies).

★ You can investigate the company's Credit Rating Information to see if it is financially stable, something essential, especially now that downsizing is becoming the norm.

Besides Google, you can check for any Annual Reports or printed materials of the company.

You could also talk with people who are already part of the company – this is why networking is so important these days.

Fresher Shoot

What kind of information about a company do you get on the company website?

Most of the information that you need to know when it comes to a company's philosophy and history will be available on the company website.

Is there any company slogan you have to memorize? Watch out for that.

What does the company provide – products or services? Learn something about these.

Try to align your objective with the mission statement of the company you are applying to. That doesn't mean cutting and pasting the company mission as the objective on your resume! Include some qualities the company stands by as part of your skill sets.

How do you research the post?

The best way to do that is to read your job ad thoroughly. You can ask friends who have worked in that post about relevant details. You can do a google search on the designation and watch interviews of people who have prominence in the industry you are pitching for.

Do recommendations matter?

Once you have researched the company, spruced up your resume, and created your cover letter, you need recommendations to make your application seem more credible. We live in a world where assertions made by the more experienced are considered important.

The resume and cover letter reveal your work history and intellectual capacity. Recommendation letters reveal what others feel about you. This carries a lot of weight during an interview. Just as you do company research, the company does its own research on you. Knowing what others have to say about you is part of that research.

What do recommendation letters contain?

★   How the person recommending you knows you

★   Key attributes you possess

★   Other skill sets and some background demonstrating these skills

Who should give me recommendations?

★   At the fresher level, a Professor, preferably your Head of Dept, could give you a written recommendation on the college letterhead.

If you have worked as a trainee in a company, you will need to get an experience supervisor or manager of the team.

Recommendation Letter Example

Name of the Recommender

Name of the Institution

Address

Telephone Number:

Date

To whom it may concern

It gives me great pleasure to introduce XXX who studied at ABC University from ……….to …………….. During this period I was her Professor in Economics.

Throughout my dealings with XXX, she has come across as focused, hard-working and knowledgeable. She is a team player and demonstrates strong inter-personal skills and commitment toward project completion.

Besides academics, XXX displays a strong interest in debating. She led the college team to win the televised National Debate on Water Pollution in 2009. I highly recommend XXX as she will be an asset to your company.

Sincerely,

XXX

Head of Economics Dept

Fresher Shoot

What is the difference between references and recommendations?

References are verbal forms of recommendations. All you have to do is call the concerned people who you think will recommend you and get permission to mention their names and contact details to your employer. The referrers may be contacted by your prospective employer via phone.

Send your referrers your detailed resume and explain to them that you are sending your application to companies that might need their validation. Give your referrers advance notice that they could be contacted.

Always thank them for their cooperation.

► Interview Rounds

Fresher Shoot

Why do I have to go through so many rounds before the main interview?

Rounds of tests constitute the shortlisting process. All your lives you have been preparing for tests and exams in school. What is a test or an exam? It is just a method to understand how good you are at time management and organizing your thoughts. Compete with yourself, not others, and then you will find tests and exams easy enough.

A technical test checks technical knowledge, verbal tests reveal your editing skills, psychometric tests show your mental ability and personality. Offices conduct hosts of tests even after you join work, so no need to get intimidated by the test-taking process.

☑ The written test

Before you attend the written test, try to understand what kind of test you will have to take. Finding out is also part of interview preparation homework. The best part is that you can practise tests of this sort and improve your scores. Where do you get these tests? Well, you can download tests of this sort from the internet and source books as well. Once you practise, you have more chances of passing the preliminary round of assessment and getting into the next round.

How good are you at written tests?

Many companies provide the usual run of the mill on the spot test. This is to see whether you have the patience to meet deadlines and have the confidence to demonstrate your written skills in a particular environment.

Are you good at writing exams?

_____

_____

_____

If you have butterflies in your stomach at the thought of exams, then change this attitude. Exam phobia is common among students. Fear of exams is unnecessary. Be prepared for the exam and see it as a challenge. A challenge is an opportunity to succeed, just as it is a possibility to fail. Both outcomes can happen – it is your job to be prepared as best as you can for the best possible outcome.

Are you able to complete your paper within the allotted time?

_____

_____

_____

If you are not, this is an area that you will need to concentrate on. You need to be able to organise your thoughts within a few lines. Sometimes students are prepared in one area and answer an essay question in 6 – 8 pages, leaving behind the rest of the answers. Your marks are distributed across several questions, so why waste all your energy on only one question?

Write at a decent speed. Try to write as quickly as you text message! The examiner only wants to know whether you have the required time management skills to complete your task. Time management is crucial in a work environment governed by deadlines.

Do you check your paper before submission?

_____

_____

_____

If you check your paper, you will find many spelling mistakes or typos and other errors. An answer paper full of spelling mistakes will not get you to Round 2. So make a habit of rechecking, for the simple reason that once you join an office you will have to run through all the business communication you make on a day-to-day basis.

☑ **Facing it: Group Discussion**

What can you expect at a GD?

Group discussions show the employer that you are capable of interacting effectively in a team – a trait that is important when you work in a company. Conflict resolution is an important part of your career and for that interaction has to be good with all individuals from day one. If it isn't, well then there is a problem.

In both situations, interview and group discussion, the oral skills required are the same. You need a lot of clarity when you speak. This means you must have a clear thought process and be able to articulate what you think clearly. In a group discussion, it helps to speak in a louder voice.

These questions enable you to understand a little more about what the GD constitutes:

★ **Are you able to assert yourself and give your views on a subject?**

_____

_____

Whatever the subject is, a GD is challenging as you are expected to put forward your views with a sensible, level-headed approach. Every candidate must speak at length and justify his or her stance with a pleasant smile and calm posture. Asserting yourself does not mean that you gesticulate or move your hands wildly. It also does not mean that you interrupt another speaker. Asserting yourself simply means being heard and understood.

★ **Are you comfortable talking to a group of strangers about general topics?**

_____

_____

Not always. The entire situation seems awkward and strange at first. Why would you want to discuss the benefits of creative writing or the importance of case studies as part of your coursework? Initially, it is artificial. However, once you get into it, the strangers will be strangers no more. Just view it as an opportunity to hear the sound of your voice being heard. It's a nice feeling!

★ **Do you listen to others or only talk?**

_____

_____

Only listening is not enough. A group discussion gauges your confidence to speak up. When you work in an office, there will be times when decision making and taking responsibility are part of your contribution. If you find it hard to speak up, that means you will also find it difficult to take important decisions when required. By voicing yourself, you are taking responsibility and being accountable.

Only talking is not good either. During a discussion, you are expected to agree or disagree with the candidate who spoke before you did. You cannot emphasize on your point of view alone. In an office, multi-sided communication is essential. So you listen and speak, listen and speak.

★ **Can you speak sensibly with others even if they have different views? Are you a tolerant communicator?**

_____

_____

_____

An example is your stand on the global warming debate. Do you get worked up about policies or are you open to dialogue? As a student, you are not expected to take sides. Whatever topic you discuss, you must leave behind your affiliations at home and try to speak in a logically controlled manner. There are various other candidates alongside you. They are from different parts of India; so be sensitive and tolerant. There is no room for personal prejudice in the corporate space. Remember that you are aiming for the job; so speak accordingly.

★ **Do you take credit for what you do or do you let others take the credit?**

_____

_____

_____

Be your own person. Take credit where it is due and don't let others walk away with credit for your work. Reason: It hurts and is not a professional thing to do. In a GD, acknowledge the previous statements made by your peers. Work from their ideas. You will then come across as involved and willing to be part of the team, something essential for corporate life. If you take all the credit, you will not be liked in the industry and even if you are selected your career will be an exercise in bullying.

So to sum it up these are some essential GD skills:

★ **Interpersonal skills or how good you are at communicating with others**

When you speak with others and want to be noticed, it is important to make eye contact with all those in your group. You must also be well-groomed and maintain a confident posture.

You have to treat everyone around you with fairness. Don't act too superior or too inferior.

★   **Problem-solving skills**

When you are given a topic, you have to think about the subject in a clear and systematic manner. Didn't we discuss the note-making exercises you did in high school? Under a general topic, you have various sub-heads which are then further expanded. Every problem can be understood if you break it up into parts, the way you solve a math problem. Being systematic and organised helps you to solve problems.

★   **Leadership skills**

How good are you at starting a discussion? Initiating a discussion is a bonus point but that doesn't mean you just say anything at all. Credit is given to the sensible speaker.

A good leader is able to persuade others in the group and make sensible decisions. You can get other people to follow your lead by making your voice firmer and your attitude more confident. Make sure you are heard – no soft voices in a group discussion.

A good leader is also a motivator and helps others in the group to articulate their ideas as well.

★   **Subject knowledge**

Speak about what you are sure of. If you are asked to discuss a topic, note down any points that are relevant to the topic as you would do for a high school debate. Don't speak for the sake of speaking and if you really don't know what to say, take your cue from a more reasoned speaker. State then why you agree with him or her, or what other thoughts you have on the topic.

★   **Listening skills and reasoning ability**

A candidate who talks too much can come across as a know it all. You have to talk in response to someone else. Listening helps you form a view and get some more points to expand. If you listen to various points of view, you will come across as more open-minded, sensible, and cooperative.

Don't try to monopolize the discussion – in a successful GD, every candidate gets to share their point of view. Do not keep interrupting when others speak.

When you are the listener, do not only look at the speaker. Also look at the others in your group. This way you become more accepted as part of the group.

★   **Ability to take criticism**

You may be a good speaker and listener but you may not like criticism. When you are in a group, do not expect everyone to agree with you. Disagreement does not necessarily have to be due to dislike. Take negative comments with a pinch of salt. Do not react angrily and conversely do not let the critic take advantage either; that makes you a better candidate.

After you ace the GD, you will have more confidence to face your employer one to one. Some jobs don't require a GD at all.

Group Discussion No-nos

★ No manipulating others – this means you don't assert yourself by controlling others.

★ No depending on someone else to give you a cue. You have to stand up for your opinion and get it out there. No one else is going to speak on your behalf.

★ Don't speak with doubt in your voice. Even if you are not sure, sound positive. The employer is more interested in how you handle the situation than how much you actually know.

Before the real thing you can try out your own mock version. You have mock exams all the time!

How do you prepare for your mock exams?

_____

_____

_____

Honestly, do you make a mockery of it? Many of you do. Mock exams may seem unfair and a waste of time, but mock interviews are not. These prepare you for the big day. Mocks are all about recreating the real situation. If you take your mocks seriously, you give yourself a lot more time to be prepared and also more time to gain experience that you can put on your resume. If you start early, you get more time to make mistakes and you succeed earlier on in life. If you wait till the last minute to prepare yourself, you will be the last in queue to gain success.

Doing the Teleconference

All job interviews begin with the phone call. You can do mock phone interviews to rehearse the situation.

Fresher Shoot

Why should I worry about phone interviews – I talk on the phone all the time, so it's no big deal, right?

You give away a lot about yourself when you speak on the phone, maybe more than you realize. Since you talk on the phone most of the time to friends or relatives, you could sometimes be very casual while talking on the phone for business reasons.

Remember a business conversation is always about business and so a casual tone should be replaced by something more formal. You must sound professional even if your employer sounds friendly. If you are too chatty, you give away too much about yourself.

Why do interviewers do interviews via phone?

The telephone interview is usually the initial stage of the screening process. Some employers feel it is easier to narrow down candidates by just observing their telephone conduct. The problem with phone interviews is that these are short notice affairs. If you have sent in your resume, don't be surprised if you get a call out of the blue.

Telephonic interviews are useful for the employer as they can avoid wasting time by determining early on whether or not you are a good fit for the company.

Suppose I miss the call?

In case you are unable to attend the call or you have missed it by accident, make sure that you have a professional sounding greeting on your voicemail or answering machine.

Is it okay if I don't do so well during my telephonic interview?

No.

Every call you get from a recruiter is a potential screening. You will be asked to provide some details about yourself and maybe be asked yes-no questions like, "Are you interested in full-time employment? We work from 9 – 6."

Before you post your resume online or provide your resume to recruiters, go through your own self-screening so that you can answer these questions straight away, without much hesitation.

How do I test my voice – is the interviewer going to judge me on the basis of just hearing the sound of my voice?

One easy way to test your voice is to record your voice so that you can assess your tone, pace of speech, accent, vocabulary, and fluency. Too many pauses must be avoided. Your voice must come across as friendly and likeable.

Doing a mock phone interview is a good preparation for the real thing.

Sit down, backs facing, and do your question-answer sessions. Pay attention to the volume and pace of speech. Do you know that you have to smile even when you speak on the phone?

Introduce yourself the same way you would in a face - to - face interview and listen to the employer carefully. Take notes and answer correctly. Just because you are at home or on the phone, don't take the phone interview too lightly as this could be the first step in short listing you for the face - to - face interview.

Remember to be very clear as during phone conversations there are several chances of being misunderstood. Also you can't take your words back. So watch what you say and remember that the person on the other line during the real phone interview is not your friend, only your employer. Speak accordingly.

Calculate the time you need to answer each question and what you need to do to make your answers as crisp as possible. A little bit of preparation can help you appear as a focused individual.

One advantage of the telecon is that you can have a list of prepared answers right before you on your notepad. You can also have a copy of your resume before you when you answer.

You can always ask your recruiter to fix the interview time that is convenient for you so that you can make the necessary arrangements to maintain a peaceful and quiet environment around you. Interviewers will not entertain the blaring TV and radio in the background.

When you speak, remain as calm as possible. Don't make any demands via phone. The telephonic interview is a warm-up that will ultimately lead to the face - to - face interview. If you jump the gun even before you are selected, you narrow your chances of getting selected drastically.

Things to remember during a teleconference

★   No chewing during the interview. When you talk on the phone with food or chewing gum in your mouth, it is quite obvious. Just because you are not face - to - face, it doesn't mean you can do the interview in any way you want.

★   If the interview has been scheduled, remember not to do your interview in your night wear. If you don't feel professional, you won't be able to sound professional either. Since you are a fresher, you won't have the expertise to act like a pro in your pyjamas!

★ Experts advise you to do the interview standing up so that you adopt a more professional approach. Haven't you noticed how different your lecturers appear when they sit down and when they stand?

★ When the phone rings, pick it up by the third ring, say a polite Hello, I'm ....

★ Keep a glass of water before you in case your throat becomes raspy.

★ Don't interrupt the interviewer. Let the interviewer complete the question. If you keep interrupting, it sounds rude. If you don't understand what is being said, just say, "pardon me."

★ If you get a tough question, no need to be nervous. Just take a moment to give the best response that comes to you.

★ Don't forget to thank the interviewer. A little bit of grace on your part can go a long way.

The Interview

➤ Your Interview Quotient

An interview is a face - to - face discussion. You will be asked questions by one or a panel of several employers. Interviews can also be part of your academic life. Once you complete your thesis, you will be interviewed by a panel of academicians.

Are you confident while talking to strangers? If not, why?

_____

_____

_____

Being confident is key. If you are not, remember that confidence comes with practice. The more interviews you give, the easier the whole experience becomes. Make it a habit to interact with people around you–college mates and colleagues. Don't always wait for them to make the first move. Keep tackling your fears as we discussed with Gaurai. Confront and get over it. This is the only way to deal with fear.

Do you fidget in your chair or play with your hair during question-answer sessions in class?

_____

_____

_____

If you do that, you come across as nervous. The next time you are asked a question, observe your own response. Many times, you will find yourself automatically becoming self-conscious and fidgeting around, tapping your feet, looking distracted, touching your face and hair. All these are signs of nervousness. Observe your reflexes and work on them. Any fidgeting on your part will distract the interviewer and bias his or her view of your conversation skills. Have you ever seen a good speaker fiddle around with his or her hair?

Do you like the sound of your voice?

_____

_____

We did a voice warm up earlier on, remember? If you are asked to read a lesson in class, do you read with enthusiasm? Do you feel the sound of each word coming out of your lips and resonating in class? Or do you just read in a dull monotone while the rest of the class is distracted? Your voice is your fingerprint to success. Why do you think Big B is still big on the radar all over the world? His baritone voice, of course.

Are you nervous?

_____

_____

_____

Well, all coaching classes tell you one thing. Being nervous is not a crime. Rule number one before you enter the corporate space is to convert all your negatives into Positives.

Nervousness ahead of a presentation or event is like adrenalin pumping. It makes you excited and can actually give your talk or performance energy. The whole idea is to keep your nervousness in check.

You control the nervousness; the nervousness cannot control you.

Are you able to speak fluent English?

_____

_____

_____

This is must for the interview and the reason why we did an oral and written skill overview in the previous chapters. You don't have to speak like President Obama. All that is expected of you is that you speak grammatically correct English in a reasonable neutral accent. A neutral accent makes you appear much more sophisticated.

Are you able to fill your answers with good anecdotes and examples?

_____

_____

When you go for an interview, you are judged based on how you present yourself. If you are good in academics, how does it show in your speech? If you are enterprising and have accumulated work experience even as you pursued a college degree, how do you show that you are highly motivated?

The interviewer does not ask only yes-no questions. If the questions are open-ended, the answers should also be elaborate. Think of how you can use your own life examples to make your profile seem more attractive.

For instance, if you are applying for the post of content writer and you have worked as assistant editor for your college magazine, you could speak about your experience. How did you collect the stories, what software did you use to do the layout, how were interviews conducted and how successfully did you meet deadlines? Nothing beats real life experience. If you speak about your experiences with pride, you have more chances of being accepted.

If even for a moment you start speaking negatively about your own achievements, you will fail. Remember the interview is not a counseling session. No negativity please.

Have you checked your resume?

_____

_____

_____

Do a quick fix of your resume. Stick to one page and make it simple. Make sure that key words are part of your resume. Use paragraphing and bullet points, so that your resume is clear. Make sure that you stick to the same style throughout. If you have used bullet points for one internship section and paragraphing for another section, the resume becomes inconsistent.

Doing the mock interview

Even when you attend job-oriented courses, you might have to go through a verbal examination. Haven't you heard of the viva? Many of you think that you don't need to practise verbally before the test. Contrary to that idea, practice gives you the necessary confidence when you walk - into the waiting room.

Fresher Shoot

What should I do during the mock interview?

The same things that you would do for a regular interview! You will be more relaxed so you can prepare better.

For a mock exercise, you will need the help of a few good friends. You could create a panel discussion environment and ask your peers to frame stock questions. Ask one of your friends to record your mock session. Use technology to benefit you. When you see your recorded interview, you will better understand your shortcomings and try harder to correct it.

Most of the time you will goof up in the first attempt. Try to hold several sessions of mock interviews until you have the confidence to deal with the real thing. Stick to the same script even when you are doing your mocks. If you repeatedly say the same information, it comes automatically to you during a real interview.

The dummy interview gives you the feedback you need to know, which areas you are weak in, and the areas where you excel. The best part about a mock session is that you get genuine feedback. Maybe your body language was too casual, maybe your pace of speech was too racy. If you don't have any friends to help you out with a session like this, look into the mirror and rehearse; you'll learn a lot about your body language in the process.

Be a STAR

Have you heard of the STAR approach? This helps you answer your questions in around one and half to two minutes. STAR is an acronym standing for Situation Task Action Result.

Before you speak, mentally rehearse what you are going to say.

S: To show your competency, you use a **situation** first. If you are asked to show your team spirit, demonstrate in which circumstance you were able to achieve it.

T: What **task** were you able to complete as part of your teamwork?

A: Action is a description of the task itself – you don't talk about others in the team, only your contribution.

R: The **Result** should be the natural outcome of your hard work and diligence.

You can't use words like luck and chance – an employer wants to see how you are able to achieve your objectives and thereby how you will achieve company targets as well.

Fresher Shoot

How do I gear up before the interview?

★ Confirm dates, time, and location! Remember dates can get rescheduled. So always keep your mobile on and be alert about any last minute changes.

★ Do you remember your grooming exercise? Dress your best, guys have a shave, and be squeaky clean when you leave home. The interviewer has to feel that you spent time preparing for the interview. If you are well groomed, you give the impression that you are interested in the job. If you go shabbily, you show your lack of interest.

There is an interesting scene in the movie *The Pursuit of Happyness*. The protagonist of the movie arrives at the office for his important interview wearing a faded blue jeans and a vest. His body is covered in paint. The reason? He had spent the previous night in jail over an unpaid speeding ticket. How does the protagonist handle the interview?

I advise all job aspirants to watch this movie to see the perfect body language that job seekers look for in a good candidate.

★ Make sure you have had a good breakfast and have taken everything – your phone (on silent mode), your resume, resume copies, certificates, any interview letter you may have, recommendations, etc.

★ Before you leave, have you worn your watch? This is one accessory that you must have strapped to your wrist. All employers need to know that you take time seriously.

★ Punctuality is key. Be half an hour early. It gives you time to mentally prepare yourself and get used to the surroundings. If you get stuck in traffic, just intimate the office and let them know that you will be late. Preferably avoid this situation. Why don't you locate the office the day before the interview? Figure out the best route you have to take to be there. Know the landmarks that will help you get there without too many hassles.

Don't be an hour early. This means you don't take the employer's time seriously. Be on time. Not too early, not too late.

In the reception area

Raj is a fresher on his first stint with the interviewer. He sits anxiously in the reception and waits for his interview call. The first rule of interview decorum is to introduce yourself at the reception desk. This is how Raj should do it.

I'm...................... . I'm scheduled to meet Mr/Ms xyz for the interview. This is the interview call letter I have received.

You will be scrutinized from the moment you enter the office. So be polite with the receptionist and don't spend your time in the reception area chatting or texting on your mobile.

Also observe how you feel about the office staff. If they are very rude and the general atmosphere is unsuitable, reassess your choice of office. If they have impeccable manners, emulate that when you interact with the receptionist and also the employers when you are called for the interview.

When it is your turn, you will be directed to a meeting room or a conference room.

At the interview

Once Raj is in the interview room, he is nervous but he doesn't show it. This is a good way of handling stress. He smiles. His body language is comfortable. He walks into the room with a straight back and makes eye contact with the interviewer. He gives the handshake when his potential employer extends his hand in greeting. He remembers the handshake hows and shakes web to web, not too aggressive and not too weak either.

Raj is on the right track.

Interview body language and speech

★   Good posture. No slouching as it shows your lack confidence.

★   Sit when you are asked to sit.

- ★ Make reasonable eye contact.

- ★ Follow the speech rules – be clear, fluent, loud enough but not too loud.

- ★ Be confident throughout the interview even if you are not sure of something.

- ★ Continue with the smile; if you feel the smile is artificial just be pleasant, not grumpy. If the questions don't make you smile, maintain a serious demeanour with a light smile.

- ★ The rule in warfare is to never let the other side sense your fears – the same rule holds good during an interview. Stay involved in the interview and alert yourself when you get distracted. Listen to your interviewer. Think over the questions and clarify doubts. This shows how earnest you are.

- ★ Your certificates should be neatly organised and placed in an orderly, accessible manner in a file. A very important part of the interview is to know your documentation. When did you take your exam? Which month, which year? How much did you score? Your certificates are a wealth of information about your achievements. If you are unable to answer documentation related questions, you may lose out on the interview. This is such a waste of effort!

- ★ Don't place your elbows on the employer's desk. Keep your bag beside your chair, not on the desk before you. When asked to provide your certificates, make sure you are able to show them gracefully and don't end up spending your time trying to pull out your file from a bag. Also, always carry a pen that works and doesn't leak, and a notepad in case you need to jot down any important points that will help you later.

Recheck: If you are far from nervous, see if this is how you feel: The employer needs us. We don't need them. Generation Y has a new problem besides nervousness – it's the problem of over confidence. Yes the employer needs you but you shouldn't come across as arrogant. Once you get rejected in a couple of interviews for being too casual and arrogant, you may start to feel the nerves of getting rejected. Avoid that situation and just be level headed – not too nervous, not too proud.

At the interview no-nos

- ★ Don't jump to your seat until you are told to sit.

- ★ Don't flood the office desk with your materials. Keep it at the side of your chair or on your lap. Don't lean your hands on the desk. You could take notes if you are required to.

★ Don't assume anything. You never know if the job is yours until you get it.

★ Don't gesticulate wildly with your hands when you talk.

★ Don't make too many facial gestures.

★ No yawning.

★ No checking texts and answering phone calls.

Fresher Shoot

Why is being a good listener so important during the interview?

Listen hard. The interviewer wants to know more about what you can give the company, not your entire life story. Listening makes the speaker feel that you are attentive and have the focus to do the job. A person who listens usually gives value to everyone's opinion. This trait is extremely useful in getting through group discussion as well.

Questions asked at the interview

The corporate world is changing and with it the tried and tested interview techniques.

During the fresher stage of your career, be prepared for the normal line of questioning. Don't be taken aback, however, if you get questions out of the blue. Usually you will be asked to give a brief rundown of your overall resume and substantiate specific details. Nowadays companies have also started focusing not on what you have done but on what you can do for the company.

You can prepare yourself with a list of some top questions and be ready to substantiate five useful skill sets that are relevant to the job you are applying for. Sticking to the traditional line of questioning makes the process much easier, but you must also have a brief idea about what you can do with those skills to create growth from a company perspective. The idea is to be familiar with your own skills and know how your skills can benefit the company.

► Kinds of interviews

You can't bracket interviews into distinctive types as questions tend to overlap. However, there are basic trends that interviewers follow.

★ **Traditional interview:** This is probably the kind of interview that you will face the first time round. The questions are all text book predictable – Tell me your Strengths and Weaknesses is a common question. This is the kind of interview that you can go 100% prepared for.

★ **Behavioural interview:** This kind of interview is more extensive and predicts how an employee will react to a future situation at work. You will be asked to describe particular situations and why you made certain decisions. For this kind of interview you must keep some positive anecdotes handy based on your internships, achievements, volunteer work, etc. Even when you join work, keep a job log because you never know when those job experiences come in handy.

★ **Situational interview:** The questions in this sort of interview deal with your response to potential situations in the future. How would you react to a careless employee or an angry customer? You can frame your answer using the behavioural interview technique – recall anecdotes that show how you dealt with stressful individuals. Frame positive responses.

Fresher Shoot

Suppose I get a question that is weird and out of context. How should I tackle it?

Don't be surprised if the employer tries to pull your leg or fool you. You could get a question like: You have three wishes to make – what would they be? You wouldn't expect a question like that but you should just go ahead and answer with a smile. What do you have to lose? You can't be quiet as your employer is waiting for your response. You can't be dismissive or ignore the question as that looks rude. So go ahead and shoot. Use your imagination!

★ **Case interview:** MBA students are familiar with this one – you get twenty minutes to dissect a business situation. This is a sort of role play situation where you are given a business problem scenario. You will be judged based on your analytical, logical, problem solving, and creative abilities. With a little bit of case study practice prior to the interview, you will get the knack of how to deal with any problem. The company is not looking for text book solutions. They want to test your knowledge of the subject. Are you aware of which business tools you can use to create a solution? Can you think on your feet? There is no one correct solution to a business problem. What you need to demonstrate is your enthusiasm to solve it.

★ **Panel interview:** Where do you look? Is what freshers ask when they think about a group of people interviewing them. You should greet all the interviewers with your focus on the interviewer. When you are questioned by one on the panel, you look toward him or her and scan the rest. One mistake that occurs during the panel interview is that the candidate forgets to address each and every one on board. You must make eye to eye with each decision maker.

So we can expect these kinds of questions during the interview:

★ Case questions zero in on your analytical and problem solving skills. MBA students can expect questions on these lines.

★ Behavioural or situational questions assess possible responses to different situations.

★ Role-play questions force you to put yourself in someone else's shoes to see how you can deal with a particular role. Working in the corporate sector is all about donning different roles adequately.

★ Industry-specific questions test your industry know - how.

★ Stock questions are the easiest, and the ones you can prepare for. These deal exclusively with your experience and academic scores.

Why do interviewers ask so many questions?

There is no other way for assessment to take place. Interviewers ask questions not to intimidate or scare you but to find out how you react to specific situations. At the work place, you will have many challenges, interactions, and deadlines. You must be alert and prepared at all times.

By shooting tough questions the interviewer tries to find out whether you have the spunk or coolness quotient to handle it. If you get cold feet or frightened during question time, you probably are not ready for the job in the first place.

Do I need to prepare answers or be spontaneous?

Like you prepare yourself way ahead for a presentation, you must prepare for the interview. Most of the interview questions are predictable. Be familiar with your resume. Know what achievements you have made; the tenure of your work experience and education; and your likes and dislikes. A job hunt is an extremely good preparation for good living as it helps you assess yourself completely and also helps you recall your actions. Self-observation and self-analysis are positive steps when you go out into the world to earn and win.

Know how to present aspects in your resume as benefits. If you have worked as magazine editor for the college magazine, you could say that "Since I've been editor of the college magazine, page layout and article procurement come to me easily and this will benefit your press."

Create answers to every challenge presented on your resume. If you have played team leader during a college-hosted corporate event, assess your role, responsibilities, requisite skills that helped and skills that you gained in the process. Also assess the challenges you faced. Turn every negative into a positive.

I know the kinds of interviews – what are the kinds of interviewers out there?

There are as many kinds of interviewers as there are people.

★ **Very prepared interviewer:** This is the kind of employer who has read your resume several times. To impress this kind of employer you must be thorough with your own job experience and academic qualifications. You can learn a lot about yourself, the nature of the job, and company from this kind of interviewer.

★ **Unprepared interviewers:** These interviewers could be as nervous as you are. They may not even have examined your resume. So it is up to you to elaborate on all aspects of your career.

★ **Rude interviewer:** Maybe the interviewer is testing your nerves or maybe she or he just had a bad day. Be positive and guard yourself against any kind of negativity.

Interview answer do's and don'ts

★ No beating around the bush. Answer the question you have been asked. Don't talk about an unrelated theme. Give brief answers that are at most two minutes long. Make your answer concise and to the point. No speaking non-stop as that conveys the impression that you are nervous.

★ Don't say negative things about the college you went to and the bosses you may have worked under. Even if you had a negative experience, the interview is not the place to share it.

★ No lies please. It's very easy for an interviewer to see through your dishonesty. An employer appreciates an honest candidate. Even if you don't have enough credentials, an employer needs someone who can be trusted. If you say one thing and your resume something else, you lose your credibility. Don't forget that if you have fabricated documents, it is just a matter of time before you will be caught.

★ Don't be defensive. If the interviewer mentions that there are certain skills you have to improve on, don't retort or get defensive.

★ Don't contradict your resume. Be consistent. Be familiar with your own resume. Instead of fully entrusting a recruiter to make it, make it yourself. This way you will be thorough with your own list of competencies.

★ Don't be spaced out. Be alert! Don't forget your resume dates. Diya, now employed with a BPO, recalls an interview experience when she had to list whatever she had achieved date-wise. She was a candidate with some work experience as well. However, she was confused about the dates and ended up sounding like she had faked her resume. Avoid such a situation by asking yourself pointed questions about your own resume during your mock interview sessions.

★ Do not get discouraged if you don't get through. It's for the best! It gives you the time to sharpen and acquire more skills to present yourself better.

★ Never make the mistake of talking to your employer like your friend. Professionalism counts. The minute you treat your employer like your friend, misunderstandings can crop up and you may give out unnecessary information that should remain with you in the first place. Even if you are comfortable talking to someone, you must keep a distance. This applies even during telephonic conversations.

So challenge your resume. Once you create your resume you have to know exactly what you did and how you achieved your goals and fulfilled your responsibilities.

► Stock Questions

Here are some questions Jaya Narayan, Executive Coach, has charted out. You can go through the answers and rewrite them to suit your course detail and job application.

★ **Tell us a bit about yourself.**

_____

_____

_____

This is the top question that you will usually get, so be prepared for this one. It's difficult to answer this question without some preparation. Use the self-introduction we have done earlier on in the book. A self-introduction is a biographical sketch of who you are. If you are a brand, this question is the commercial that will sell you.

★ **Why do you want to work for this company?**

_____

_____

_____

_____

This question translates as let us know what you know about the company. This question presents an opportunity to stress on your research skills, qualifications, competencies that you have for the job, and your enthusiasm. It is your chance to talk about all the company research that you did and let them know that you have done your homework. What do you know about the company and its products or services? How do you illustrate that in your conversation with the employer?

Ans: This company is a leader in the industry. Based on my research, the company has an impressive portfolio. The company is headed by people like Mr XYZ, a social entrepreneur and innovator. It would be a privilege to work in a company where innovation and social skills are encouraged.

★ **What accomplishments are you proud of?**

_____

_____

_____

The answer to this question showcases your positives.

Ans: My biggest achievement is that I scored 98% in Psychology. I did my internship at NIMHANS and gained experience tutoring blind kids as part of my volunteer efforts.

★ **What are your top three strengths?**

_____

_____

_____

Your strengths are what you are truly proud of. They should not be qualities that you have created for the interview, but real qualities that you have understood about yourself after your self-assessment. Strengths include patience, tolerance, commitment, thoroughness, interpersonal skills, etc. You would be advised to illustrate your qualities using an anecdote.

Ans: I had an opportunity to work with ABC media during my third semester. As a newspaper intern, I learnt to do reporting and vox pops. I worked as part of a team to create several extensive reports within a short deadline. From this experience I learnt that my strengths lie in interviewing people, creating features, and taking useful pictures. I did a short course in photography as well after my internship.

★ **What are your weaknesses/what is the scope for developmental opportunities?**

The trick here is to answer your negative question positively. The interviewer is not looking for an honest confession of all your faults. What she or he wants to see is your presence of mind. Usually, you will be uncomfortable to talk about things you do not like about yourself. Don't ever talk about your physical characteristics. Avoid I'm too fat, I'm too thin. Avoid I eat too much, I have allergies all the time.

Don't say you are a workaholic or that you are a perfectionist because you are a fresher and you wouldn't be too sure about those aspects of yourself until you enter the corporate culture and know more about your own work ethic.

Ans: The one time my test grades took a toss was during the IPL season. My biggest weakness is my weakness for cricket.

Why this industry?

This question is self-explanatory of course, e.g., you are interested in accounting as you have a degree in Commerce. You can mention why you took accounting as a core subject in the first place.

Ans: I come from a family of bankers and numbers were always my first love. Even as a child I used to keep ledgers in my uncle's supermarket. I've been tallying numbers for a while and that is why I didn't have any doubts about doing accounts for my degree. Working in this company under the designated role would give me a chance to learn more about the accounting field and hone my skills as well.

★ **What are your career goals in the long term?**

This is a trick question. Most of us don't know where we will be in the next five minutes, let alone five years. The idea behind this question is to find out what kind of person you are. If you are a person who has taken your course seriously and have a definitive goal, you will be a more responsible person and therefore a better candidate to employ. You may want to start your own business or start a freelance service, but these are your own personal goals. These are not goals that you can share with your potential employer. Your goals stated during the interview should be employer-centric. In your answer you must focus on remaining employed and getting promoted to a better position.

If, on the other hand, you have no clue about your life's goal, then the employer might not want to take the risk of employing you.

Ans: Five years down the line, I hope to be working in a more responsible position. I will want to head my team to solve challenges in the workplace. My goal is to learn from my work experience and use that knowledge with maturity in a higher and more challenging role in office.

★   **What are your salary expectations?**

_____

_____

Be reasonable. Base your answer on your research on the industry. This is the one answer where you can use your negotiation skills – What's in it for you and what's in it for me? Work is worship and if you are offered a poor salary, you don't have to take it. Many freshers underestimate themselves and say yes to any salary amount proposed. If you do your homework right and find out what kinds of salaries are offered by similar bracket companies, you can provide a reasonable enough figure. This will impress the interviewer as you have done the right kind of research.

If you are made an offer, don't agree or disagree immediately. Sometimes in desperation you say yes to any offer that comes your way. Avoid doing that – don't forget that shopping smart is about bargaining. If you don't bargain in markets, you get fleeced.

Your salary = Your worth. So think about your worth and then respond.

★   **Do you have any questions?**

_____

_____

This question should never be answered with a, "do you give holidays on these festival days? When is the sign out time?" Questions like these put you in a very bad light and reflect your unwillingness or inability to do the job. When you are briefed on your role, you are expected to respond to the challenge by asking the questions that will help you meet the challenge.

Better than saying you have no questions at all, you could shoot the following questions:

★ What kind of challenges can I expect during the first six months?

★ How will my performance be assessed?

★ Do you support training to keep your employees updated on new developments in the field?

Fresher Shoot

What do I do after the interview?

★ Thank the interviewer for having spent valuable time with you. Take a business card. Send a thank you email once the interview is done. Make sure that the email is spell-checked and grammatically correct. Employers usually appreciate this kind of effort and sometimes a simple thank you note can make a big impression on an employer.

★ If you really think that you clinched the interview and you can't wait for the job, ask about getting a formal written offer letter and exactly when the company requires you to join. If it is too soon to ask, clarify the rest of the steps required to complete the interview process.

★ Size up your experience. What positive experiences are you taking with you? What negative feelings are you leaving behind?

Suppose I don't pass the interview?

Be prepared to fail. Rejection is a normal part of the job hunt process. If you take your interview results with an open mind, you will find it easier to deal with rejection. Different companies have different criteria for employment. If you are not the right fit for the company, the employer would not risk taking you in. Don't get disheartened. Just apply elsewhere. Every interview you attend adds to your personality and builds your confidence. Sometimes recruiters can tell you things about your personality that you weren't aware of. Instead of defending yourself, every negative that has been highlighted is actually a lesson that will aid you in self improvement. Also, even if you have submitted your resume to a career consultant, remember to follow up on the proceedings, and continue looking for jobs in different avenues.

Be prepared to succeed as well. Once you ace the job interview, you will have to make many changes in your lifestyle.

Keep track of the number of interviews you attended. Always record the interviews you have attended and the companies you have previously applied in. Some companies do not take your resume a second time around or they will impose a gap before they reconsider your application.

Is it a good sign if I'm called for a second interview with the same company where I completed my first one?

Yes, experts believe that now you are halfway there. Some reasons for you getting called again is that someone else has turned down the offer or maybe the interviewers want to understand 'Brand You' a little more and see if you are the right fit.

For this interview, you will have to go much more prepared. Don't be repetitive, try to add on new experiences and anecdotes. Do a little more in-depth industry research. It's your second interview so you are experienced already! No need to fear, you have nothing to lose.

What do I do if I don't get a response?

Follow up within ten days. Enquire about your employment status. In the meantime continue with your job search. Attending several job interviews helps you negotiate salary scale better as you are a brand that wishes to move to the better company.

Don't see rejection as failure – it's actually a beginning. It prepares you better for the future. Don't pin all your hopes on one interview either – things may or may not pan out as you expect it to. What matters is the experience you have gained – possibly even new references for a future job.

Don't see success as the supreme achievement either; it is also a beginning and you have to sustain growth. Preparation has to continue.

So here are your interview essentials

★ **Clarity**

You have to be clear when you speak. Not too fast as though you have to catch your breath. Not too slow as though the employer cannot understand. Many times, students mumble or slur. Remember you are not talking to your friends in the canteen area; you are speaking to your potential employer.

★ **Response**

You need to introduce yourself well. Prepare a decent introduction that you can use at any venue. Work on the self-introduction exercise we discussed. Remember when you are asked about yourself NEVER say, "You can find it in my resume." What the recruiter wants is to hear your story from You.

Answer the questions you are asked as sincerely as possible. Speaking from your heart can win you brownie points!

★ **Neutral accent**

Articulate with a neutral accent. Remember you are not speaking your native language. Try as far as possible to follow the pronunciation rules we discussed earlier. You must leave behind your native language when you switch to English. The consonants and vowels in vernacular are pronounced differently as compared to English; differences also extend to timing, tone, and rhythm.

★ **No chatter**

Don't talk too much. If you do, you come across as nervous. You only have to answer the questions that are asked. When you talk too much, you could give away a little too much information about yourself. Not a good idea during interview time.

★ **No unnecessary conversation**

Like salary talk. You may be good but that does not mean you can start negotiating the salary you have in mind. Talking about salary is always the last part of the interview; so don't bring the conversation to it unless the employer does and be clear about expected salary from Day 1.

Recap

Understanding the job market.

Learn to read the job advertisement accurately.

Create an effective resume and cover letter.

Get over your fears.

Understanding what the employer wants.

How to prepare for the interview.

What kinds of interviews are there?

What kind of interviewers could you meet?

How to nail the telephone interview.

Interview stock questions.

After the interview?

SECTION 5
CORPORATE ETIQUETTE

What to Expect at the New Job
Navigating Day One

Etiquette and How
    Introduction Etiquette
    Business Card Etiquette

    Wining and Dining Etiquette
    Tech Etiquette
    Phone Etiquette
    Cross Cultural Etiquette
    Professional Etiquette
    Work Relationship Etiquette
Moving ahead: Keeping the Job
Assertive You
Climbing the Ladder

1

What to expect at the new job

You got the job! Congratulations.

How did you get here?

You assessed yourself, polished your skills, made a resume and created cover letters, attended interviews, and improved 'Brand You'.

Now what?

You passed the interview. Breathe in and out. Yippee! Now what's in store?

You need a lot of motivation and consistent enthusiasm to make the most out of your interview success. Remember how hard you worked to get here?

It's your job to keep this job. You may have a brief idea about your role and the

space, that you get a better picture.

of you and how you will show results. You will also be a little upset that you have to leave behind the college routine that you loved and start a completely new schedule.

In Section 1 we met Ephin, a Post Graduate student who works with a high-end company as part of her internship programme. She believes that friends, teachers, assignments, and exams are things students can manage easily. Corporate life is nothing like that. "Work is all about reporting to the boss daily, doing work correctly (no experimental college approach), and being responsible. All the hard work you did to get through the interview comes into action now. It's a continuous show of professionalism and performance."

Ephin says "corporates demand different aspects of the individual and make us act differently. In college we learn, relearn, and unlearn. At work we put our learning into practice. It may or may not be the same theories which we absorbed from classrooms."

Rule number one is you have to get it right from day one – if you do then rest assured, you will have something to look forward to in the company.

Corporate life is not about impressing your peers – it's about impressing the higher ups. This doesn't mean you have to keep giving your boss compliments. It just means add value to the organization by doing your work well. You have to exhibit confidence all the time and be willing to work as part of the team, rather than backing off at the last minute or making excuses.

Employee Shoot

When I join a new company what should I expect?

_____

_____

_____

_____

Ephin describes how smoothly her first day at work went: "I was welcomed by my onsite supervisor. Though I didn't do many things during the first two days, she started giving small tasks with proper explanations which I paid close attention to."

Go back to your first day in college. How did you deal with it? Were you nervous?

Write down what kind of experience it was. What positives do you remember and what negatives?

_____

_____

_____

_____

The first day in college is a day of finding classes, meeting new lecturers, making new friends, getting a feel of the campus and syllabus.

What would you change if you had a chance?

_____

_____

Maybe you would be a little friendlier or a little less nervous. Think back to what you could have done to make your first day at college more useful and apply it in the office.

You can avoid the mistakes you made when you first joined college. Joining work is an opportunity to restructure your life and give it a better sense of direction. Think about why you wanted this job in the first place and try to see the positives of your new workplace. Instead of saying, "My work desk is too small", you could say "They have an excellent refreshment area."

If your job has no positives, then it is a positive chance to think of a job change.

What kind of routine do you have? Do you wake up early? Is exercise a part of your daily life?

_____

_____

_____

_____

Having a routine is a must. One thing about work life is that it is extremely regimented and structured. Every moment is valuable and if you waste your mornings, you cannot make the most of your day. Try to maintain some kind of exercise schedule as you are gearing up for a day of work and need the energy and alertness to get through the day. In office, prioritize your work and avoid distractions as far as possible. Save time and you get a head start.

Employee Shoot

How do I make the transition from college life to corporate life easier?

We dealt with this transition in the Introduction. Now we will explore this question in a little more detail.

★ Polish yourself till you shine. If you are low on company protocol, then even if you were the best student on campus you don't stand a chance. Keep improving yourself – be it in language, general knowledge, interpersonal skills, etc.

★ Learn the company goals. Every company has procedures that you will be expected to pick up within the first couple of months. Working in a company is actually like learning all over again – so don't come to office thinking that you'll never have to study again! The truth is you will have to read the fine print more than ever before.

You also learn from the rest of the colleagues about how things are done in the institution you work in. Intelligent employees ask questions about when they get appraisals or promotions. They make friends with the achievers in the office; they know how to interact with the senior managers and other clients. They are listened to in meetings. Watching them helps you improve your career.

★ Don't be so passive that you forget who you are. Freshers are the life blood of a company and they keep the energy levels high. Listen to what the rest of the team says and give your input without hesitation. Unless you speak up, no one is going to give you a chance. Make sure that your contribution is noticed.

★ Take the in-house training programmes seriously. Joining office is preparation to improve your learning curve dramatically. Keep adding up on skills. Don't think that you landed the job and you can slow down. Every day you accumulate a variety of skills. Note it down and try to improve on areas where you feel there is more to understand. Take advantage of any opportunity your workplace gives you to improve your skills – be it making a presentation or attending a seminar. It may be time consuming but the whole idea of getting a new job is not to think about rushing back home. If you work hard in the initial phase of your career, it makes the future much better.

★ If you are a hard worker, you will make more good contacts with people who trust you. Good networking means a better experience of corporate life.

Navigating Day One

There is nothing like having a new experience. On your first day what you must remember is that though the first impression is the best, you must sustain the impression that you have made on people. Post interview, you will have to sustain the impression that you made during your introduction. This impression extends across all office activities like chatting with colleagues, talking on the phone, sending emails, etc. So what little things can you do on day one in your office?

★ **Get to Know People**

Who is the boss and where are the colleagues? Lots of introductions on day one and the days ahead. Get everyone's names into your head. Remembering names soon is a credit to you as it shows that you are interested in other people and that you care.

★ **Watch**

You learn a lot about company etiquette and work culture by just watching colleagues interact. Have your lunch with them, network with them; being a loner tends to make office politics hard to handle. Watch, learn, know, and grow.

★ Show your interest

Once you get the job, your enthusiasm should only double.

Let your boss know that you are interested in learning the rules. Always be enthusiastic on your first day even if you are feeling a little nervous. Keep up the enthusiasm as the first couple of days is when people will be at their best with you – take advantage of that honeymoon period and learn as much as you can.

You'll probably have a one - on - one with your boss after joining. Take notes and ask questions. What is expected of you? How much clarity do you have about your role in the company?

★ Find your way

Locate your seat. Where's the bathroom, the lunch break area? You'll find out soon enough.

★ Know the rules

Do you need to punch in and punch out? Any photo id? New company email to be made?

You'll probably have an orientation programme – this programme is held to convey organizational policies and expectations. Be attentive during an orientation. Take notes. It's not like your fresher's day in college! Don't get overwhelmed by the PowerPoint presentations and lectures. It's important for a fresher not to make too many assumptions on the first day and the first week. Your goal is to integrate yourself with the company and that takes time. Be patient and attentive – the rest will follow.

Also find out about rules and regulations, employee perks, etc. Make sure you can get your information about the company and developments there, along with the work you have to do.

★ Be nice!

Be nice to the people you meet in the first week – particularly the HR personnel and IT dept folks, people who get you wired and connected to your PC.

Small talk is good to get to know everyone. Gossip is not.

★ Ask

Start doing your homework. Read the company literature. Follow instructions and ask questions. Ask as much as you can throughout the beginning stage of your career. Let people know that you mean business. Ask until you understand – no short cuts from day one.

★ Work hard

You'll have to work extra hard the first couple of months to party harder later. Working is not just about getting paid; it's really about performance. So late hours will be in but make sure that you don't give the impression that work is your only priority. You may not get that much time for yourself – be prepared for erratic timings, but also remember that you are your own priority.

Day one tips fast track!

★ Keeping time is important but don't keep glancing at your watch as it makes you look impatient and eager to leave.

★ Dress well and carry an organised briefcase or handbag.

★ Never be idle – no sitting idly texting, chatting on the phone, or yawning loudly.

★ Take as many pointers from seniors as you can.

★ Read whatever company material or literature you find.

★ Get to know your team members and be nice to all of them.

★ Do the tasks you are assigned with eagerness and pleasantness.

Etiquette

➤ What is it?

Etiquette is a code of conduct relevant to a specific situation. There is an ideal behaviour or a set of social skills in every sphere and situation – be it classroom or boardroom. You behave differently at a wedding and a funeral; you eat differently at a fine dining restaurant and a pizza joint. To survive in cold clime, you need to wear really warm padded clothing and to survive in hotter places, you dress in lighter cottons.

The same changes apply to society – different societies have different social structures. Each community has certain rules when it comes to oral communication, table manners, grooming, gift giving and receiving, and other social interactions.

What is etiquette in one culture may be considered improper in another. When you get through your interview, your etiquette training has just begun.

Fresher Shoot

How can you learn manners?

Manners are social habits you acquire by observation.

Etiquette is something that you can learn. It helps employees of the company to wine, dine, interact, and succeed gracefully. "Corporate etiquette is about adjusting your cultural lenses in acceptance with the globally accepted protocols," says Kauser Khan, Managing Director at Protocol, a corporate etiquette and grooming organization.

It is about knowing how to behave in a situation-appropriate manner. How do you maintain civilized behaviour at the workplace? If you expect good behaviour from others, then first you have to set the trend. Do unto others as you would have them do unto you.

★ **Your manners quotient**

There is absolutely no substitute for good manners. Many potential employees have been rejected because of poor manners. Being polite is an excellent way to create an impression. Are you courteous with your superiors? You may think you are but think again.

Say your good mornings, thank yous, and please. It is good to be polite to people you meet on a daily basis. That way it becomes a habit. Being chatty with your colleagues is important. Ignoring them will not help at all – who knows if you need someone to back you up tomorrow?

Etiquette is so important in today's office culture. You will have to interact with people across different cultures. The way you behave is crucial to your success. It's no use being a good worker. You need the grace to make a good impression.

There are so many things you have to learn about yourself. In college, you can hang around with your friends and the people who will make you feel good about yourself. In the office, you may not meet your best friend. You may have to work with your biggest enemy. How do you deal with it? Politely, of course.

The rule is to be nice, not a door mat. You have to balance the attitude. Assertive and polite at the same time. That can only come with practice.

Do you make comments about people around you? What kind?

_____

_____

It is quite normal to comment on people but in the corporate sphere it is best to keep your opinions to yourself. No need to make negative comments on a person's looks, personal life, and accent. It is rude. No need of too many positive comments either. Just do your job.

Do you use abusive language if you are offended?

_____

_____

_____

If you have the tendency to get worked up when you are criticized then watch your tongue. In the corporate sphere, you are expected to deal with all kinds of people across time zones. You will be expected to be punctual and deliver the goods. If you fail to do so, face the music. Getting abusive can cost you your job. The Hari Sadu ad is a dream that is hard to pull off you can't call your boss an idiot as it just goes against protocol.

Do you take credit for everything even if someone else contributed to a project? When have you done this?

_____

_____

_____

Don't be childish. This is not kindergarten where you are trying to get a star from your teacher. Give credit where it is due. When you do your research paper, don't you make a reference section where you write down the names of the books you referred from? Same when you work in a team. Snatching the credit shows that you are not confident about your own abilities. Similarly, allowing someone to snatch credit is a failure on your part as well.

Do you litter or make your surroundings dirty in any other way? How?

_____

_____

_____

Learn basic manners first. No use putting lipstick, talking on your android, and having the perfect resume, if you litter your neighbourhood and work space. Try to maintain personal hygiene not just in you but wherever you go. Don't leave a mark of your *chaltha hai, yaar* attitude.

Do you chew gum or have supari during class hours?

_____

_____

_____

Chewing gum is quite a common habit. However, it is not in good taste. This habit also

Kauser Khan: Freshers have to leave their Student Image behind them in college.

and this affects their performance.

So chewing the cud is just not acceptable.

the X factor does not mean that you should be too casual. You have to act according to the place you are at. This is etiquette. Drop the habit and become more respectful of others.

Do you respect your lecturers or are you casual with them?

_____

_____

_____

Be respectful always. This will develop into a habit and you will carry the same

fail to meet your deadlines.

When you drive, do you respect lane discipline?

_____

_____

_____

You have petrol in your engine and the road ahead of you is utterly jammed. You think you can drive in any which way to win the race. First of all, if all those who are driving adopted a more disciplined approach, there would be less congestion. If you are disciplined while driving, you will also be disciplined in other things that you do.

Do you try to push your way through a queue?

_____

_____

_____

_____

Dealing with queues is something we do all the time. Try to be ethical about staying in queue and not jumping into the middle of the queue pretending that no one is behind you. This is childish behaviour.

Are you a good listener?

_____

_____

_____

It's no use if you are a good speaker and a poor listener. While in office, you will need to be all ears at all times. Listening is the bedrock of all relationships – personal and professional.

Do you have table manners?

_____

_____

_____

You need to know how to eat South Indian and Italian with the same style in today's world. While you eat dosa with your fingers, you have pasta with a fork. Depending on the place that you are in and the people you are dining with, adjust your eating etiquette a little. If you work in an MNC, you may have to be familiar with cuisines from all over the world. You will have to work on your eating etiquette - how to eat with fork and spoon, how to make a toast, etc.

Do you boss people around?

_____

_____

_____

If you do, then it's a bad idea. No one likes to be bossed. Do you? The best way to become a leader is to become an example to others. If you become a role model to others, then people will automatically treat you like a leader. Leadership doesn't come from being bossy, making threats, and raising your voice.

Do you respect other people's privacy?

_____

_____

_____

You should. If you touch other people's things, invade their space or touch people while in queue, you could be making an etiquette error. Every culture has a certain rule when it comes to introductions. In Arab countries, men can stand in closer proximity than in countries like Japan where a larger distance should be maintained between two people.

Do you yawn loudly in public?

_____

_____

_____

Conceal the yawn as it looks very rude. If you keep yawning loudly at office every day, you give the impression that the job doesn't interest you.

Do you talk and text even when you are in class?

_____

_____

_____

You may have an important issue to clear with your girlfriend or something terribly important that you have to address in class hours. However, talking on your mobile or texting while in class or even when your superior is walking past can be considered as bad manners. Find other ways of dealing with the crises. Even if the class is boring, you must not waste your time and the lecturer's. Use your smart phones instead as a learning tool – to pass notes or google concepts. Talk later, after class.

You can't develop good manners suddenly at the time of interview. Use your phone when it is appropriate.

Are you polite at home and with your neighbours? What kind of person do you come across as?

_____

_____

_____

What about at college? Are you able to carry the same persona to college or are you different? In what way?

_____

_____

_____

When you answered those questions you may have wondered how you can adopt different kinds of behaviours in different situations. It is quite normal. People can easily adapt to different situations. Ideally, if you are polite and helpful at all times, it will reflect in your character when you most need to create a good impression. The best place to start changing your negative behaviour is at home. Change is not something that can happen overnight, so start at home where by trial and error method you can improve on negative aspects like laziness, rudeness, lack of routine, etc.

Beginner's Office Survival Guide

★ Create a priority list: Underline your priorities. This is very important. Why have you chosen to work in this office? What are your goals? If you are clear about what you want to achieve, you will find that distractions will not cloud your path as much.

★ Be ready for the attention: Your boss and colleagues will notice many things about your mannerisms and the way you dress. Don't worry. The attention will only last a couple of days.

★ Attentive attitude: The first couple of days and months require a lot of attention.

You have to be attentive about the goals you must achieve and understand with clarity the nature of your work. You also have to observe the hierarchy in the office. Who calls the shots? Who doesn't?

★ Target mania: If you can meet most of your deadlines and be punctual then you are considered as a reliable employee and this is a great point scorer.

★ Punctuality: Most recruiters affirm that the most difficult quality to find in India is punctuality. There are excuses galore – traffic jams, bandhs, processions, all kinds of excuses that make being on time an impossible goal to achieve. The best way to maintain a good impression in the first few months of your career is to be consistently punctual. Make it a habit to get out of your house early, so that you don't get into the manager's bad books from day 1. If an emergency comes up, ring up your team leader or manager and explain the reason for the delay.

★ Cleanliness: Being organised and keeping your desk entirely clutter free will make people respect you. You will not spend your time searching for things and you will appear to be a more reliable person.

★ Confidence vs nervousness: Handle targets positively and then you have nothing to worry about! During the first phase, many freshers are bogged down by a lack of confidence. This affects their grasping power and performance as well.

Have you ever watched a recorded video of yourself at a public gathering with your friends and in a more professional environment? Observe your own gestures and clip the gestures that are too suggestive of nervousness. There's nothing wrong with being nervous. The only wrong is showing that you are.If you are nervous before a big presentation go to the rest room and stretch. This is where knowing a little bit about yoga and meditation helps. Taking deep breaths is the best stress reliever available.

★ Goodbye slanderous gossip: No indulgence in gossip. There is simply no time to waste criticizing others. Change yourself first. Listen to what is relevant to your growth and the growth of the company; listening to idle talk can jeopardize your career.

★ Minding your manners: Politeness is in. Be nice to others and you can expect the same in return. Know when to say what. Speak according to rank. This means being argumentative with your boss is only going to be a setback. Being over friendly with the peon is also going to delay your work; dominating your subordinates is not ethical either.

Be uniformly polite. Always remember that when you behave badly with someone, you have made yourself an enemy and that doesn't help you at all. Earn respect with your courteousness. It takes time but it is worth the effort!

No chewing gum during office hours. It is okay to use a mouth freshener after meals, but no conversing with gum in your mouth. It is extremely unprofessional.

★ **Preparedness:** Always be ready for a face - to - face meeting with your supervisor. If you have developed your competencies this should not be a problem. Many times what spoils an employee's self-image is lack of self-esteem due to lack of preparation. Update yourself on a day - to - day basis.

★ **Goodbye slang:** It pays to keep your slang to yourself and your circle of friends. Slang has a tendency to show up in answer papers as well. Avoid it as the corporate world is filled with people from all walks of life. Many of them are senior to you and don't like slang one bit. Unless you are in the media industry or work as a copywriter, slang cannot be part of your work life – oral or written. Copywriters use slang to create effective ad campaigns but when they talk to their managers they don't tell him to get a life, at the fresher level anyway. When you write business emails in the office, no sms text message styles. Your words should be correctly spelt. No shortening of words – remember to keep the vowels in there.

★ **Grooming:** All the homework you did for the interview day must stay with you. Get a couple of formal outfits and two to three pairs of shoes, and accessories that you can afford. Build on your collection.

In the beginning avoid overtly loud colours and flashy get-ups. For the ladies, even the colour of nail polish says a lot about you. Safer shades are nude, light, or subtle colours.

Never put very strong deodorant as there could be people who have allergic reactions to strong smells.

★ **Communication:** Try to blend into the office atmosphere and show a bit of your personality as well.

Don't try to promote your business at work. If you are selling products at the office you work in, you are jeopardizing your own work prospects.

You should know the best mode of eliciting a response – call or email. For very serious issues, better to call or do a face - to - face meeting. Before you send out an email, check your content thoroughly; try to avoid simple grammatical errors.

Etiquette

Etiquette differs on a social occasion and in the office. Remember that you are no longer in college – start being formal.

► The Basics of Office Etiquette

We worked on the basics of self-introduction, be it at a job fair or for an interview. The principles of self-intro are the same wherever you go.

If you do not know anyone at a gathering, no need of turning into a wallflower. Don't hesitate to introduce yourself. Get a background of the people at the function so that you know what to speak about.

Don't say, "What's your good name?" No need of an adjective. Just say, "What's your name?"

To introduce yourself, you walk up to the person, make eye contact, smile, say Hello, I'm ...., and do the handshake, a 2 – 3 second web to web contact.

If you know the person already, properly pronounce the name of the person you greet. In case, you get the name wrong, apologize sincerely. People hate to hear their name mispronounced.

Etiquette requires that you stand up when you are being introduced.

Also remember your handshake hows – the eye contact, the smile, the web to web contact (two to three shakes).

The name game: During introductions people tend to forget the names of the people they are introduced to – this happens because of distractions. How do you remember?

★ Pay attention to the person you are being introduced to.

★ Keep addressing the person throughout the conversation. This way the name will stick.

★ The best way to continue a conversation is by asking open - ended questions. Keep following cues that you get from your colleagues or clients. Stay away from topics like religion or politics, and maintain a helpful tone.

Fresher Shoot

What is corporate body language? Is it different from regular body language?

Body language is a barometer of your personality inside office and outside it. At the corporate level it is best to keep your body language positive.

Body language and voice have to be modulated at all times, not just during an interview. Work culture is continuous tense – it's a process that should continue throughout your working hours and even when you talk to clients from your home.

Corporate Body Language: Do's and Don'ts

★ Avoid the headshake from side to side, which means yes in some cultures and no in others. From the shoulders up, try to avoid too many actions.

★ No waving hands and legs about too much.

★ Learn how to greet clients from different cultures with gestures that are appropriate, like bowing in case of the Japanese and shaking hands with Americans. Watch how other people around you behave and take your cues from there if you are not sure about how to conduct yourself.

★ Ladies don't tilt your head too much when you listen as it gives an impression that you are flirting! Girls are taught to hide their hands, fold them neatly on their lap, but that means that you may be hiding something. No folding your hands in front of you all the time, as it gives the impression that you are insecure.

★ Do you smile too much? Problem there as well. Be pleasant but don't show all your teeth all the time.

★ No fiddling with your hair, clothes, or accessories. Every gesture can be interpreted.

➤ Business Card Etiquette

★ Attach your business card to your portfolio.

★ Make sure your cards are neatly maintained and conserved in a card holder rather than a wallet.

★ Business cards are never presented during meals.

★ Learn how to exchange business cards efficiently. If you have a meeting scheduled with clients make sure that your business card is in an accessible place like your pocket (man) or in a holder in your handbag (woman). You provide the business card only after you have introduced yourself. You must give it with eagerness and enthusiasm.

➤ Office-Specific Etiquette

Be considerate. When you use the toilets, office equipment, and elevators, remember that you are not at home.

A woman was once caught eating bananas in the restroom of a corporate office – her excuse was that she was not allowed to eat at her desk. What should she have done? Using the cafeteria downstairs would have been a better option.

Elevator Etiquette

★ Don't push yourself into a lift. Get in and hold the lift open for the persons outside. Make way for people who want to move in or enter the elevator.

★ Wait for everyone to exit before you do. No pushing yourself out of the lift - this is not a crowded bus.

★ Elevator no-nos include no staring, no shouting, and no smoking.

Door Etiquette

★ While opening a door, you have to be careful not to slam it or push someone who may be standing near you.

★ The person who arrives first holds the door open for the person behind.

★ Normally younger people hold the door open for senior citizens – follow the system of hierarchy to open the door. Subordinates hold the door open for clients.

Office Equipment Usage

★ If you have a larger assignment and people are in cue to use the photocopying machine, give way.

★ When there is a problem with the equipment, alert the department that deals with solving these kinds of problems. Take the initiative – don't wait for the next person to fix it.

★ Avoid using office equipment for your own needs.

Travel Etiquette

★ Traveling by air is not like traveling by train. Since the airplane is a confined space, be careful about the way you handle your hand luggage.

★ Plane departures can be orderly affairs if all people respect the queuing system.

★ Try as much as possible not to inconvenience others. Some travelers are indecent with stewardesses and endlessly intoxicate themselves throughout international flights. It is best to remain sober and talk to your co-passengers only if they are interested.

Hotel Etiquette

★ Carry your booking confirmations with you.

★ Remain polite and civil at restaurants. No need to carry hotel cutlery, towels, and books when you check out.

★ Make decent tips as required.

► Wining and Dining Etiquette

We go to restaurants all the time but when you go on business you have to maintain the right amount of balance between formal and informal.

★ No need to be intimidated by a fancy restaurant. The first thing you need to do is make a call and book a table for the prescribed number of people i.e., you have to make a reservation.

★ Read the menu carefully and take the waiter's opinion on the best dishes to choose from. Start with starters and the main course. Desserts afterwards.

★ If you are not a wine connoisseur or an expert on wines take help from someone in your group to make the right choice. With fish and poultry, white wine works better and with red meat, red wine is the better fit.

Fresher Shoot

How do I know how much to tip?

If there is no service charge, pay 5 – 10% of the bill as tip.

The Toast

Making a toast is a sign of elegance – a successful toast is the highlight of every successful formal fine dining experience. The host usually makes the toast in honour of his guests, to bid farewell or to celebrate a brand new launch.

The host makes his remarks, looks at his guests and the guest he is raising his wine glass to, and then says, "to so-and-so." All other guests follow suit, except the person who is being honoured. You don't toast to yourself! Before dessert, you can return the toast with a short thank you expressing your appreciation.

The Basics of Dining

Napkin:

★ Your napkin is placed on your lap when you sit at the table.

★ When you need to leave the table, you must loosely fold your napkin and keep it to the left or right of your plate.

★ When you finish you place the napkin on the left side of the plate. Not on the chair.

Cutlery Rules:

★   Knife is on the right (as it is easier for a right handed person to cut with the right hand) and fork on the left hand side of the plate.

★   When you finish using the cutlery do not put them on the table.

★   Imagine a clock. After your meal, your knife and fork handles should point to five o'clock and the blade and tines should point to ten o' clock.

Eating Decorum:

★   No chewing loudly.

★   No slurping your soup.

★   Cut small portions and then eat. Don't stuff large chunks into your mouth.

★   Do not talk with food in your mouth.

★   Thank the waiters every time they attend to you.

Body Language:

★   No elbows on the table.

★   Eat with you mouth shut.

★   No picking teeth.

Mobile Decorum:

★   Keep your phone on silent or vibrate. This is how the mobile should be kept during formal occasions.

★   You can use the phone only once you excuse yourself from the table.

Employee Shoot

I'm Indian - why can't I eat with my fingers?

If you are eating Indian, eat like an Indian. In fine dining restaurants follow the norm. It's not so hard once you get used to it.

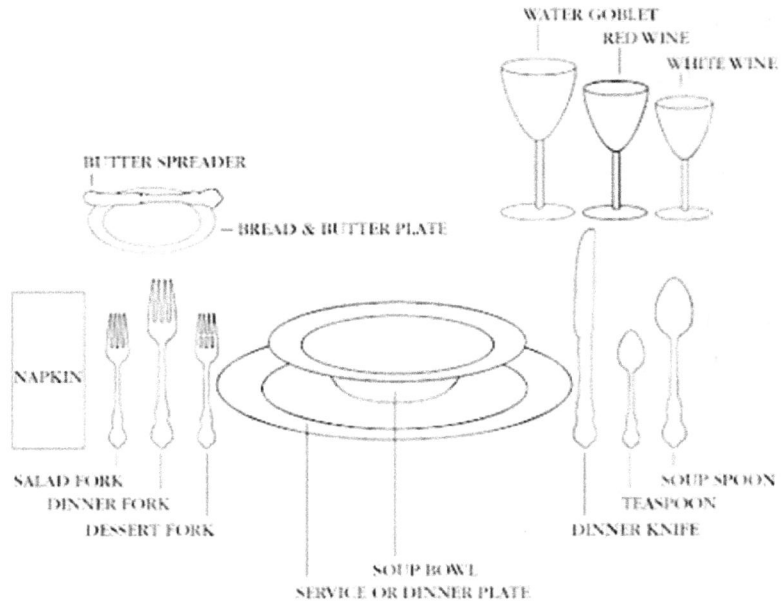

Diagram of formal place setting with labels: WATER GOBLET, RED WINE, WHITE WINE, BUTTER SPREADER, BREAD & BUTTER PLATE, NAPKIN, SALAD FORK, DINNER FORK, DESSERT FORK, SOUP SPOON, TEASPOON, DINNER KNIFE, SOUP BOWL, SERVICE OR DINNER PLATE

► Tech Etiquette

Talking politely on the phone and sending polite emails is also an important part of corporate life. When you write or speak formally, you cannot become offensive. You need a formal vocabulary to deal with all kinds of situations. It is hard to separate your emotion from your professional life, but with time it is possible.

Online Etiquette

Email:

★ Avoid all-caps, slang, and one word responses. Remember emails are not text messages. No FYI, R U Free?, THNX, LOL!

One email response to a requirement for post of content provider: m a riter…wil rite copy 4 u….

Do you think that such a response to an opportunity will give you a job?

★ Format your language while sending the email. Make sure you use the correct line spacing. Unequal formatting makes your email look unappealing.

★ Do your grammar and spell check every time you send out the email.

★ Use the Bcc to share information with several people without sharing email contacts and Cc option to copy messages to others.

Social Networking:

★ While you are at work, remember that you have to comply with confidentiality protocols at the workplace. You should not share office information with friends or on networking sites.

★ Most offices don't encourage you to use computers for your own personal purposes. So even if you are a computer whiz with a knack at being a great social media geek, don't waste your time poking and liking on Facebook, sending out chain mails to multiple friends, tweeting on Twitter, and gaming when you think the boss is not looking.

The boss may not see you – remember how your lecturers never could catch you texting in class? However, the down side is that you could get caught, you could get distracted and your productivity will go down. This affects your promotion big time. Now tell me which of those friends you liked on Facebook is going to help you now?

★ Be Net Nice! Once you get a job, be careful about what you blog or put up on Facebook. No complaints about your job or boss. Even if it is done in good humour, it is best avoided.

➤ **Phone Etiquette**

★ Make your ringtone and receiver ringtone simple and professional. How would you feel if the ringtone on your boss's phone resembled a croaking frog? Wouldn't you judge your boss's personality based on the sound of the ringtone you hear?

★ If you get a personal phone call, speak outside the office area. No personal phone calls in office.

★ No picking up phones during meetings with the boss. Answer the calls afterwards.

★ Receive calls quickly. Pick up the phone within three rings. Give a smile when you say Hello.

★ If you made the call, mention your first name, last name, and state your purpose as introduction.

★ Throughout the conversation be clear and precise. Don't ramble on in the conversation. Only state what is necessary.

★ End the conversation with a wrap up. Say, "Thank you for your time." Thank you and no slang goodbyes.

➤ Cross Cultural Etiquette

India is a melting pot of cultures, and so is the world. You have to know how to deal with people from different parts of India and the world. Be accepting of differences and keep your comments about their accents or looks to yourself. Remember you are as different to others as they may be to you.

How do you usually react to people from different cultures within India? Are you comfortable, nervous, amused, or irritated?

_____

_____

_____

In the chapter dealing with phonological aspects of speech, we saw how Indians from different parts of the country make grammatical mistakes unique to their mother tongue. Even though we are Indians, we have very different languages, manner of speaking, and mannerisms.

How do you react to people from the rest of the globe? Are you more nervous or more respectful? Why?

_____

_____

_____

Dealing with people from different communities is a mixed affair. Sometimes you are enthusiastic to meet people from cultures different from your own; sometimes it is frightening that you will misunderstand them and they you.

Long ago, all these misunderstandings turned into casteism, racism, and segregation. Today many of those barriers have started to fall apart thanks to globalization. There is no reason to be afraid of or biased towards people with different kinds of upbringing. If you all work in the same company, your goals are the same and so any kind of prejudice only slows down the company from achieving targets.

People from China, Japan, and different parts of Europe each have behaviour and mannerisms different from their Indian counterparts. Within India the diversity is only too obvious. Do you know how to deal with people within your own country?

Each person is a combination of geography, culture, individuality, circumstances, etc. So be very careful when you talk to people whose cultures you are unfamiliar with. Avoid making general statements and be courteous, i.e., be polite. Making a faux pas or a mistake can be avoided if you keep yourself informed about alternate cultures. It is a balancing act that must be mastered in these cross cultural times.

Fresher Shoot

I'm used to interacting with people from one fixed area – how can I adjust to an MNC environment?

The famous writer R.K.Narayan writes about his delightful travels in the US – in spite of being a vegetarian with an obsession for the typical South Indian coffee, he enjoys his trip. You can remain who you are and adjust to new surroundings.

Just appreciate people who come from different cultures and who look different from you. Today the office is every man's land. People come from all over the country and even the world. There is zero tolerance for being prejudiced. Instead of laughing at or being scared of people from different cultures, try to learn to communicate with them.

Why is there so much multiculturalism nowadays?

Because people looking for work are migrating to cities on a massive scale.

Schools in cities are becoming case studies of different parts of India coming together in one classroom. Different cultures mean different mannerisms and different foods and habits. Cultural diversity is a reality you have to get used to.

The internet has led to the world becoming a smaller place where everyone is interconnected. People communicate continuously on a face to face and long distance basis. Distance is not a barrier any more. This is why knowing English is so important – it has become the language of commerce of the twenty-first century. If you are in the Voice section of a BPO you will be introduced to the nuances of accent training so that you can effectively communicate with native speakers of English.

I know English but I still can't follow my foreign colleagues' speech – why?

Accents differ and the contexts they are spoken in. However good you are at English you won't be able to enjoy a good joke in England because many times the joke makes sense only in a particular context that can be understood if you live in the UK and know the slang and the politics of that particular region. Knowing English is not enough for effective communication. You also have to know about the person you are sending a message to or receiving a message from.

How can I prepare for an official trip to a foreign country?

If you are being sent to a foreign country, the US for example, you will be given adequate preparation – an overview of the history, government, and basic manners that are expected of you like punctuality and positive body language. Whichever country you go to, people have certain traits.

In the US people don't like it if you are too curious about their personal lives.

Do a little research of your own. Find out more about the country you are being sent to. Understand the accent used there, the formal dress code, code of conduct rules, and acceptable topics of conversation.

While the US is much more liberal, the UK is still a little stiff upper lip or conservative.

It is difficult for an outsider to understand the jokes and dialects used in foreign countries. If you prepare yourself a little, the transition will not be as difficult in English speaking countries. In case you have to work in a non-English speaking country like Japan, learn a little about the culture, etiquette, and history of the nation. Learn a few basic phrases, and you will be appreciated if you show your willingness to adapt to a new culture.

Cross Cultural Etiquette Tips

★ Be tolerant of all team members regardless of their identity. Tolerant doesn't mean putting up with people – it means being genuinely understanding.

★ Don't allow personal prejudice to get in the way of team work.

★ Never hurt other people's feelings and if you do so by accident apologize immediately.

★ No funny jokes about a person's appearance or accent, unless you are close with your colleague and have an understanding with each other.

★ No religious comments.

★ Speak and interact using simple, not complicated English and you will find the work is done much faster.

Culture Facts

★ **Greeting Peculiarities:** Arabs kiss their male friends from cheek to cheek. In the US a handshake is the ideal greeting.

- ★ **Yes/No?:** If someone from US shakes his head from side to side, it means no, and when someone from India does the same it could mean yes.

- ★ **Eye Contact:** If you don't look eye to eye, a European may find you deceitful; in the subcontinent if a woman keeps her gaze away, she is just being respectful and sending out a clear signal that she means only business.

- ★ **Proxemics:** Even how close you stand to your client is culturally determined. Someone from the US could stand 5ft away from you and be comfortable; the same distance would make a Japanese client uncomfortable as he would prefer to stand further away.

Fresher Shoot

Any pointers to deal with people from specific cultures?

According to Ranjini Manian, CEO of Global Adjustments and author of *Upworldly Mobile*, while dealing with Westerners it is better to stay away from discussing topics like health issues, age, marital status details, and faith, as these are considered extremely personal matters.

She describes how each culture has its own particulars.

- ★ With the Japanese you must bow and be courteous.

- ★ With the Koreans you must try not to be distracted as they consider lack of focus as a sign of disrespect.

- ★ With the Germans efficiency helps and makes a strong impression.

- ★ With the Americans, situational humour is a plus.

Ranjini Manian explains how the first step to knowing another culture is knowing one's own. There are many aspects of cultures – from your name, greetings, meetings, body language, hierarchies, cuisine, etc. To build bridges between cultures, you must be observant, be willing to learn from new cultures and learn from your mistakes as well.

➤ Professional Etiquette

In an office you must come across as Professional – that is the word that should guide you in all your career moments. Professional implies many qualities and not just getting the work done.

Ask yourself these questions when you join:

What skills do I have to work on? Each office presents a new opportunity to work on different aspects of yourself.

Interpersonal skills   Knowledge base   Communication skills   Grooming

_____

_____

_____

_____

Depending on the kind of workplace you are in, you will have to relearn many of your skills. You may say I've already worked on polishing most of my skills, my wardrobe, my goals, etc, then why should I relearn? Learning is a continuous process and each office has its own goal posts. See your new workplace as an opportunity rather than a challenge.

What should I know now to handle my role?

Team members   Procedure   Goals   Company procedure

_____

_____

_____

Every company has certain procedures and rules. Study the material you are given and follow instructions to the tee. Follow company protocol.

▶ Work Relationship Etiquette

Having a good **People Quotient** is good news. When you start out your career you don't go into the office trying to make a best friend. You do your job as best as you can and make friends as you go about it. Sometimes you will be advised to stay impersonal and not get too involved in other's lives especially when you are starting out and are in the process of learning the job. This is because corporate offices are not designed for true friendship – the competitive atmosphere does not allow it.

This doesn't mean you can't have good friends. Usually it is the people with the good interpersonal skills who do well at work.

There are etiquette schools where you are taught aspects about how to behave. You will be told not to ask someone to their face why they are upset. Be compassionate and help if your help is required; don't poke your nose into someone else's business just to contribute to office gossip.

It is easy to understand the nature of your job and how to time manage it and organise your tasks. It is not as easy to handle relationships at work. Since you work in an organization, you will have to deal with people all the time, sometimes through email, via phone or, face to face. Your people skills need to be good if you want a future in the corporate sphere.

Employee Shoot

How do you speak with the boss?

First analyze your relationship with authority figures at home.

_____

_____

_____

_____

In college?

_____

_____

_____

_____

If you have trouble dealing with authority, then look at authority differently. In the initial phase of your career, it is good to have someone tell you what to do. This is part of the learning process. Once you become an expert in your line of work, you can move up the ranks. If you like being told what to do, challenge yourself to go one step ahead of your superiors. Being too submissive will lead you nowhere. There has to be a balance.

Every boss is not a Hari Sadu! Start out the relationship with respect and support, not stress. When you join work, your boss will help you learn the ropes of the job. Just remember that no one is perfect and that more senior individuals in the organization have many tips and tricks that will make your first couple of months much easier. So be courteous and avoid any kind of unnecessary back talk as that can create many problems later on. Your boss is the key to your promotions and salary raise. Keep that in mind during your interactions.

Dealing with the boss

Before meetings or face - to - face interactions, write down your doubts. Don't keep asking questions – make a list and ask these questions all at once.

expected of you.

name calling, especially in India. It goes against regular protocol. It does help though to know a little about the boss, if she or he has children, other interests, etc. It can break the ice a bit.

How does your boss communicate with you? Follow the cue. If your boss uses email, follow suit.

Being a good employee does not mean being a slave. Initially buttering up and

your eyes and ears open. If you are being sidelined, be clear about your stand. Be pro-active and not reactive.

Don't take everything your boss says or does too personally. Dealing with the boss is just part of your working life. Remember bosses come and go; so don't divest too much energy on one.

Be helpful. It is time consuming of course but putting in that extra effort will make you

is a necessity, do it with grace and not hesitation. If you are hesitant your boss should be the last to hear of it. Every action of yours is weighed, so act with grace.

If you need help from your boss, ask for help. Saying, "You never helped me" at the last minute" is a negative approach. Always be open for compromise and as far as possible steer clear of arguments. If your boss feels strongly about something, no need of lowering your head and feeling bad about it. Maintain eye contact and

manner.

Expert Tip: Says Kauser Khan, "The new member of the organization should be receptive, approachable, and open to learning all the time. The interaction that she or he has with the boss should be one of honesty and integrity."

Employee Shoot

How do you deal with colleagues?

First ask yourself:

How do you come across to your friends?

_____

_____

_____

If you were popular and had a good time with friends, you can expect much the same in office as well. If you find making friends difficult and usually keep to yourself, don't expect office life to transform that. Wherever you go, you take 'Brand You' with you. If you want change, then the first instance of change should come from the way you think and the way you behave.

Most of the time freshers come to office with a lot of expectations about making friends and generally having a lot of fun. You may meet your best friend in office but most of the time it would be unlikely! There are many targets to meet at office and although someone may be good company, it is always better not to mix work with friendship. Maintain good relationships with all your colleagues and if you are really close with a colleague, hang out after office or during the weekends.

★ Relationship building is based on people. It is always good to maintain healthy conversations with your peers. It lessens your stress and anxiety, and makes the whole experience of going to office something you look forward to.

★ Talking also helps you to solve problems that are taking you to a dead end. Sometimes when people talk, they automatically generate solutions. So speak positively and yield positive results.

★ At meetings, make sure that you put in your contribution and that you are heard. Listen to the points being discussed and stick to the topic when you speak. No need of getting over excited, don't be disinterested either. Do not gesticulate or wave your hands too much.

★ When you are in discussion, different ideas are bound to come up. Better not to disagree every time you hear new ideas. Hear them out and then provide your alternative. If you disagree at every count or reject other people's ideas, you spoil the mood of the entire meeting. Negative body language results and spreads to other colleagues at the meeting. Brain storming is an opportunity to hear different ideas, not to poke fun at others.

Dealing with colleagues:

★ Treat your colleagues as you would treat yourself, with respect.

★ Appreciate the good will gestures of other colleagues.

★ Listen to your colleagues and stay impartial.

★ Find a mentor, someone who can guide you and advise you, not do your work for you!

★ Even if you have problems, don't share it in the office with your colleagues. Your colleagues are not your sounding boards or people who want to listen to your sad stories. If you keep sharing your problems, you spread a lot of negativity in the air and lose respect.

★ Be prepared to meet difficult people. Be civil with them, not passive and not aggressive.

★ Be prepared to meet with criticism. There may be truth in it, so take it with a pinch of salt. Listen and ask your critic to be specific and guide you toward a more acceptable solution.

★ Watch the players in office – they often teach you how to survive office politics.

★ Build an atmosphere of trust around you by being thorough in your work and transparent in your dealings.

★ Take gossip with good humour. For some people, gossip is a way to de-stress. If you are gossip averse, don't participate! Simple as that.

★ Avoid groupism, a common term used in India to describe the group forming mentality of most office goers. The groups are usually based on the use of a common language. Avoid using your native language to make negative comments about someone you don't like. Nowadays Indians understand several languages and you don't want to make comments on somebody and then get caught, do you?

Employee Shoot

How do you deal with the opposite sex?

This depends on the following:

How do you deal with the opposite sex in your college life?

_____

_____

_____

If you are very shy while interacting with the opposite sex, then work on building your confidence levels. Shyness can be the result of many things – your upbringing, situation, circumstances, etc. The key word to remember is respect. If you are polite and respect of your colleagues, man or woman, your corporate life will sail smoothly.

Don't try to mix business with pleasure at the office. It can lead to unpleasant situations later on. When you join a new company, you could get carried away by the freedom but keep all relationships healthy as you are building your career now. Distractions later!

How do you confront your colleague if he doesn't give you credit or takes full credit for your work?

This is a sticky area but the situation always happens. Even if you don't want to, you must confront the person who takes credit and make yourself very clear. If you are not clear about your stand from Day 1, you are inviting trouble. Make sure that you voice your opinions in a group and not on a one-on-one basis. This way you are sure to get credit where it is due.

How do you deal with clients?

Clients come in all shapes and sizes. There is no one-for-all solution to handle them as each client approaches your company with certain specifications. You will have to be very flexible and keep taking cues from the client as to how you should behave with them.

★ Whether on the phone or email or face to face, your job as an employee is to build the client's trust with the organization. Since you represent the company, any contact with you should give the client confidence. Have you noticed how good shopkeepers sell their wares? They make you feel important and you leave the shop feeling good about yourself and making the purchase as well. Make the other person feel good.

★ In order to give the client or customer confidence you need to have confidence in yourself. The minute you are doubtful, you put others in doubt.

★ Respond to customer or client queries patiently. Take every call and reply to every email.

- ★   Get a clear picture about the nature of the work that you have to do before you start work. Lack of clarity about additional details as the work progresses changes the way the project works out. Be clear about achieving timelines.

- ★   No criticism of clients please, unless you want to chase them away.

- ★   Use your negotiating skills to the maximum.

How do you deal with conflict situations?

Conflict of interest is common in an organization. Be prepared to deal with conflict situations. Rather than getting frustrated and angry about conflict, what you need is preparedness to deal with any situation.

How do you usually deal with conflict at home?

_____

_____

_____

_____

If you find that your conflict handling situations result in a lot of shouting and slamming doors at home, then you'll have to rethink of better ways of coping with stress in the office.

How do you deal with conflicts with your peers?

_____

_____

_____

_____

_____

If you can't handle criticism from your peers, then you will find it hard to deal with criticism in office. With politeness and a smile, you can override most difficult situations. Getting worked up will only make the conflict worse.

Why do you think conflict happens?

_____

_____

If conflict is a common feature of your life, then you will have to review your problems and take help either from a good mentor or professional help. Is it something about your behaviour that provokes conflict?

Conflict starters

★ Gossip

★ Laziness

★ Buttering up

★ Disagreement

★ Criticism

★ Inability to communicate

The reasons for conflict could be many – lack of confidence in each other on both sides and different ethical viewpoints. All these are ego problems that can be nipped in the bud if you are careful.

It is always better to approach your boss with your issues. Complaining to another higher up in the organization has to be a very last resort approach. If you just sit down and talk to the boss, the situation may brighten up. Fear can spoil your relationship with the organization.

Moving ahead: Keeping the job

Here are two kinds of employees.

Pavitra is punctual to office. She has a pleasant personality and posture, and commands respect with her seriousness and good humour. She takes her responsibilities seriously and works to achieve targets. She participates in grapevine talk only if the conversation is harmless to co-employees. She treats every colleague with immense respect and when she brings up her concerns during meetings, her words are weighed. She follows the corporate ethic in her office and knows how to deal with her boss as an equal.

On the other hand, Aruna is always preoccupied with her personal problems. She greets only selective colleagues. She is at loggerheads with the boss and loses no opportunity to criticize her boss behind his back. She completes tasks half-heartedly as she thinks her boss will put her into trouble whatever she does. She does not enjoy her time at office and worries about her responsibilities at home continuously.

Which employee do you want to be?

It is quite obvious. Aruna must first take stock of her personal issues. Just as you made a self-assessment when you started reading this book, you must continue assessing your goals and problems throughout your work life. Aruna must find solutions for her problems at home. She must then try to resolve the differences she had with her boss. If she wants to survive in the company, she must put aside any ego hassles she faces and stop back biting as it is an unproductive exercise. She must look at new ways of making her job more agreeable.

Keeping your job is all about disciplining yourself to handle each day at work as productively as possible. Remember the economy is fluctuating all the time these days. Do not make any effort to lose your job, only to KEEP it.

Here are some tips to keep your job once you get it.

★　Behave confident even if you are not and gradually confidence will become part of your everyday life. There is a first time for everything. After that, each task can only get easier. Give your first presentation in office with confidence, then people will look up to you. Keep working on your Confidence Quotient, take every opportunity to make an impression. Work with reasonable confidence, over-confidence puts people off as much as shyness.

★　Tailor your actions at work to meet the vision and mission of the company. You tailored your resume objective to meet company requirements. When you are getting paid, keep in mind that your professional goals and company goals should match.

★　Know your customers or clients and act in key with their expectations. No use losing your cool with the people you work for. Always be the reliable guy in the office. This will take you a long way. In office, it's not just about your excellence quotient – it's also about how good you are at handling people situations and the level of trust you generate.

★　Learn to appreciate your colleagues. Every interaction you make with your colleagues has the potential to teach you something. Suppose your colleague is better than you at something, accept it and learn from him or her. Take the best from a person and profit from it.

★　Meet deadlines by preparing in advance. A little preparation will take you a long way. Life throws up a lot of surprises but if you are prepared for work-related pressures, then you will not react negatively to pressure. In the corporate world, what people admire and respect most is a person who can remain calm even in the most difficult situations.

★ Be punctual – set your watch a little ahead if you have to. Be punctual for interviews and be punctual while at work. A person on time is a person who knows his place in the company and values everyone's time including his own.

★ Don't apply for leave at the end of the month when you are most needed. Especially in the financial and banking sector, the end of the month is a crucial time. For the first two years of work, avoid taking long leaves unless you have a really serious emergency.

★ If you are part of a team, be a committed team player and make your team strong. Team building and interactions within the team are what make the company grow. You participate with enthusiasm, not because you have no choice.

★ If you want to speak up against something, speak with tact. No losing your cool. It doesn't always pay to be very open about what you feel. Analyze the situation on the ground and then voice your issues. If your problems have no ready solution in sight, then do a rethink on how you can adjust to the situation until possibility for change at the work place arises.

★ Make no sacrifices – be focused about your personal goals and your professional goals. Both are important. Work but do not work to death. Take care of your health and don't turn into a donkey.

★ No borrowing and lending money from colleagues please – it is unprofessional.

★ Don't use office technology (Facebook, phones, etc.) for your personal benefit. I've repeated that time and again in this book. Many employees think that the office pays them to use office technology any way they like. Use your own smart phone if you have to.

★ Be patient. Career advancement is slow. The first couple of months are all about getting settled in the job and learning the ropes of interactions with colleagues, customers and clients. This is the time when you turn from a fresher to a PROFESSIONAL. Don't get disheartened by any failure during this time as this is your learning period and when you learn mistakes are bound to happen.

Assertive You

What do you think the biggest setback to success is? Diffidence is a serious problem with many newbies.

You deserve the job or deserve to retain the job only if you can offer your employer what he wants.

Take these four steps to improve your self-awareness at the workplace:

★ Understand what the employers want. Get this knowledge by talking to your seniors and having casual conversations with managers.

★ Understand the gaps between employer's expectations and your skill sets.

★ Can you fill these gaps with additional certification through career management profilers, etc?

★ For proper career management track your progression in a regular manner. Keep yourself updated with the latest skill sets and know your SWOT.

Self awareness makes you more assertive as you will be more aware of your potential and limitations.

Another problem freshers face beside diffidence is the inability to say No.

How good are you at saying No?

_____

_____

_____

It's one thing saying No to your family and friends and quite another being honest about whether you understand things or are willing to take things up. Be assertive from Day 1. Don't say yes to everything. Somehow we feel that saying No to someone is rude. We just don't know how to say we don't know in real life.

Mahesh says okay to sitting late nights and working weekends. He says yes to extra workloads. He says yes even when he doesn't know the job and takes a longer while to get the job done. He thinks that by agreeing to everything his higher ups say, he will make a good impression. He is also frightened of saying no as he comes from a family where respect for elders is the rule and saying no is considered rude.

Mahesh carries his home baggage to the office environment. He says yes to everything, whether he knows the job or not and whether he has the time or not. Does he succeed?

Not really. Mahesh is not working smart – he does not get a promotion, he ends up getting burn out and ultimately he quits his job.

He was unable to do justice to his work and additional projects he had been assigned.

Two NO rules to remember

★ You show respect to yourself as well as to the person who asks when you say No to the things that you don't know. Think about it: If you take up a job and don't execute it properly, all that you are doing is wasting the other person's time. So, when you are supposed to clarify, clarify.

★ When you are saying No, do that in the most polite manner. Explain why you don't understand or why you need help. Be gentle and firm.

Climbing the Ladder

Once you join and learn the ropes, you have to stick on. Before you think of jumping jobs, not a good trend when you are starting out, learn how to stay in your new work place.

Employee Shoot

I'm not a player - how will I survive?

Know that office politics is in. Most of the problems you are likely to face in office will be because you are not good at handling office politics. Politics is everywhere – it can be positive ways of influencing people, and also put to bad use. There are offices where politics is minimal and offices where a heavy dose of politics is the norm. The ideal attitude is to stay away if you are not that type and if you play, play the game well. Stay ethical. Don't take it too seriously and put more focus on your work.

I can't stand my boss. What do I do?

Well there are good bosses and there are not so good bosses. If you want to climb the ladder of success, you need to maintain a communication channel with your boss. If you are scared, irritated or indifferent to your boss, no amount of work that you do is going to get you ahead in the company.

I hate my job. Now what?

Already? A common problem that many freshers face is the monotony of going to work and doing the same things every day. If your work bores you, find ways to make it interesting. Make to-do lists, check targets, set personal goals, learn something new every day. Interest is something that you create. Maintain a sense of humour to get you past the most boring day and be flexible in your expectations. Look at what your job profile gives you in the long run.

I like having fun all the time, work or no work. How do I keep the fun factor alive in my work?

Gen Y knows how to have fun. Your generation knows how to empty the wallet and go on a high as you only have one life. Fun is good as long as it doesn't turn into a fuzzy focus. You need a good corporate ethic in the way you conduct yourself to survive in any industry. Living for the weekends will not motivate you enough to climb the ladder of success.

You'll have to redefine fun – fun as in achieving goals and targets; making friends out of colleagues, and learning on the job.

I get stressed out easily. How do I handle that?

If you do then you need to rethink the way you handle situations. Work pressure means that you don't know the art of balancing. Initially you will be learning on the job. Be prepared for a bit of stress. Do some physical exercise to make the work pressure ease a bit. The whole idea behind accepting work is being able to accept the challenge.

We discussed methods of tackling stress. What is stress doing to you? Laugh at your shortcomings and there will be no hard feelings against you. At work, you will encounter all kinds of stress – deadline stress, inter-personal ego problems, office inconveniences, etc. Be geared up and from day one ACCEPT problems, delays, ego ups and downs. DEAL with your problems head on. The more you postpone dealing with issues, the more chances of that problem growing beyond your reach. Solve the problem when it is a seed, not when it has grown.

To solve problems, you need to be a good decision maker. One instance is when you are loaded with a lot of work that is not really part of your assigned role or of any importance to the company. Remember what leadership thinker Sangeeth Verghese said – Say no when it is hard to comply. At the fresher level, saying No often is not advisable as every task you perform is an opportunity to learn. However, if you find that you are doing more favours than work, then stop. Stress happens when you don't know the right moment to say no.

Am I focused enough?

If you know your own personal goals, no matter what the circumstances, you will attain success. Many times people are pressured by their home situation, marriage plans, financial ambitions, etc. These distract them from achieving job-related growth. When at work, focus on achievable targets. Leave home out of work and friendships for after right amount of time to your personal and professional life, one of these suffers.

Am I doing the job or task right?

There are many ways of knowing this. You will get positive feedback from your boss

Typically it takes around 21 days to get your brain wired in to learn a new task. So be patient and you will learn.

Am I prepared to grow?

Jayashree Joglekar, Director at Door Step School and former Head of Wipro, Pune:

Be prepared to take on any job. You will learn no matter what the assignment is.

This is extremely valuable advice. What is important is your will to grow as all experience ultimately leads to growth. Are you willing to invest time in any task you are given? Then you will grow to your full potential. Are you willing to understand

fresher, you may be overwhelmed by the things you do not know, but it is the things that you do know that has made you pass the interview. Never underestimate your worth and how you contribute to company growth.

Am I aware of the new competencies I am gaining?

track of your assignments, the people you interact with, the meetings you attend, the assignments you complete. Keep a private journal or a personal blog. Keeping track of what you did and who you dealt with is useful in knowing your new competencies.

Am I handling time right?

We have an estimated 112 hours every week if you minus sleeping time. A successful person is one who uses those 112 hours to effect. When you work, you should utilize

Am I adapting myself to my new environment?

This is where all your etiquette skills come in. If you work in a government institution there are a different set of rules. In a corporate setting, again the rules are very different. Watch what your other colleagues are doing to get a feel of your environment. Will you be able to tune yourself to the crowd? Have you been able to make a few friends? If you isolate yourself, you will find your work environment impossible to deal with.

Ok. I've been working for three months now and I'm already feeling complacent. How do I sustain the growth curve?

Jayashree Joglekar believes that knowledge is power. "You need knowledge to grow. Do you know the business your organization is in? If you don't, find out. If you do, find out more about the industry. Can you build a capable team? This is another way of growing in the organization and the industry."

Skill building must be a continuous activity, mainly because the skills we gain now will be outdated five years from now. So keep learning and figuring out the job climate even while you are at work. Read the news either in print or on your smart phone - don't say I've got my job and won't be preparing for another interview for a long time. Watch the news. Improve on your oral and written skills. Improve your grooming. You've just begun – the way to make this journey interesting is to keep working on self-improvement.

Am I waiting for good things to happen?

Stop waiting and start acting. If you are positive, there are more chances of positive things happening. This is more because being positive leads you to make positive decisions. Many times people get worked up because they accept defeat even before they are defeated. This attitude slows down the work and demotivates. When the motivation is lost, the work suffers.

How do I stay motivated?

To grow in the workplace and to enjoy what you do on a daily basis, you need MOTIVATION 24/7.

Some people are motivated by money, others by responsibility, still others by deadlines. You have to find reasons to be motivated if you want to climb the ladder. Be excited about 'Brand You' and continue building on the brand. If your office work is monotonous, take an interest in yourself, continue skill building, do distance courses, make new friends, invest in your wardrobe or any activities that you love. Just because you get a job, there is no need to put aside your life. Balance is the key.

Way Ahead

I leave you to decide your future. The future is like clay – a possibility that you can mould with your own hands. We saw how getting a job involves polishing 'Brand You' and how keeping a job is a continuation of that. Keep aside all your negatives. Diffidence or lack of confidence, disappointment, regret, inferiority complex, superiority complex, boredom, obsession, and laziness all keep you away from success. Then why do you want to chase these emotions and states of being?

Your parents and your lecturers tell you the same thing. Work hard. Be positive. Love your job and it will love you. Be responsible. Have faith in yourself.

These are not just words. These are ideas that can make you successful in your corporate life and turn you into professionals sooner than you think. If things are bad in the work place, tell yourself I can handle this, can't I? And if you are praised ask yourself: What more can I do to improve myself?

Continuous self assessment and listing out the pros and cons makes you a good

yourself and you will be there if you take the steps in the right direction.

"Once you start working, what you earn is proportionate to the amount of responsibility you take up. You are not only a learner but completely accountable. It's altogether a different feel. It can be as great as college, if you want it to be." Words of wisdom from the enterprising student and intern, Ephin couldn't have been more spot on. Having a good work life depends on how much you are willing to learn and understand about your work and yourself.

Good luck on your job journey!

Recap

What can you expect at the new workplace?

All things etiquette.

SECTION 6
CHANGING CAREERS

Rethinking your Career

Career Change Interview Questions

Career Graph: The Four Stages

1

Changing Careers

Rethinking your Career

How was your job journey? Now you have reached that stage of the book when you are mature enough to understand the implications of job change.

There is a story about a frog who lived in a well (you must know this story). All his life the frog only knew about the contours of the well, the familiar well smell and the insects that lived there. When another frog accidentally entered the well, he was astounded.

"You live in this hole?" he asked the frog, looking at him with a disapproving smile.

The frog proudly showed him every nook and corner of the ancient well.

"Have you ever thought of the world outside?" the newcomer frog asked his ignorant friend to which he croaked an emphatic no.

When the two frogs went out into the world, the frog in the well could hardly open

became clear to him – the big blue sky, the wispy clouds, the lemon green grass. He never went back into his well again.

Don't be the frog in the well. If one job doesn't work for you, there are so many other options for 'Brand You' – you will be amazed by the opportunities that experienced candidates have today.

Changing careers is becoming a staple part of the professional life. In the olden days, careers were permanent. Once you were employed you stuck with the company for life. All that has changed. Although you are expected to remain loyal to your company, if your interests change and expectations increase, you have no choice but to look for better options.

Change can happen within your career when you are promoted or given a different designation.
with as you have to relearn your way through corporate life to suit the needs of your

new office. You'll have to adapt.

Employee Shoot

Should I really leave my job to grow?

_____

_____

Not really.

If you are not sure about whether you need to change jobs just yet, then look for opportunities to grow in the current job.

Grow in your Career

★ Do a daily Job Log and assess your SWOT on a monthly basis. Check which strengths you have gained and which weaknesses you have overcome.

★ Take up new projects and new challenges. Don't be a lurker – take charge of your career.

★ Sign up for new training programmes.

★ Update yourself on the industry you are part of.

When is the right time to think about job change?

★ When your company is downsizing or going bankrupt.

★ When you wake up every day and feel upset about going to work.

★ When all your efforts to stay don't work.

★ When there is absolutely zero growth financially and personally.

★ When you lose respect for the organization.

Is it wise to change jobs?

Why not? The first job that you take usually helps you to build your portfolio. Not all freshers get their dream job. What you do get from your first job is transferrable skills.

My boss is not going to tell me what I should do next. Sometimes I don't know either. How do I decide?

Identify the pros and cons of your job.

Pros: The positives of your job could include good pay, good location, good boss or supervisor, good work ethic, stimulating work, possibility of promotion, good team, etc.

_____

_____

Cons: The negatives of your work could include lousy pay, remote location, difficult higher ups, poor work ethic, boring work, stagnation, etc.

_____

_____

Weigh your pros against the cons. If your work gives you happiness and you see a possibility of growth in the company, stick with it. But if all avenues are shut, no matter how hard you work, then you should rethink your goals and restart your job search. Spending a lot of time in the wrong work place can lead to a lot of heart burn and career stress. No need to tolerate an unhappy job. Never think that you are stuck in a rut and if that feeling comes, it is time to move on.

Pros   **Cons**

_____

_____

_____

_____

What do I do before I apply for a new job?

Reassess

Start from scratch. If you are unhappy about your first job and don't think that you have much of a future in your assigned role, you are now more equipped to re-do your assessment tests. You know the ropes now, you are no longer the wide-eyed fresher straight out of college. Your assessment of yourself will shape out much better.

You know what you can offer a company. So check how far those skills and values have improved.

➤ **Reassess Skill Sets**

What skill sets do you have now that you didn't have when you were a fresher?

_____

Along with the skill sets you acquired at the college level and identified at the beginning of the book, you will also have gained an entirely new set of skills from your first job. If you started out as a mass communication graduate and ended up working as an editor, your language skills have been sharpened and your accuracy levels when it comes to quality control have shot up dramatically. Even if you didn't like your job that much, every job offers you unique skills sets that can make your career graph a more positive one.

► **Reassess Values**

What must you change about your values in your new office?

It's easy to read about what is expected of you at work. It is far more difficult to practically adapt to corporate culture. In spite of your research and preparedness, there are many mistakes that you made when you joined work – how can you fix those?

You follow the company values – this helps the team move forward with a common goal. When you think about rejoining a new company, list the values that have been strengthened in your time at Office #1. These values will help you make the transition to Office #2.

► **Reassess Experience**

What is your job experience now?

Go back to the time before your first interview. You were worried about how limited your experience was. Your resume had too little to say about your contribution on the work front.

Now you don't have that worry. Highlight every bit of experience you have received on your former job, particularly if your job change is within the same industry. If you are picking a different industry altogether, you will be starting from scratch – you wouldn't need to give too much emphasis to your previous experience then. So identify if your new job depends on your previous experience.

► ## Reassess Knowledge

How much do you know now that you didn't know before?

_____

_____

If you have continued with your GK building exercises, then you will have widened your knowledge base. You will also have a clearer knowledge about your own SWOT.

Rediscover

► ## What do you want now?

_____

_____

What you want as a fresher and what you want later on mid career are two different things. You may have struggled a great deal to get through your first interview. Now all that effort has gone to waste, you say. Yes?

Of course, not. Every stage of your career is different.

► ## What are your short - term goals now?

_____

_____

These will be different too. Find out what skills you should develop to achieve your new goal. Don't get stuck to lists and ideas you made yesterday. If you want to change careers, you have to change your entire approach. So start from scratch.

Rework your resume

Job change or not, it is a good idea to keep preening your resume and not leave it dull and static. Update your resume and list out your new experience skill sets and transferrable skills that you have accumulated on the first job. A Functional Resume works best – skill sets on the top, actual experience below it.

Your resume is your marketing instrument. Creating a fresh resume takes some time and thought.

Check if your Personal Details have changed – any change in phone no. or location?

Rewrite your objective to suit the needs of your new job profile.

Rewrite your Work Experience section:

Latest Experience

Date (specify the time frame)

_____

Job Title

_____

Company

_____

Responsibilities you had on the job:

★　_____

★　_____

★　_____

Your achievements on the job, if any

★　_____

★　_____

★　_____

Date (specify the time frame)

Previous Experience

_____

Job Title

_____

Company

Responsibilities you had on the job:

★ _____

★ _____

★ _____

Your achievements on the job, if any

★ _____

★ _____

★ _____

Add any additional skill sets or educational qualifications you have gained in the interim period.

Now you are ready to upload your brand new resume on to job sites and send out your resume to potential recruiters.

Spread the Word

Networking is an important tool in the career world. When you meet people in the industry, you learn more about jobs in the market that fit 'Brand You'.

For example, if you have a Linkedin account, you could be discovered by a potential employer just on the basis of your updated resume.

Network with people you know. Let friends and family know that you are on the look-out for new opportunities. Many employers now appoint via networking as it is much easier to appoint someone whose profile you are comfortable with. Networking is a money-and time-saver as far as an employer is concerned.

Employee Shoot

What do you say during networking meetings online or face to face?

★ First thank the person for taking the time to connect with you and if it is relevant mention the person who referred you to the contact's name.

★ Introduce yourself and mention the line of work you were in.

★ State your objective, for example if you are in HR and want to move to sales, mention something like, "I'm doing some research on opportunities in the sales field and I found out that you are the best person to talk to."

★ Don't ask for a job – just impress the person you are talking to with the power of your personality.

★ Find out how the person got into the present job slot, which sectors of industry are worth getting involved in, which headhunters give you the best opportunity – ask intelligent questions and listen patiently. Sometimes during conversation, opportunities are mentioned.

Write down your networking objective.

_____

_____

When you network, you learn more about presenting yourself and showcasing your own abilities. Many times, there is a tendency to underplay achievements. Showcasing yourself improves your confidence levels and helps you to get noticed.

How do you plan to do your networking?

_____

_____

Building contacts is a gradual process that must be planned. Always keep business cards and contact nos. of important people you have met in the industry and your previous colleagues and bosses.

Get your Recommendations

Make sure that you keep good relations with most of your previous employers – it helps you to get good references and also paves the way for better opportunities.

Career Change Interview Questions

The fresher interview is the simplest. As you gain more and more experience, you might have to encounter some more tricky questions. Here are a few:

Why did you leave your previous job?

_____

_____

There are many reasons you may have left your first job. You could have had personal constraints, health issues, problems with the management, problems with co-workers, etc. Your employer does not need to hear the real details of why you left. Just be pleasant and explain that you seek a better opportunity.

What do your colleagues say about you?

_____

_____

Try to recall a positive comment that your supervisor made about you, e.g., she is a focused and dedicated employee. It helps if you have a recommendation letter to prove it.

Did you have any problems with your previous boss?

_____

_____

You'll have to diplomatically answer this one. Even if you had problems best not to elaborate on problems you had with your previous boss. Saying nasty things about your previous boss shows zero integrity on your part.

Have you been fired?

_____

_____

Layoffs are quite common these days. If you were fired, admit it and give a convincing explanation. Maybe the company was restructuring itself or was relocating. Maintain positive body language the whole time you answer this question.

Employee Shoot:

Is there any difference in the interview the second time round?

No need to be nervous as you have been here, done that. Just think of your second interview as a chance to discuss the possibility of a better job with better perks. You will be asked the question: Why the job change? If you are changing your stream altogether you must be prepared to answer why you choose to do that.

I'm nervous about changing my job mid career. Do I stand a chance?

Of course you do. Youngsters are an employee favourite because they are willing to do all aspects of the job with enthusiasm. As you grow older, you start finding your comfort level and decide to stick to it. However, what you have is a whole bunch of skill sets that freshers will not have. You will be better at negotiations, handling deadlines, problem solving, and stress management.

I want to change my stream completely. What do I do?

If you want to change your stream, you obviously know what you want. There are candidates who have been in sales for over five years and want to switch to HR – that's workable. You'll have to network with people you already know within the industry and outside it. Networking with people you know and expressing your desire to be a part of a different industry gives more opportunities.

If you are a doctor and then wish to get into creative arts, it is possible but as far as possible use your professional acumen. It is a gift that you should not throw away. Look at the bestselling author Deepak Chopra. He worked as an endocrinologist once. His books still reflect his interest in healing. You can stay in your field and use your talents to give a different spin on it.

Ask yourself why you are leaving your course or job. Is there any way you can grow in your present career? Do you only see a dead end or is there a possibility that you can integrate your interest with your profession?

Take on challenges within your own present career. Learn as much as you can. Create circumstances to excel within your field. See if your contribution is valuable. If you still feel that career change will help you grow then it is a risk that might set you free.

You are responsible for your decision. Even if you change careers or jump streams, happiness is not guaranteed. Before you do make the jump, make sure that you know what you are getting into. One cannot be a substitute for another. So even if you like catering and you are in the finance sector, maybe finance gets you better returns and helps you lead a more comfortable life. Which priority works for you – money or self-satisfaction? You have to answer all this when you think of changing jobs.

Career Graph: The Four Stages

#1: Fresher

Higher on Knowledge Quotient and armed with information and data, the fresher must transfer these skills into practical experience. When a teacher teaches for the first time in a demo class, she is nervous. She knows the subject but does not have the body language to match it – that comes with experience.

The first phase of your career is usually the most difficult and challenging. The teacher who cannot control a noisy class must have an open mind and try to find out how to keep her students occupied.

There are so many ways in which a teacher can get her students' attention – using anecdotes, jokes, and even grooming as tools. She develops self awareness and uses out of the box solutions to solve problems. She develops effective ways of communication and learns to deal with her emotions and her students' emotions.

The first part of your career is the time when you get your LIFE SKILLS.

You also learn that being a professional does not mean you only excel in your line of work. A professional is an all-rounder. A teacher not only educates – she is also a guide, a comedian, a philosopher, a mentor, a listener…a teacher has so many roles to fulfil. Whichever organization you go to, your relationship with the people and the organization is important. You acquire FUNCTIONAL SKILLS.

In the first phase of your career, you learn about your ORGANIZATION. Each organization is unique, with a distinct set of rules and hierarchy. What works in one organization need not necessarily work in another. In each organization, there will be a certain group who is influential. You have to know who the movers and shakers are. You have to master the PROCESSES in your company – then you succeed faster.

FOCUS is the name of the game – no distractions about salaries and designations! Just keep learning as much as you can. Be a sponge and work hard. Don't pay much attention to others. Just work on your life skills and work skills and you are ready to climb the ladder.

#2: Specialist

This stage of your career is the time when you develop EXPERTISE. Every medical student today knows that a degree in medicine is not enough – you have to specialize.

Even after you get a job, make a JOB LOG – keep a diary of your daily SWOT or strengths and weaknesses. This helps you identify which functions you excel at and which you have to improve on.

Once you are familiar with your work, many tasks come automatically to you. Now you have to learn how to work smart. Work hard but do not over work as that could lead to burn out. You are responsible to yourself as well as the company you work in. So learn to BALANCE as you become better at time-, conflict- and stress-management.

Keep the INTEREST. How do you stop your job from being monotonous? Update yourself with the latest tools and tricks in the trade. It's no use saying you are not tech-savvy. If your job requires it, you will have to learn about social media marketing. The more updated you are, the easier it will be for you to adapt to new circumstances.

#3: Relationship Builder

Now you are comfortable with your work and know how to keep the job as interesting as possible. Focus on building strong relationships that will build your reputation in the company and help the company grow.

How you deal with people is a measure of your success. It is people who will give you recognition and people who will criticize you if you fail. Work is worship but do not forget to value the contribution of people around you. If you truly VALUE your boss, colleagues, and subordinates, they will RESPECT you.

Failure is a part of growth. Don't focus too much on getting everything right. If things fail because of your short sightedness, you will be blamed. You will feel disappointed that the people who supported you earlier now do not care. This is the way the world works. Take failure as a learning tool – behind every success there are many failures. This is the time when you have to RESPECT yourself and develop a POSITIVE relationship with yourself.

#4: Leader

You have succeeded and failed – you have learnt the career game. You are now comfortable in your own skin. This is the best time to become a guide to others. With experience comes responsibility. Sometimes 'seniors' like to monopolize data and bully juniors. This only shows how insecure they are. The more experience you have, the more you have to share.

The new trend this century is 'Like' and 'Share'. On websites like Facebook, you can paste links and people in your network can share your post. The more 'followers' you get the more popular you become – your ratings increase. Always help, train, go out of the way to help others and you will feel GOOD! To succeed, you must lead and to lead you must be open.

Being helpful does not mean you must spoon feed and do someone else's work for them. It means you must guide a person to be self-sufficient and instead of laughing at mistakes, correct errors and help change the fresher into an expert.

This is what a career is about – satisfaction in what you do and how much you can reach out.

Employee Shoot

I have work experience. What reasons would there be for me not getting hired?

There are several reasons for not being selected.

Too little experience: You are just out of the job and you don't have the relevant experience for the new one. Maybe you don't have the experience in years but if you can make a strong case for your portfolio, you can cross this hurdle.

Too much experience: Ironic, isn't it? Many companies prefer hiring young dynamic freshers who are willing to take lesser salaries. Make sure you have posted your application for a more senior position. If you apply for a similar post to your initial position, your employers will question your decision.

Unrealistic salary expectations: Negotiate salary as per industry rates unless you have good reason to be offered a much higher salary.

Job-hopping: If you have changed jobs several times in the last couple of years, employers will be hesitant to employ you. Nowadays, changing jobs is quite normal. There was a time when one was married to the job for life – now people

If you maintain a sound business ethic, you will succeed in the long run. Think in the long term, say the next twenty years. It is a long beautiful journey ahead, no need to crowd it with disappointments and disillusionment. Be positive, pragmatic, decisive,

Write down where you see yourself once you have retired.

_____

_____

_____

Now move toward that goal!

Recap

Why do you need a job change?

Job change related interview questions.

The four stages of your career.

SECTION 7
TEST YOURSELF

Assessment Tests
Verbal Reasoning
Logical Reasoning
Personality Test
Career Motivation

1

Assessment Tests

There are many things that you do not know about yourself. You base your actions on ideas you have of yourself, but how many of us really know what our potential is and what we are truly capable of?

Fresher Shoot

I don't need tests. I already know what I'm like.

Do you?

which areas you need to improve and which areas you are good at.

These tests provide you the feedback you need to be more prepared.

Doing tests is preparation for future tests and exams when you are in the job hunt process.

Assessment tests are used for:

Career Planning

Personal Awareness

Empathy

These questions give you a brief idea about assessment tests in general.

You can solve the questions in any order.

Verbal Reasoning

Match the word that fits the relationship

1. PIT: ABYSS :: HEIGHT: ?

   a) Altimeter   b) Altitude   c) High   d) Above

2. SKY: EARTH :: GROUNDLESS:?

   a) Base   b) Ground   c) Justified   d) Baseless

3. HAPPY: SAD :: STEM:?

   a) Bud   b) Seed   c) Root   d) Stem

4. UGADI: KARNATAKA ::VISHU:?

   a) Andhra Pradesh   b) Rajastan   c) Bengal   d) Kerala

5. Water: Thirst :: Money:?

   a) Wealth   b) Bank   c) Finances   d) Bankruptcy

6. CHAPTERS:BOOK ::?: RECIPE

   a) Condiments   b) Measure   c) Ingredients   d) Parts

7. LAND:REAL ESTATE :: Computer:?

   a) Information Technology   b) Information Testing

   c) Information Tendency   d) Information Trends

8. TUSK:ELEPHANT :: POUCH:?

   a) Rhinoceros   b) Tiger   c) Octopus   d) Kangaroo

9. DEATH:LIFE :: ZENITH:?

   a) Below   b) Depth   c) Nascent   d) Nadir

10. HERD:ELEPHANTS :: ?:Geese

    a) Group   b) Bunch   c) Gaggle   d) School

11. EXEMPT:SPARED :: PRICELESS:?

    a) Expensive   b) Extravagant   c) Prized   d) Cheap

KEY:

1. b   2. c   3. c   4. d

5. d   6. a   7. d   8. d

9. c   10. c

Logical Reasoning

1. Abhay and Binny are a married couple. Raj and Jai are brothers. Raj is the brother of Abhay. How is Jai related to Binny?

   a) brother-in -law   b) brother   c) son-in-law   d) cousin

2. Dinesh said to Nandu, "That boy playing cricket is the younger of the two brothers of the daughter of my father's wife". How is the boy related to Dinesh?

   a) son   b) brother   c) cousin

   d) nephew   e) brother-in law

3. Chandu is Ajit's father's nephew. Dipu is Ajit's cousin, but not the brother of Chandu. What is the relationship between Dipu and Chandu?

   a) cousin   b) sister   c)nephew

   d) cant' say   e) none of these

4. A and B are brothers; C and D are sisters. A's son is D's brother. How is B related to C?

   a) father   b) brother   c) grand father

   d) uncle   e) none of these

5. Vijay saw the picture of a lady and said, "She is the daughter of my grandfather's only son." What is Vivek's relationship with the lady?

   a) brother   b) uncle   c) father

   d) can't say   e) none of these

6. Radhika pointed to a man and said, "He is the brother of my uncle's daughter". How is Radhika related to the man?

   a) son   b) brother-in-law   c) nephew

   d) uncle   e) cousin

7. Kareena said this of a man, "He is the only son of my mother's mother" How is Kareena related to the man?

   a) mother   b) aunt   c) sister   d) niece

8. A said of another man, "His son is my son's uncle". How is A related to the man?

   a) brother   b) uncle   c) father

   d) grandfather   e) none of these

9. X introduced Y saying, "He is the husband of the granddaughter of the father of my father". How is Y related to X?

   a) brother   b) son   c) brother-in law

   d) son-in-law   e) nephew

10. Sudhir introduced Rajiv as the son of the only brother of his father's wife. What is their relationship?

   a) cousin   b) son   c) uncle   d) son-in-law

Key:

1. a	2. b	3. d	4. d
5. a	6. c	7. d	8. c
9. c	10. a		

Personality Test – Who are you?

1. Are people honest with you?   Yes/ No

2. Are you confident about your appearance? Yes/No

3. Do you know your SWOT (Strengths and weaknesses) Yes/ No

4. Do you lose your temper easily? Yes/ No

5. Do you like to spend time with people? Yes/ No

6. Are you a good listener? Yes/ No

7. Do you like to advertise your achievements? Yes/ No

8. Are you always worried about what others think? Yes/No

9. Do you give free advice even when no one asks for it? Yes/No

10. Can you handle criticism? Yes/No

Key

1. People will be honest with you when you are honest with them and have an open, welcoming body language. If you don't make much eye contact, then people will not open up to you as much. People mimic each other - if you are honest with them, they will almost always return the favour. Of course there are exceptions.

2. If you are, people will automatically respect you. Your thoughts are mirrored in the world - if you feel inadequate about your looks then others will voice that bias. You may have weight problems or complexion issues, but if you groom yourself adequately many flaws can be reduced. If you want others to like you, like yourself first.

3. Find out your strengths and weaknesses. We will get into this in detail in Section 2. It's only when you know what you are good at that you can find out where your opportunities lie.

4. Everyone has a threshold level - with experience you will find that your threshold level keeps increasing. If you lose your temper easily, take it as a challenge. Find out which situations cause you to lose your temper. Can you avoid those situations or are they a part of your daily life? If the situation is avoidable, then stay away. If you have to deal with negatives every day, then watch your response. Can you avoid reacting? If you can remain an observer, you will stay calm. (If you are in serious situations when you lose your temper for good reason, then get HELP.)

5. If you are comfortable dealing with people, then life is easier. There is nothing wrong with being an introvert - just see people as an opportunity to learn new things.

6. Good listeners are good learners. Work on this skill as it is useful.

7. Branding yourself is one thing - but there is a time and a place to sell yourself. Talking about your achievements is one thing but bragging is another.

8. Thinking about what others think of you is a waste of time and energy. Present yourself well and speak confidently - then you don't have to worry about what others think.

9. Don't have all the answers for personal problems - that is not etiquette. Wait for people to look up to you for solutions and then give advice.

10. Criticism is an important part of growth. Take praise and criticism in your stride - they are two sides of the same coin. Beware of flatterers and befriend your critics.

Career Motivation

1. Are you able to make decisions quickly and correctly?	Yes/No
2. Does challenge interest you?	Yes/No
3. Can you work under pressure?	Yes/No
4. Do you have the stamina to meet deadlines?	Yes/No
5. Do you have good inter-personal skills?	Yes/No
6. Are you able to meet targets?	Yes/No
7. Are you tech savvy?	Yes/No
8. Are you willing to learn every day?	Yes/No
9. Can you change?	Yes/No
10. Do you plan your goals?	Yes/no

Key

1. Being decisive means being responsible. Delaying a decision is counter-productive.

2. The corporate space offers challenges on a day to day basis - start liking it.

3. Enjoy your work and pressure changes into opportunity.

4. Physical health = 100% productivity. So stamina is important.

5. Communication with your peers and seniors is key to your survival. So brush up your communication skills.

6. You must learn to meet deadlines - otherwise you could lose your job.

7. Tech savvy is in, so spruce up your tech skills. The hi-tech whiz always keeps the job.

8. Be naturally curious and learn on the job all the time.

9. You have to say goodbye to every trait that makes you stick out and learn to adapt.

10. Planning is an integral part of meeting goals – it is part of preparing yourself for the task, be it an interview or a job target.

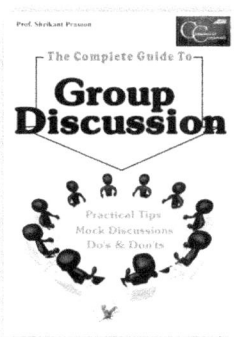

This comprehensive guide book on GD helps you clear the fog surrounding GD and by following its step-by-step instructions you can become a winner in GD.

This book includes:

Practice for GD

Go Ahead, Enjoy Reading and Be a Winner!!!

This dictionary explains corporate-related terms that all job seekers should know. Terms have been arranged in alphabetical order to make searching easy and convenient. You'll invariably come across these terms while searching for a job or during the interview. It will be of immensely help at the time of writing your exit interview.

What does the term career objective signify? What is an aptitude test? What do employers mean by relevant experience? How do you define customer satisfaction? What's the difference between an assistant manager and an assistant to the manager? How do you explain the term product life cycle? And so on...

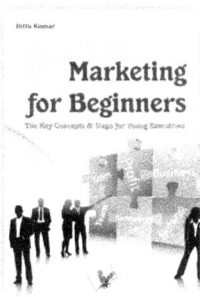

---

him and sells itself, "

— *Peter F. Drucker*

The book, Marketing for Beginners gives an exhaustive explanation about the key concepts of marketing, its strategies, and defines the important terminologies, such as Brand Selection, Distribution Channels, Vendor Selection, Pricing, Sales Process, Customer Relationship Management(CRM).

It's different and exclusive from other Marketing or Management books as it not only gives the detailed description of the various components of Marketing, but also cites examples to explain each of them, making it crystal clear to the readers.

The book has been supplemented with many case studies and examples to make it more interesting. The book comes accompanied by an interactive CD containing a PowerPoint Presentation for better understanding. The book will act as a valuable guide for all its readers to remove the barriers of effective communication.

Some of the highlights of the book are:

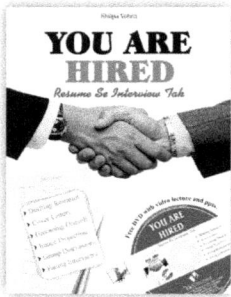

Have you ever applied for a job and not been called for the interview? Have you ever wondered why? Well, don't be discouraged! This book explains in

dream job.
The highlights of the book are:

This fascinating book authored by Dr. Aparna Chattopadhyay offers you a new vision of self-awareness which would enable you to assess your feelings, capabilities and aptitudes. As you develop self-awareness, you will not only be able to identify the emotional patterns in your life and will manage them well, but will also be able to activate all-round personality development.
This book enables you to:

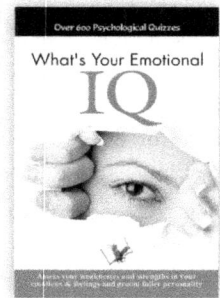

    Generate fresh enthusiasm and ambition in your life

    Build self-confidence and develop inner peace
    Enjoy better interper-sonal relationships

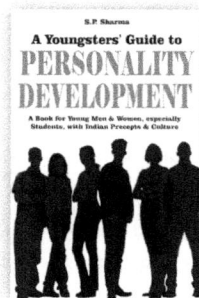

In a world marked by competition, personality is the key to success — whether it is social or business or personal or political arena. Interview

addressing a public rally, or delivering a speech in an international conference…if you have a confident and pleasing personality, you will surely make your mark! This book seeks to motivate young men and women, particularly students, to make conscious and continuous effort to build character and develop good personality.

do you do if you are faced with a situation in life for which you were not

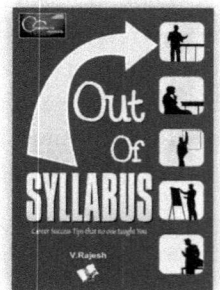

Career is one area where one is expected to know and manage situations. After all a person is paid a salary to be able to handle things and deliver results. The reality is that most people get a lot of academic and conceptual inputs relating to

academic learning.